ONCE UPON A TIME IN
FLORIDA

Stories of Life in the Land of Promises

Edited by Jacki Levine

Foreword by Nashid Madyun

St. Petersburg

Copyright 2023 by Florida Humanities

All rights reserved

Published in the United States of America. Printed in Canada.

28 27 26 25 24   6 5 4 3 2

Library of Congress Cataloging-in-Publication Data

Names: Levine, Jacki, editor.

Title: Once upon a time in Florida : stories of life in the land of promises / edited by Jacki Levine ; foreword by Nashid Madyun.

Description: 1st. | St. Petersburg, FL : Florida Humanities : produced by the University Press of Florida for Florida Humanities, 2023. | Includes index. | Summary: "Curated from the archives of FORUM, the award-winning magazine of Florida Humanities, this anthology presents 50 often surprising and always intriguing stories of life in Florida by some of the nation's most talented writers and scholars."—Provided by publisher.

Identifiers: LCCN 2023012996 (print) | LCCN 2023012997 (ebook) | ISBN 9798987660805 (cloth) | ISBN 9798987660812 (pdf) | ISBN 9798987660829 (epub)

Subjects: LCSH: Humanities—Florida. | Florida—History.

Classification: LCC AZ513.F6 O53 2023 (print) | LCC AZ513.F6 (ebook) | DDC 001.309759—dc23/eng/20230413

LC record available at https://lccn.loc.gov/2023012996

LC ebook record available at https://lccn.loc.gov/2023012997

Design by Louise OFarrell

Frontispiece: *Briny Breezes Trailer Park, Delray Beach*, circa 1952, by Stevan Dohanos (American, 1907–1994), oil on masonite. Courtesy of the Samuel P. Harn Museum of Art, University of Florida, Gainesville; the Florida Art Collection, Gift of Samuel H. and Roberta T. Vickers. Photo by Randy Batista. © 2023 Estate of Stevan Dohanos / Licensed by VAGA at Artists Rights Society (ARS), NY.

Pages vi, vii, ix, and x: Photos by Carol M. Highsmith. Photographs in the Carol M. Highsmith Archive, Library of Congress, Prints and Photographs Division.

Distributed by the University Press of Florida for Florida Humanities

Florida Humanities
599 2nd Street S
St. Petersburg, Florida 33701

To the tellers of Florida's stories—past, present and future—who capture the complexity and true magic of this state.

This project was funded in part by the UNITED WE STAND initiative of the National Endowment for the Humanities (NEH). The NEH was established by the National Foundation on the Arts and the Humanities Act of 1965 to provide for the establishment of the National Foundation on the Arts and the Humanities to promote progress and scholarship in the humanities and the arts in the United States.

Here is one point that emerged from this act that reflects the merits of the UNITED WE STAND initiative and the values of Florida's contribution to what it means to be an American.

> An advanced civilization must not limit its efforts to science and technology alone, but must give full value and support to the other great branches of scholarly and cultural activity in order to achieve a better understanding of the past, a better analysis of the present, and a better view of the future.

NATIONAL ENDOWMENT FOR THE HUMANITIES

Contents

Foreword xi
Nashid Madyun

Acknowledgments xii

Introduction 1
Jacki Levine

Part I. Beginnings

1
The First Floridians 12
They survived many millennia of a changing environment until disease and deadly conflict came from across the sea.

Jerald T. Milanich

2
Who Started the Myth of the Fountain of Youth? 20
Exploring the murky beginnings of Florida's most enduring fable.

J. Michael Francis

3
The Real First Thanksgiving 25
Half a century earlier—and 1,200 miles south—a feast of gratitude.

Michael Gannon

4
Uncovering Fort Mose 28
In America's first free Black town, enslaved Africans found sanctuary and liberty.

Kathleen Deagan

5
He Persisted 34
Francisco Menéndez escaped slavery, became a militia leader, and then did it all again.

Darcie A. MacMahon

6
How Seashells Saved St. Augustine 37
This modest mollusk displayed a secret strength.

Michael Gannon

7
On the Backs of the Enslaved 42
How Middle Florida and its planter class built wealth and power.

Larry Eugene Rivers

8
Florida Gives Its All to the Civil War 46
Whatever their loyalties, few Floridians were spared the conflict's costs.

Robert A. Taylor

Part II. Florida Comes of Age: Promise and Paradox

9
The Eye of the Beholder 54
Swampy hellhole or perfect paradise, travel writers have portrayed visions of vastly different Floridas.
Casey Blanton

10
Taking the Waters 60
For Victorian-era visitors, Florida held the promise of miracle cures.
Rick Kilby

11
The Florida Century 67
Through boom and bust, this outback became a megastate.
Gary R. Mormino

12
Along the Backroads, 1930s 77
Remembering when Zora and I chased the vanishing folklife of Florida.
Stetson Kennedy

13
Dear Honey 82
Wartime life and letters of Marjorie Kinnan Rawlings.
Betty Jean Steinshouer

14
When the WACs Came Marching In 89
How Mary McLeod Bethune—and the Women's Army Corps—rescued struggling Daytona Beach.
Gordon Patterson

15
The Mighty Orange Faces Its Uncertain Future 94
Changing tastes, stubborn disease put the squeeze on a beloved state symbol.
Gary R. Mormino

16
Recollections of a Space Traveler 99
Former congressman and astronaut Bill Nelson shares the perils that lurked before, during, and after his historic mission.
Interview with Bill Nelson
by Rick Edmonds

17
Memoirs of a Child of the Space Program 105
Blasts from the past, in a time and place like no other.
Andrea Brunais

18
Florida's Fields of Dreams 112
How sports have boosted our fortunes and, at times, healed our divides.
Steven Noll

19
The Mouse That Roared Quietly 122
With secrecy worthy of a spy novel, Walt Disney set his sights on Orlando.
Richard Foglesong

20
How They See Us 128
The small screen portrays a Florida you may not recognize.
Eric Deggans

Part III. All Things Unequal under the Sun

PARALLEL LIVES 138

Growing up in Florida in the 1950s and '60s, two Floridians, one white and one Black, describe wildly different experiences.

21
Raised with Love, Schooled in Cruel Realities 139

In childhood, he learned the harsh lessons of Jim Crow and, finally, the power of being seen.

Bill Maxwell

22
A Sheltered 1950s Childhood, Then an Awakening 149

All this minister's daughter knew was segregation, but slowly her eyes opened to the damage and the loss.

Beverly Coyle

23
That Summer of '64 157

Martin Luther King Jr. and the fight for racial justice in St. Augustine.

David R. Colburn

Part IV. When a Deadly Pandemic Strikes

24
A Lesson in the Pandemic 168

Teaching our young daughter to cope when Dad was on Covid-19's frontlines.

Nila Do Simon

Part V. We Were Strangers Here Ourselves

25
Finding Florida 172

Out of so many puzzle pieces, how can you create one state identity?

Stephen J. Whitfield

26
We Are Here to Enlighten, Not Accuse 177

A Seminole historian urges accuracy as Florida commemorates the Spanish landing.

Willie Johns

27
Observations of a Native Son 183

Former governor and US senator Bob Graham on the "Cincinnati Factor" and why Florida remains the "State of Imagination."

Ron Cunningham

28
Adiós a los Niños 186

Parents waved farewell in sadness and hope, as their children were secreted out of Castro's Cuba.

Jon Wilson

29
When Life Takes Flight 190

Thirty years after fleeing Cuba, Ileana Ros-Lehtinen made history in the US Congress.

Dalia Colón

30
Sweetness of Memory 192

Photographer Andy Sweet poignantly captured the waning days of South Beach's elderly Jewish community before his own life was cut short.

Bill DeYoung

31
What You See When You Look at Me 198

A Haitian immigrant meets her neighbors.

Maude Heurtelou

Part VI. This State of Inspiration

32
Finding a Literary Path Home 204

Learning to love Florida, through the writers who knew it first.

Lauren Groff

33
Many Voices from Afar 206

For 500 years, Florida's literary life has thrived on the state's complexity.

Maurice J. O'Sullivan

34
Echoes in the Wind 212

In search of the poetry of Florida's Native people.

Maurice J. O'Sullivan

35
Harriet Beecher Stowe, Florida Snowbird 217

Winters in a Mandarin cabin transformed her writing and sparked a tourist boom.

Michele Currie Navakas

36
Lift Every Voice and Sing 225

James Weldon Johnson's song for Jacksonville schoolchildren became an anthem for the ages.

Craig Pittman

37
Jack Kerouac's Florida Farewell 232

He found a fertile place to work but no escape from his demons as his road reached its end.

Thomas Hallock

38
Muse over Miami 240

How a hopeless kid from New Jersey became South Florida's "Queen of Crime."

Edna Buchanan

39
Once Upon a Time in Key West 246

Writer Philip Caputo laments what's been lost and what still stirs his soul.

Philip Caputo

40
The Highwaymen 254

Painting fast and selling their dreamy landscapes cheaply, these young Black artists created a lasting vision of a Florida Eden.

Gary Monroe

41
Singing the Songs of Florida 259

A White Springs festival celebrates the elusive music that is Florida folk.

Peter B. Gallagher

42
The Great State of Rock 265

A star-studded group of Florida guitar masters electrified rock and roll.

Bob Kealing

Part VII. Roots and Rivers

43
The Wondrous Gulf 276
How its bounty and its bluster have shaped the story of Florida.

Jack E. Davis

44
The Tales They Tell 283
Fish camps preserve the soul of a vanishing way of life.

Charlie Hailey

45
The Marvelous, Misunderstood Mullet 291
Tracing the storied past of Florida's least respected and most important fish.

Terry Tomalin

46
Florida's Deep-Blue Destiny 296
From the depths of a spring it is clear, we lose connection with the state's waterways at our peril.

Bill Belleville

47
Remembering Bill Belleville 303
His storytelling celebrates the mystery and glory of our state's waterways.

Cynthia Barnett

48
River of Grass 309
How a New England transplant came to champion and name an unloved but extraordinary wetland.

Jack E. Davis

49
Clyde's Quest 316
Neither snakes nor alligators nor giant mosquitoes can keep this photographer from his beloved Everglades.

Jeff Klinkenberg

50
And on to the Sea 322
Thinking of Uncle Cooter, on the banks of the river he gifted to me.

Harry Crews

Index 326

Foreword

WE EACH HOLD A VERSION OF FLORIDA inside ourselves, its sense of place, its story of home.

But how do you define "home" when it comes to Florida? So many of us were neither born here nor have a long family history here, so we must create and build this story ourselves, in our own time and way.

Generation after generation, Florida has been a collection of cultures, thoughts, and ambitions brought by people from around the world.

Since 1973, Florida Humanities, the state affiliate of the National Endowment for the Humanities, has endeavored to help Floridians—whether they be first generation or the latest in a long line of state residents—understand their home state through programming and grant making illuminating the state's literature, history, environment, architecture, and civic issues.

One such avenue is the award-winning *FORUM* magazine, this nonprofit's state-wide publication, which shares the stories of Florida produced by a wondrously eclectic blend of Pulitzer Prize winners, scholars, literary giants, famed journalists, artists, photographers, and thinkers. Through their work they have contributed to decades of inspiration and joy in helping us define our own visions of Florida.

And that's part of what we celebrate in this anthology as we mark the fiftieth anniversary of Florida Humanities. Just as the music of our lives strikes the same perfect tone every time we listen, this is a collection of best resonance. These essays and stories were published in *FORUM* over the past thirty-five years. Together, they tell a story of Florida and reflect the mission of Florida Humanities itself, to help us understand the complex richness that is Florida.

These fifty works from decades of excellence could have easily been five hundred or a thousand chords or a full symphony. Carefully curated by award-winning editor Jacki Levine, this collection stands on the shoulders of all the grand work that has come before it by those who have so thoughtfully chronicled this state.

Nashid Madyun
Florida Humanities Executive Director

Acknowledgments

THIS ANTHOLOGY to celebrate the fiftieth anniversary of Florida Humanities would not have been possible without the treasure trove of stories published over the years in *FORUM,* Florida Humanities' magazine. We are deeply indebted to all of *FORUM*'s contributors and particularly to the writers and photographers of the fifty stories of Florida included here. Their insight, scholarship, and detail-rich observations make these pieces timeless.

Many thanks to the executive directors of Florida Humanities with whom I've had the privilege to work: Nashid Madyun, who took the helm in 2021 and whose enthusiasm for the humanities and this project has been crucial, and Steve Seibert, whose steadfast belief in the humanities is inspirational.

A special thanks to the Florida Humanities staff, who work tirelessly to ensure the humanities are shared in every corner of the state: Stephanie Chill, Lashonda Curry, Brenda O'Hara, April Myerscough, Sheila Plew, Patricia Putman, Andrew Quintana, Roseanne Smith, and Mara Utterback. And thanks, too, to the rest of the extended Florida Humanities team: Janet Scherberger, David Meek, Lena Juarez, Pam Daniel, and Gary Mormino. And deep thanks to Barbara Bahr, former director of operations, whose kindness helped smooth my way as *FORUM* editor.

Gratitude to the Florida Humanities Board of Directors: Lester Abberger (emeritus member), Frank Biafora, Tina Bucuvalas, Peggy Bulger, Dan Denton, Olympia Duhart, Kerry Edwards, Reginald Ellis, Maria Goldberg (vice chair), Alex Hamrick, Joseph Harbaugh (past chair), Matt Hudson, Sue Kim, George Lange (treasurer), Thomas Luzier (chair), Jordan Marlowe, Patrick Morris, Randy Noles, Susan Towler, Timothy Schmand, and Glenda Walters.

Thanks to the former executive directors of Florida Humanities, which began life as the Florida Endowment for the Humanities in 1973: Donald R. Eastman, William Brennan, Ann Henderson, Francine Curro Cary, Janine Farver, and, as noted above, Steve Seibert.

Thanks to former *FORUM* editors Barbara O'Reilly and Rick Edmonds, whose talents ensured a legacy of excellence and are reflected in these pages.

Thanks, as always, to the National Endowment for the Humanities, the State of Florida, Department of State, Division of Arts and Culture, the Florida Council on Arts and Culture, and the National Endowment for the Arts, for their crucial support and partnership.

A sincere thank you to the University Press of Florida team: to Romi Gutierrez, director, for her important help with this project; to Sian Hunter, senior acquisitions

This color postcard offered would-be tourists a guide to the pre-Disney Sunshine State, with cities identified with a descriptive graphic. Courtesy of Orange County Regional History Center.

editor, for her guidance; to Michele Fiyak-Burkley, associate director, for her organization and shepherding; to Tana Silva for careful copyediting; to Sue Baldwin for proofreading; and to Louise OFarrell, for making this book beautiful and engaging.

To Jessica Newman, whose editorial and organizational skills and calm were a gift; to *FORUM* designer David Meek for help digging up photographs; and to former *FORUM* designer Russ Kramer for retrieving an illustration he created twenty years ago.

To Cynthia Barnett, gratitude for introducing me to the Florida Humanities team in 2016 and for insightful editing of this anthology's introduction; to Diana Tonnessen for casting her careful eye on the introduction; and to Della McMillan Wilson, for sharing her proposal-writing expertise.

Thanks to the University of South Florida St. Petersburg campus Nelson Poynter Memorial Library, for creating and maintaining the invaluable *FORUM* digital archives, and to Kathy Arsenault, Carol Hixon, Catherine Cardwell, and David Shedden, from the library, and Lisa Lennox, formerly of Florida Humanities.

Special thanks to the Florida Museum of Natural History and Darcie MacMahon, Kristen Grace, and Jeff Gage; to the staff of the Special and Area Studies Collections, George A. Smathers Libraries, University of Florida, and the State Archives of Florida, for generously sharing images that bring Florida's history to life.

Deep gratitude to Lee Anne Chesterfield, Dulce Román, and Jessica Uelsmann of the Harn Museum of Art for enabling us to feature wondrous works from the museum's Florida Collection, a gift of Samuel and Roberta Vickers, on this anthology's cover and throughout its pages. And thanks, always, to the Vickers for their priceless Florida legacy.

Gratitude always to the readers of *FORUM;* to Florida's teachers, who share the true stories of this state in their classrooms; and the many Floridians who support Florida Humanities to ensure this important work continues.

On a personal note, thanks to my husband, Alan Agresti, for unfailing encouragement, and to my family: Bonnie Seegmiller, Barry Klein, Brad Grossman, and the entire Klein, Grossman, and Agresti families. And, always, to my late mother, Sandi Klein. And thanks to the dear friends who walked with me through this process.

And finally, to my own "first Floridians," Jacob and Bessie Levine and Tess and William Ratnoff, who crossed an ocean from Eastern Europe to New York by ship and, years later, boarded the Orange Blossom Special to Miami to complete their journey under the sun.

Introduction

Jacki Levine

As the 1950s inched toward its close, the American decade ahead promised to be a golden age of science, fueled in part by a diminutive metal orb with a catchy name.

On October 4, 1957, the Soviets launched the first artificial satellite to orbit the earth. Sputnik I was a beeping, blinking reminder that the Cold War competition had now truly slipped the bonds of Earth. And much to the dismay of the American earthlings below, the Soviet Union appeared to be ahead.

Throughout the '50s the United States had launched small rockets from an isolated stretch of Florida coast at Cape Canaveral. But Sputnik supercharged a sense of urgency.

In Washington, a powerful Texas senator named Lyndon B. Johnson championed and chaired a Special Committee of Space and Aeronautics. Almost a year to the day of Sputnik's launch, President Dwight D. Eisenhower debuted the National Aeronautics and Space Administration (NASA).

Then, in 1961, came President John F. Kennedy's prophetic promise: the United States would "put a man on the moon" before the end of the decade. The following year, on February 20, 1962, John Glenn became the first American to go into orbit.

At the hot center of it all was Florida's Cape Canaveral, ground zero for launch operations. As aerospace technology companies, engineers, technicians, test pilots, and their families descended by the thousands, motels with whimsical names like the Sea Missile, AstroCraft, and Starlite buzzed with sightings of visiting astronauts and legendary journalists such as Walter Cronkite. It was boom time, in more ways than one.

Science and technology reigned in schools and universities and in hefty federal research grants through the National Science Foundation (NSF).

As Sputnik's three-month orbit propelled a competition in space, the nation's humanities scholars watched the resources driving the country's commitment to science and didn't want to be left behind. Wasn't an understanding of literature and history, ethics and philosophy, culture and each other as essential as science to the nation's path forward?

Florida, from a distance. This photograph, taken by an astronaut onboard the International Space Station, shows the peninsula's deep relationship with water, which has shaped its history and way of life. Courtesy of NASA.

We in America have not always been kind to the artists and the scholars who are the creators and the keepers of our vision.
—Lyndon B. Johnson

Inspired by the success of the NSF, educators and scholars from around the country formed a National Commission on the Humanities, led by Dr. Barnaby Keeney, president of Brown University. The group lobbied Congress and the White House to create an entity to strengthen humanities scholarship as the National Science Foundation had done for science, as a grant-making agency that could touch America's communities large and small with eye-opening programs to enlighten and engage the citizenry.

Just as the nascent space program had a few years before, the group found a powerful ally in Lyndon B. Johnson, a former teacher, now the US president.

On September 29, 1965, Johnson signed the National Foundation on the Arts and Humanities Act, establishing the National Endowment for the Humanities (NEH) and the National Endowment for the Arts.

"We in America have not always been kind to the artists and the scholars who are the creators and the keepers of our vision," Johnson told 200 guests assembled in the White House Rose Garden. "Somehow, the scientists always seem to get the penthouse, while the arts and the humanities get the basement."

One condition of the humanities' release from "the basement" was the promise that the NEH would bring civic and cultural literacy directly to the American people, in classrooms and community centers, in libraries and the smallest of museums, over the airwaves and on the printed page.

How best to do this? Nonprofit NEH affiliates in each state and US territory.

From its very beginning, Florida Humanities, celebrating its fiftieth anniversary as a state affiliate of NEH in 2023, zeroed in on Florida itself. The Sunshine State affiliate would preserve and share in every corner of the peninsula, even the most remote, its history, its literature, its diversity, its foodways, its wondrous and fragile environment, and its contemporary issues of inequities and public policy. And always, the stories of its people.

"This has everything to do with the state we are in," says Janine Farver, the fifth executive director of Florida Humanities. "There is no state more in search of its own identity than Florida."

Indeed, from the wishful fable of the Fountain of Youth to the worn-out trope of the hapless Florida Man, the state has been portrayed as a sunny paradise or a temple to all that's crass and pretentious. But the complex reality has been harder to fathom.

That's what Florida Humanities tackles through the programs it sponsors with community partners around the state and its own initiatives. And that's why, unlike most other state councils, the Florida Humanities lens is sharply focused on its home.

"There was a real decision in Florida that because we are a state where two-thirds of us were born somewhere else, because we're so diverse, we need to be more place-based, and that's how we'll attract your average Floridian into our programs," says Farver. She joined Florida Humanities in 1992 from Tampa's nonprofit radio

station WMNF, a Florida Humanities–funded partner, and was executive director for the last dozen of her twenty-five years with the organization.

"It's really kind of a different feeling if you were raised in Miami Beach or raised in Pensacola. I think back to the topic of 'how do we make the humanities accessible and tangible and relevant to people?'" she says. "It's by diving into something people care about, and just about everybody cares about where they live and why they live there."

Steve Seibert is a longtime board member, board chair, and Florida Humanities executive director from 2017 to 2021. "Florida is a hard entity to put your head and heart and hands around," he says. "It's so complicated. As it relates to European settlements, it's the oldest state in the union; at the same time it has some of the newest residents. It's old and new; it's intensely urban and intensely rural. It has a stunningly deep legacy of literature but not well known—better known now in part because of Florida Humanities."

"I see Florida through my own experiences. We all do," Seibert says. "But it's such a broad and complex state that the only way to really understand it is to try to see it through other people's eyes."

Lester Abberger was named to the Florida Humanities board in 1992 and served as chair before becoming an emeritus member. His interest was first captured the year before joining when he came across a story about the writer Peter Matthiessen in an issue of *FORUM*, the magazine of Florida Humanities.

His roots run deep as a fourth-generation Floridian, yet even for the Florida native there's a lot to learn. "If you are open enough to it, there are always opportunities to learn more about the place we call home, and the humanities is a wonderful way to do that," says Abberger, who was also a board member and chair of the NEH's State Federation of Humanities Councils. "Whether it's architecture or art or history, all the disciplines of the humanities help us better understand what a very special place this is."

Florida Humanities "is a cultural and historic guardian of Florida," Abberger says. "Without understanding the history and the culture you can't build a meaningful sense of community in the state."

As Florida Humanities celebrates its fiftieth anniversary, it has awarded more than $20 million to nonprofits to support humanities-based public programs around the state. During the first years of Covid-19, Florida Humanities was also tasked with quickly distributing $2,753,000 in federal relief funds for general operating

Top: Zhaedyn Hodges Sigars, reciting poetry in the state Poetry Out Loud competition, previously sponsored in part by Florida Humanities. Sigars went on to win the competition in 2019 and 2020. Photo by Scott Purks. *Center*: Natalie Schimek, winner of the 2018 Poetry Out Loud competition. Photo by Chris Zuppa. *Bottom*: Judges listen intently to the Poetry Out Loud contestants. Courtesy of Florida Humanities.

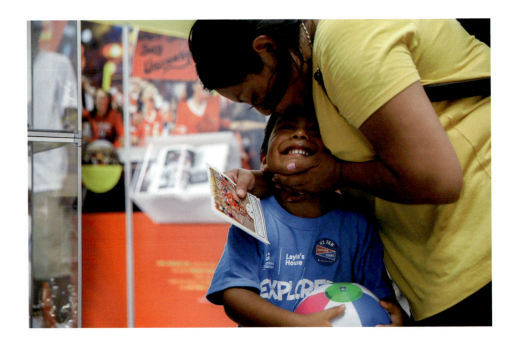

A moment in Sulphur Springs at the Smithsonian Institution Traveling Exhibition Service's Museum on Main Street exhibition, *Hometown Teams: How Sports Shape America*. MoMS is a collaboration between the Smithsonian Institution and state humanities councils nationwide. Photo by Chris Zuppa.

> *Each funded program—and there have been thousands—opens a small portal into a larger understanding of the state.*

support to cultural organizations that were financially impacted by the pandemic in 2020–2021.

As a grantmaker, Florida Humanities funnels the fluctuating resources it receives from the NEH, the state of Florida, and donors to programs run by nonprofit community partners from the Panhandle to the Keys.

Each funded program—and there have been thousands—opens a small portal into a larger understanding of the state: from a powerful traveling presentation on the 1920 Ocoee Massacre, to the Voices of Florida Bay project, which captured video interviews with many whose livelihoods depended on the fragile waterway, to a Key West exhibit of Cuban "chugs," the makeshift watercraft in which countless refugees risked their lives to cross the Florida Straits. And Florida Humanities has collaborated with the Smithsonian Institution Traveling Exhibition Service's Museum on Main Street program to bring Smithsonian-quality exhibits, with names like *Water/Ways*, *Hometown Teams*, and *Voices and Votes*, to even the smallest communities, each adding its own content.

The nonprofit has also created its own programs to enlighten and educate Floridians. The Florida Stories free walking tour app features illustrated guided tours of thirty-six historic Florida places, from Miami's Little Haiti to the Panhandle's DeFuniak Springs, created with a partner in each area. *FORUM*, the organization's statewide magazine, highlights stories about Florida by the state's top writers and scholars. The Florida Talks program, with a speakers bureau of thirty educators, scholars, journalists, and others, offers dozens of public talks, from mermaid and music history to heritage and environmental programs, and much more. During the pandemic, Florida Talks ramped up online offerings and became Florida Talks at Home!

> "The most meaningful program in my time was the Telling Project," says former Executive Director Steve Seibert. "That moved me and everyone who attended so deeply. We had veterans of different wars and that was in itself important—to have a veteran from Vietnam talking next to a veteran from Iraq or even Afghanistan about their experiences in a very personal way."

One powerful program, the Florida Center for Teachers, brought public school educators together for a week or weekend to immerse in Florida topics such as archaeology, literature, history, and the environment.

"It covered a variety of things. We did literature. We did programs on Marjorie Kinnan Rawlings and Marjory Stoneman Douglas and looked at women writers in the state," says Farver of the program that launched in the early 2000s. "We did a lot of programs based on environmental issues so that teachers could be enriched and energized and excited and bring more Florida content and the humanities into their classrooms."

Over ten years, Farver says, the program served thousands of teachers and by extension, thousands more students. "You have to really think about how you're going to serve a state of twenty million people," she says, "and it seemed always to me that teachers were a target audience. They are information multipliers."

One of the organization's most popular programs, Parallel Lives, looked at the waning days of Jim Crow in Florida through the stories of two writers of the same age, one Black, the columnist Bill Maxwell, and one white, the novelist Beverly Coyle, who grew up near one another in profoundly different circumstances. "Beverly and Bill grew up miles apart. They are exactly the same age, and they were just a perfect way to reflect upon the civil rights movement through the eyes of a young white girl and a young Black boy during a time when their lives and education in the state were changing radically," recalls Farver of the 1990s program. "They did a beautiful job of evoking that period through stories and through their lives. It was so impactful we received so many letters and great evaluations and so many news stories about it, and again, it's really Bill and Beverly who made it what it was."

Maxwell and Coyle's stories, which are included in these pages, were adapted into the play *Parallel Lives*, still performed on college campuses and in community venues around the state.

How do you bring historical figures to light in a way both entertaining and thoughtful? Another of Farver's favorite programs was Florida Chautauqua. "Over the course of the time we did Chautauqua we probably developed as many as twenty to twenty-five different characters from Florida history," she says. "Some of them traveled as individuals, but then later on we would group those that shared a thematic history. At one point we had Governor Napoleon B. Broward, Marjory Stoneman Douglas, and Osceola together all talking about the Everglades. Broward wanted to drain it, Stoneman Douglas wanted to save it, and Osceola had actually lived there. Though they lived at different times, they all left legacies that had to do with the environment."

Veteran Taylor Urruela shares his story during a Telling Project event in Tampa Bay. Courtesy of Florida Humanities.

Introduction · 5

Farver and Seibert remember the Telling Project, which dramatically presented war experiences of Florida veterans in their own voices, as one of the most important, profoundly moving programs in the history of the organization.

"That moved me and everyone who attended so deeply," Seibert says. "We had veterans of different wars, and that was in itself important, to have a veteran from Vietnam talking next to a veteran from Iraq or even Afghanistan about their experiences in a very personal way, and the audience connection to them and the power of their experiences, which were often so very different."

The program exemplified the core power of the humanities, Seibert says: the ability to see the world through someone else's eyes. In World War II, Seibert explains, nearly 100 percent of families in America knew someone closely who was fighting overseas or working in a production plant.

"By the time you get to Vietnam that number is probably down to about 10 percent.... So you have war experiences where so few members of your community have any idea what is going on and what the experiences of these veterans are. To have people courageous enough to sit and talk about these experiences in a really thoughtful way in a curated conversation, . . . it was something. It was an honor to observe it."

For Seibert, programs such as the Telling Project and Parallel Lives encourage Floridians to find connections with one another, a key tenet of the humanities and one that is more essential today than ever.

"The answer to a functioning democracy is learning to understand each other. You don't have to necessarily agree, but we must understand each other," says Seibert. "The only way to do that is to read history, to read literature, to understand something about poetry, to have a grasp of ethics, to have a grasp of comparative religion . . . to glimpse what motivates other people, and the only path for that is through the humanities."

Nashid Madyun, who became Florida Humanities' executive director in 2021, understands the historic power and importance of the work, and aspires to make it even stronger in the digital age.

"For a half century this organization has examined, supported, created, and amplified humanities in Florida, using the brightest thinkers available to lay this immeasurable foundation," says Madyun, who came to Florida Humanities from the Southeastern Regional Black Archives at Florida A&M University in Tallahassee. "We now forge ahead in a digital age with the same purpose and set of questions: What is Floridian identity? Who is Florida now, and who is it becoming? How best can we share its story?"

Telling the stories of Florida, which is deep within the mission of Florida Humanities, can unify Floridians across this long and segmented state. Many of these stories have been captured over the more than thirty years of *FORUM* magazine.

Telling the stories of Florida, which is deep within the mission of Florida Humanities, can unify Floridians across this long and segmented state. Many of these stories have been captured over the more than 30 years of FORUM magazine.

Florida Humanities' *FORUM* magazine explores the state's history, literature, cultures, environment, and way of life, as well as highlights the nonprofit's funded partner programs around Florida.

One of the great pleasures of my four years as editor of *FORUM* was the time I whiled away in its archives, stored among the treasures of the University of South Florida's online digital collection.

What I'd promise myself would be a quick search—*What has FORUM written about Florida's cowboys?* for example—would invariably lead me through a labyrinth as bewitching and complex as Florida's underground caves. "Cowboys" might lead to a tale about the Civil War's "Cow Cavalry" or the state's Black cowboys or even a pictorial horseback visit to the Florida Wildlife Corridor Trail. I never knew where these diversions would take me, only that it would be far from where the search began. By the time I emerged, I would be convinced anew that the historical gold stowed in the archives needed to be brought to the surface.

And so, as Florida Humanities' fiftieth anniversary as the state affiliate of the National Endowment for the Humanities approached, the idea took hold to publish an anthology of gems from the archives of *FORUM*. What could be more fitting to commemorate the organization's mission to "*preserve, promote and share the history, literature, cultures and personal stories that offer Floridians a better understanding of themselves, their communities and their state*" than a collection of Florida stories published over the past thirty-five years, written by some of the state's and nation's

Introduction · 7

What unfolds in the following pages is a kind of "Once Upon a Time in Florida" narrative of our state, divided into seven parts and fifty stories spanning some 14,000 years of history to today.

most acclaimed and thoughtful writers and scholars? With such a surfeit of intriguing stories, this was bound to be a joyful, even simple task. Well, joyful, most definitely. Simple, not so much.

Too much choice leads to agonizing decisions. So please accept this disclaimer: Even with fifty pieces, there are bound to be *FORUM* stories you remember fondly or as essential and believe should have been included, or feel historical events, regional milestones, or important figures were left out in favor of others you see as less consequential. For that I apologize and say there are countless stories that we too would have dearly loved to see within these pages.

In fact, what I discovered early on, unsurprisingly, is the archives could easily accommodate at least a dozen more such anthologies—people, places, historical events, the environment, literature, growth, Florida's music and arts and food, and the list goes on. And because we chose only stories that were written especially for *FORUM* or with funding from Florida Humanities or the National Endowment for the Humanities, we also had to leave out worthy pieces published as book excerpts.

We perused the archives again and again, from the earliest newsletter-type *FORUM*s from the late 1980s to the award-winning full-color issues of today. We read and read, created list after list, culled and arranged, rearranged, added and subtracted, and turned the list over and read it upside down until a kind of narrative emerged.

What we have assembled here is a mere sketch of the Florida experience but rendered vividly thanks to the storytelling gifts of the contributors, many of whom you'll know. What it illustrates from the beginning is a state with an innate wildness some take for beauty and others chaos, inhabited for thousands of years by the earliest and most resilient Floridians before being "discovered"—and subsequently idealized, exploited, demonized, drained, paved over, longed for, adored, mocked, and in some cases loved to death.

It's a state that has mirrored the dreams and disappointments of everyone who's ever reached its shores by makeshift raft or luxury yacht, whose image is often merely a reflection in the eye of the beholder. A state with a surprising 500-year-old literary history that traces back to the impressions of the earliest European explorers. And a diversity among regions and residents, most of whom were born elsewhere, that is both a strength and a reason Floridians often identify with where they came from rather than where they live.

What unfolds in the following pages is a kind of "Once Upon a Time in Florida" narrative of our state divided into seven parts and fifty stories spanning some 14,000 years of history to today. A final disclaimer: because these pieces were written over the past few decades, you may at times notice terms that have since become outdated. For example, those held in bondage are no longer referred to as "slaves" but as "enslaved people," describing the condition under which these individuals lived as opposed to defining their identity. In some places language has been updated; in others it has been left unchanged because of the context in which it appears.

From left to right: Harriet Beecher Stowe, James Weldon Johnson, Ileana Ros-Lehtinen, Edna Buchanan.

Through these stories we see, time and again, how the state evokes intense and wildly different responses in its new arrivals and native-born who look around and absorb their own deeply personal versions of Florida.

Uncle Tom's Cabin author Harriet Beecher Stowe, who long wintered in a cottage on the St. Johns River, regarded Florida much the same way she did her Mandarin property: It is "shockingly untidy," she declares, and yet it is also "so beautiful that I am quite willing to forgive its disorder."

Native Jacksonvillian James Weldon Johnson, whose "Lift Every Voice and Sing" is called the "Black national anthem," was a Renaissance man: a school principal, lawyer, lyricist, and poet. Yet he left the city of his birth after a near-lynching in the tense period following the Great Jacksonville Fire of 1901. "For weeks and months, the episode preyed on my mind and disturbed me in my sleep," he writes. Soon after, he and his brother "decided to get away from Jacksonville as quickly as possible."

Ileana Ros-Lehtinen was eight years old in 1960 when she and her parents boarded a Pan Am flight in Havana for Miami. Less than thirty years later, she became the first Latina to serve in the US Congress. "For many generations of refugees, no matter from where they come, we see Florida as a place of refuge, a safe haven," Ros-Lehtinen says.

Pulitzer Prize–winning crime reporter and novelist Edna Buchanan recounts her first visit to Miami Beach from New Jersey: "I took one look and burst into tears.... I'd been born in the wrong place! . . . But now, home at last, I'd left behind the gritty black-and-white newsreel that was my life and stepped into Technicolor and CinemaScope where my future waited."

Whether you are native born, a transplant, or a visitor passing through, we hope you discover much to contemplate within these pages, to see our state through the eyes of others—and to consider your own place in the epic story of Florida.

PART I
Beginnings

The first Floridians adapt through thousands of years of environmental change, then are overwhelmed by disease and conflict with the arrival of the Europeans. And the colonization begins.

Artist's conception of the Calusa town Tampa (present-day Pineland). The Calusa's southwest Florida coastal culture had high population density and was dependent on estuarine fisheries rather than agriculture. Art by Merald Clark; courtesy of Florida Museum of Natural History.

1 The First Floridians

They survived many millennia of a changing environment until disease and deadly conflict came from across the sea.

Jerald T. Milanich

Jerald T. Milanich, curator emeritus of archaeology at the Museum of Natural History at the University of Florida, lives in the Catskill Mountains, where he continues to write and carry out research on a number of topics, including the people who once lived in what is now the state of Florida. His most recent books are *Illuminating Edison: The Genie of Menlo Park and the New York Sun, 1878–1880; Tales from the* Catskill Tribune: *The Mountain's Premier Source for Fake News*; and *Handfuls of History: Stories about Florida's Past.*

FROM THE SURFACE, the pond at the Windover site in Brevard County seems like a most insignificant body of water. It is small and shallow. Yet, this is one of the most treasured archaeological locations in Florida, for the pond's peat-lined bottom is a vault that for thousands of years held artifacts and remains that allow us now to form a picture of the lives and practices of some of the First Floridians, the Early Archaic people.

Careful excavations by Glen Doran of Florida State University revealed that about 7,000 to 8,000 years ago the Early Archaic people buried their dead underwater in the peat of the Windover pond. The peat helped to preserve an array of normally perishable artifacts and human tissues, including brains that contain genetic material.

Many of the tools used by Early Archaic people have been found there: shark teeth and dog or wolf teeth, to which handles were attached; pins, points, and awls made from deer bone and antler as well as from manatee and either panther or bobcat bone and bird bone. Found, too, were bones from a number of animal species presumably eaten by the Windover people, which suggest that they utilized almost every meat source available to them. The pond also revealed that these people had an assemblage of material items well suited to life in Florida. From the peat was excavated a sophisticated array of preserved cordage and fabrics whose fibers came from Sabal palm, saw palmetto, and other plants.

The Windover people were part of a continuous line of Native American inhabitants of this peninsula, stretching back at least 14,000 years and reaching forward to the early eighteenth century. But there are no direct descendants of the Windover people to be found now in Florida. What happened? The Europeans arrived, bringing with them genocidal warfare and devastating diseases.

The first settlers of Florida, the Paleo-Indians, found this a much different place than that which we know today. Sea levels were much lower, the result of so much water being tied up in Ice Age glaciers, and the peninsula was nearly twice its present width. For instance, the Gulf of Mexico shoreline was more than 100 miles west of its present location.

Florida was also drier than today. Many of our present rivers, springs, and lakes were not here, and even groundwater levels were significantly lower.

The Paleo-Indians were nomadic, seeking animals to hunt and water in deep springs like Warm Mineral Springs in Sarasota County or at watering holes or shallow lakes or prairies where limestone strata near the ground surface provided catchment basins. Such limestone deposits are found from the Hillsborough River north through peninsular Florida into the Panhandle. Most Paleo-Indian sites are located in this region, although sites have been found as far south as Dade County.

After about 9000 BCE, as glaciers melted and sea levels rose, Florida's climate generally became wetter than it had been, providing more water sources around which the Paleo-Indians could camp. These new conditions may have influenced the later Paleo-Indians to practice a less nomadic lifestyle and to maintain camps occupied for longer periods of time.

The tool kits of the Paleo-Indians were altered as the people adjusted to changing environmental and social conditions. A wider variety of stone tools began to be used, and many of the stone points originally used to hunt large animals were no longer made. These changes were sufficient by 7500 BCE for archaeologists to delineate a new culture, the Early Archaic, of which the Windover people were a part.

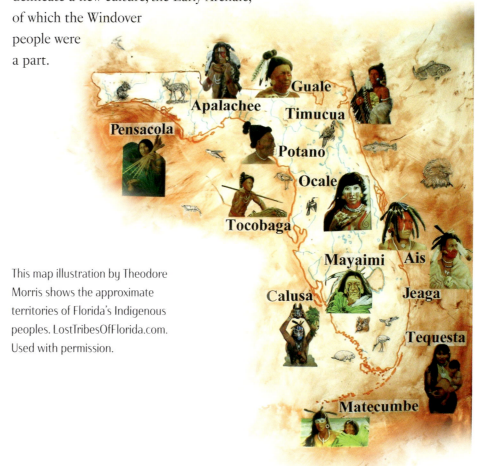

This map illustration by Theodore Morris shows the approximate territories of Florida's Indigenous peoples. LostTribesOfFlorida.com. Used with permission.

The First Floridians · 13

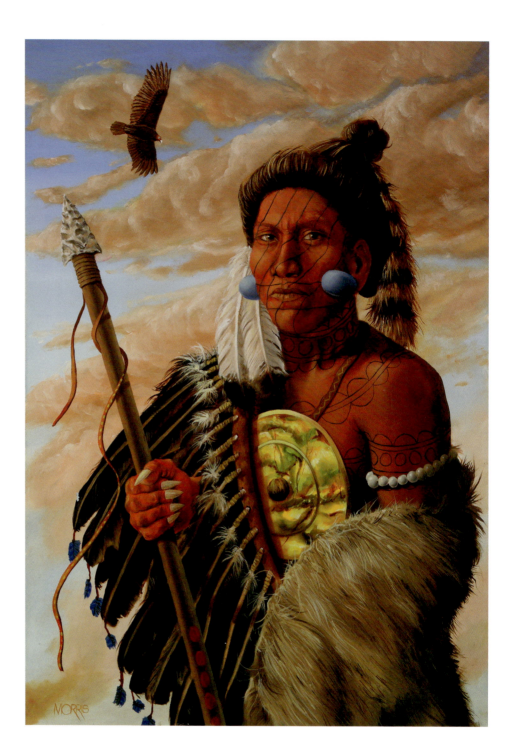

Powerful Timucua chief Outina oversaw a massive confederacy of Indians along the St. Johns River. In the mid-1560s Outina allied first with newly arrived French soldiers, then with the Spaniards who routed the French. The tattooed Outina wears fish-bladder earrings, a rare copper breastplate, and feathers of eagles and turkey vultures in this painting by Theodore Morris. LostTribesOfFlorida.com. Used with permission.

After 5000 BCE the climate of Florida began to ameliorate, becoming more like modern conditions, which were reached about 3000 BCE. The period between 5000 and 3000 BCE is known as the Middle Archaic. Middle Archaic sites are found in a variety of settings, some very different from those of the Paleo-Indians and Early Archaic periods, including, for the first time, along the St. Johns River and the Atlantic coastal strand. Middle Archaic peoples also were living in the Hillsborough River drainage northeast of Tampa Bay, along the southwest Florida coast,

Slightly before 2000 BCE, the Late Archaic villagers learned to make fired clay pottery, tempering it with Spanish moss and palmetto fibers. By the end of the Late Archaic period, 500 BCE, distinctive regional styles of pottery had emerged, a phenomenon that allows archaeologists to define and study specific cultures.

and in a few south Florida locales and at numerous sites in interior northern Florida.

It is clear that populations were significantly larger than in earlier times and that a more settled lifestyle was present. The Middle Archaic peoples also used a larger variety of specialized tools than their ancestors, perhaps a result of increased sedentism.

By about 3000 BCE, the onset of the Late Archaic period, essentially modern environmental conditions were reached in Florida, and expanding populations would soon occupy almost every part of the state. Wetland locales were heavily settled. Numerous Late Archaic sites are in southwest and northeast Florida and in the St. Johns River drainage, where sites are typified by extensive deposits of mollusk shells, the remains of thousands of pre-Columbian meals. Archaic populations probably lived all along the coasts, but many sites have been inundated by the sea rise that continued throughout the Archaic period.

Slightly before 2000 BCE the Late Archaic villagers learned to make fired clay pottery, tempering it with Spanish moss and palmetto fibers. By the end of the Late Archaic period, 500 BCE, distinctive regional styles of pottery had emerged, a phenomenon that allows archaeologists to define and study specific cultures. (In many instances we can trace, albeit incompletely, the histories of these cultures from that time to the colonial period, when their societies were first described by Europeans.)

It was during this Late Archaic period, too, that the Native societies of Florida began constructing mounds in which to inter their dead. Mounds, most made of sand, are found throughout the interior forests and coastal regions and extend into southern Florida.

Villages had leaders who helped to coordinate communal activities, including the building of mounds and the performance of burial and other ceremonies. Villagers were organized into a number of lineages or clans, each of which probably had a name and distinctive paraphernalia or other symbols of membership. When a village grew too large for its residents to be supported easily by local resources, one or more lineages broke away, establishing a new village nearby. Traditions and shared lineage membership served to tie old and new villages together and develop feelings of group identity.

Major changes occurred among the societies in the northern half of the state after 700 CE when corn agriculture was added to local economies. Farming never became important in southern Florida. Instead, the cultures of that area continued to rely on a host of wild resources as food, especially fish and shellfish and numerous plants. Although squashes and gourds and other plants earlier were grown in gardens, perhaps even in the Late Archaic period, it was the extensive cultivation of corn and later, beans, which provided the people of northern Florida with sustenance that allowed population expansion and new cultural developments.

The First Floridians · 15

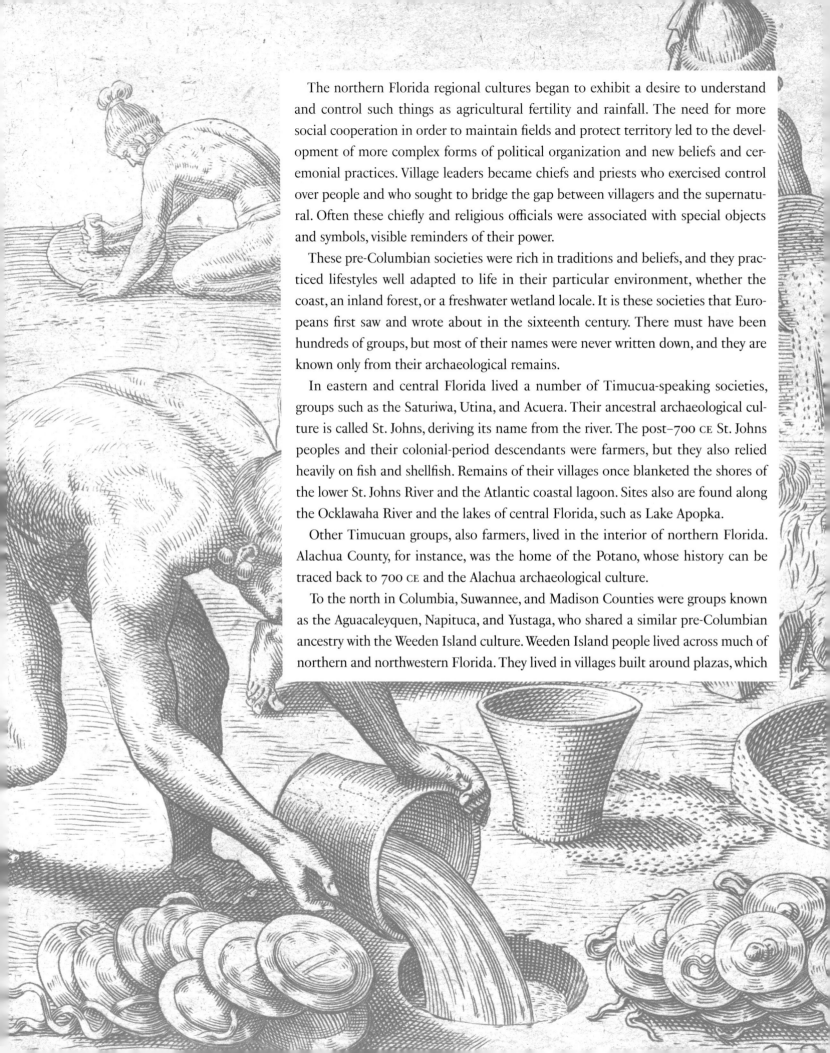

The northern Florida regional cultures began to exhibit a desire to understand and control such things as agricultural fertility and rainfall. The need for more social cooperation in order to maintain fields and protect territory led to the development of more complex forms of political organization and new beliefs and ceremonial practices. Village leaders became chiefs and priests who exercised control over people and who sought to bridge the gap between villagers and the supernatural. Often these chiefly and religious officials were associated with special objects and symbols, visible reminders of their power.

These pre-Columbian societies were rich in traditions and beliefs, and they practiced lifestyles well adapted to life in their particular environment, whether the coast, an inland forest, or a freshwater wetland locale. It is these societies that Europeans first saw and wrote about in the sixteenth century. There must have been hundreds of groups, but most of their names were never written down, and they are known only from their archaeological remains.

In eastern and central Florida lived a number of Timucua-speaking societies, groups such as the Saturiwa, Utina, and Acuera. Their ancestral archaeological culture is called St. Johns, deriving its name from the river. The post–700 CE St. Johns peoples and their colonial-period descendants were farmers, but they also relied heavily on fish and shellfish. Remains of their villages once blanketed the shores of the lower St. Johns River and the Atlantic coastal lagoon. Sites also are found along the Ocklawaha River and the lakes of central Florida, such as Lake Apopka.

Other Timucuan groups, also farmers, lived in the interior of northern Florida. Alachua County, for instance, was the home of the Potano, whose history can be traced back to 700 CE and the Alachua archaeological culture.

To the north in Columbia, Suwannee, and Madison Counties were groups known as the Aguacaleyquen, Napituca, and Yustaga, who shared a similar pre-Columbian ancestry with the Weeden Island culture. Weeden Island people lived across much of northern and northwestern Florida. They lived in villages built around plazas, which

at times were fronted with one or more earthen mounds. Villagers made ornate ceramic vessels decorated with an array of symbols important to their beliefs.

The largest and most politically complex of the colonial-period groups was the Apalachee who lived in the Panhandle between the Aucilla and Ochlocknee Rivers. Fertile lands in this region allowed the Apalachee and their pre-Columbian ancestors, the Fort Walton culture, to be the most successful farmers in Florida. Extensive cultivation of corn, beans, and squash supported large villages, many with truncated pyramidal-shaped mounds built as platforms on which to erect the temples and residences of chiefs and religious leaders. The Apalachee spoke their own language, a Muskogean tongue quite different from Timucua.

It was the Apalachee village of Anhaica, located less than a mile from the present site of the Capitol building in Tallahassee, that Spanish explorer Hernando de Soto occupied during the winter of 1539–1540. According to the de Soto narratives, the village was extensive, with some 250 large houses whose roofs were made of thatched palmetto and whose walls were made of twigs and vines woven around vertical stakes and coated with mud. Soldier Alonso de Camona described the Apalachee as being much taller than the Spaniards, whose average height was about 5 feet. De Soto's secretary, Rodrigo Ranjel, commented on the pride of the Apalachee, writing, "They gave one to understand that they would be insulted if they were thought to be of any other tribe than the Apalachee."

Around Tampa Bay, an estuary capable of supporting large populations, lived several related groups, all thought to be Timucuan-speakers. The Ucita, Mocoso, and Pohoy lived on the southern and eastern shores of the bay, and the Tocobaga were to the north on Old Tampa Bay. All of these groups were associated with the Safety Harbor archaeological culture, which is distributed along the coast and adjacent inland areas from Charlotte Harbor to the Withlacoochee River in Citrus County. Although the people living next to Tampa Bay did not grow corn, their relatives immediately to the north did.

Preparations for a Feast, by Theodor de Bry, 1591. The engraving depicting Timucua Indians preparing a feast is based on a sketch by Jacques Le Moyne de Morgues, a member of the short-lived French colony in Florida, Fort Caroline. Le Moyne served as the artist for René de Laudonnière's expedition to Florida in 1564. Courtesy of State Archives of Florida, Florida Memory.

The Key Marco Cat. The carving was discovered by anthropologist Frank Hamilton Cushing in 1896 buried in muck in an excavation in Collier County. The kneeling feline, considered one of the finest pre-Columbian pieces of Native American art ever found, was carved out of hardwood 700 to 1,500 years ago. The figurine is on loan to the Marco Island Historical Society from the Smithsonian Institution through April 2026. Courtesy of Anthropology Collection, Smithsonian Institution.

Safety Harbor sites, some with huge heaps of shellfish as well as mounds and village areas, once dotted the shoreline of Tampa Bay. But many of the sites were destroyed around the turn of the twentieth century when the shell was mined to build roads. Today only a few of these large sites exist, such as the one at Madira Bickel State Park.

The lifestyles of the various regional cultures of southern Florida also were well established by 500 BCE, the end of the Late Archaic period. Although some beliefs and symbols were shared with the cultures to the north, southern Florida cultures, including the colonial period groups, reflected the uniqueness of their environments.

The vast savannah around Lake Okeechobee, called Lake Mayaimi by Florida Indians, was the region of the Belle Glade culture and the location of a number of Native villages, some with mounds, earthen embankments, ditches, and even canals.

To the west was another distinctive archaeological culture, one centered on the Gulf coast from Charlotte Harbor south into Collier County. This was the home of the powerful Calusa Indians, who lived by harvesting the bounty of the sea. Mounds of shells demarcating their villages are found on nearly every coastal island and shoreline in Charlotte Harbor, Pine Island Sound, and San Carlos Bay. According to Spanish accounts, the Calusa were excellent seafarers, often paddling their canoes from Florida to Cuba and back.

Still another regional culture, the Glades culture, utilized the mangrove coasts and estuaries of southeast Florida, extending south into the Keys and west into Monroe County. Dade County was the home of the Tequesta Indians, who, like other Glades people, lived by fishing, gathering shellfish, and collecting plants and other animals. Just to the north were groups like the Boca Ratones and Santaluces, names given the Natives by the Spaniards. Glades archaeological sites once covered the shores of the Florida Gold Coast. Where there were once shell middens on Biscayne Bay, today there are high-rise buildings.

The initial voyage of Christopher Columbus to the Caribbean and the ensuing attempts by Spain, France, and other European powers to explore, conquer, and colonize North America brought changes to all Native societies, including those in Florida.

Post-Columbian Inhabitants of Florida and the European Invasion

IN THE SIXTEENTH CENTURY Europeans first traveled to the coasts of Florida and then through the interior. The expeditions of the Spaniards Juan Ponce de León (1513), Pánfilo de Narváez (1528), de Soto (1539), and Tristán de Luna y Arellano (1559) and the French colony led by Jean Ribault and René de Laudonnière in northeast Florida (1562–1565) provide important descriptions of the Calusa, Tequesta, Apalachee, Timucua, and other groups. But these and other European intrusions also introduced Old World diseases such as measles, smallpox, and other infections,

Map by Spanish royal cartographer Geronimo Chiaves of the Spanish province of "La Florida." Chiaves's map was most likely drawn from accounts of members of Hernando de Soto's 1539–1543 expedition. It was first published in Abraham Ortelius's *Theatrum Orbis Terrarum* in 1584. WIKI.

against which Native Florida Indians had no immunities. Epidemics swept through Native villages, killing 25 percent to 50 percent or more of the people.

In 1565 Pedro Menéndez de Avilés ousted the French from their stronghold at the mouth of the St. Johns River and established a Spanish town at St. Augustine in order to colonize the land Juan Ponce de León had named La Florida.

Menéndez arranged for Jesuit and later, Franciscan missions to be established among some of the Native groups, an effort to convert them to Catholicism and to control them so they could serve as a labor force for the colony. Missions eventually stretched westward through the Timucuan groups of northern Florida from St. Augustine into the Apalachee of the Panhandle. Missions, many short-lived, also were placed among the Timucua on the lower St. Johns River and among the Tocobaga, Calusa, and Tequesta.

But even the best intentions of the missionary priests could not counter the epidemics that repeatedly struck mission villagers. Less than 200 years after the first Europeans arrived in Florida, the Indian populations had declined from several hundred thousand to practically nothing. Raids initiated by English colonists from the Carolinas in the early eighteenth century destroyed the missions and enslaved, killed, or scattered the remaining mission Indians. Georgia and Alabama Indians also raided into the state, further decimating even the once-mighty Calusa.

By 1763, when Spain gave up her Florida colony to Britain, the Native American Indians of Florida whose ancestors had lived here for at least 14,000 years were almost gone.

But Florida would not remain unpopulated. By the 1740s, Creek Indians from Georgia and Alabama who had been raiding into Florida since the late seventeenth century established settlements in lands previously occupied by the Apalachee and Timucua. By the 1770s these Native people began to be called by a new name, Seminole.

From the **Fall 1992** edition of *FORUM* magazine, "Florida's Native Americans."

Author's 2022 Addendum

During the three decades since this essay was published, archaeologists and historians have continued to uncover new information about the Florida Indians. Were I to write this essay today, I would note that the Seminole, Miccosukee, and other Florida Indians rightfully view themselves as descendants of the Indian societies who preceded them in Florida. It also is important to acknowledge that the entire state of Florida exists atop the ancestral lands of the Indians who lived here in the past and who continue to live here today.

2

Who Started the Myth of the Fountain of Youth?

Exploring the murky beginnings of Florida's most enduring fable.

J. Michael Francis

J. Michael Francis, Hough Family Chair of Florida Studies at the University of South Florida, St. Petersburg, is author of numerous works, including five books. He is executive director of La Florida: The Interactive Digital Archive of the Americas. He was a research fellow at the American Museum of Natural History in New York and a Jay I. Kislak Fellow at the Library of Congress in Washington, DC. He was curator of the traveling museum exhibition *Imagining La Florida: Juan Ponce de León and the Quest for the Fountain of Youth.* In 2021 Francis received the Officer's Cross of the Order of Isabella the Catholic from King Felipe VI of Spain.

IN 1575, NOT LONG BEFORE HIS DEATH, a Spaniard named Hernando de Escalante Fontaneda drafted a remarkable memoir chronicling his seventeen-year ordeal as a captive among Florida's Calusa Indians. Escalante was enslaved by the Calusas in 1549 after he survived a shipwreck in the Florida Keys. At the time, he was just thirteen years old.

Escalante's unique account is widely considered one of the most important documents on early colonial Florida history. But perhaps it is best known as one of the earliest written references to Florida's most enduring myth: Juan Ponce de León's quest for the Fountain of Youth.

According to Escalante, Indians in Cuba and Santo Domingo were convinced that a magical river existed somewhere on the Florida peninsula and that bathing in it turned old men young again.

Large numbers of these Indians went in search of the elusive waters, he wrote, and many died in the process. He derided the Indians for believing such a foolish legend and added that while he was a captive, he had bathed in many of Florida's numerous rivers. Yet "to my great displeasure," he wrote with a hint of sarcasm, "I was never able to verify the fountain's existence." He then mocked the lone Spaniard naïve enough to believe such a tall tale. "It was simply laughable," he wrote, that Juan Ponce de León would set out on such a quest.

It might be easy to understand Escalante's contempt if it were not for one small matter: *Ponce was never searching for a Fountain of Youth.*

There, I said it. Ponce de León was never searching for a Fountain of Youth. Escalante was simply repeating an apocryphal story that had appeared in a work published more than two decades after Ponce's 1513 expedition to Florida and more than a decade after Ponce's death. There is no historical evidence to suggest that Ponce was even aware of the fabled spring, let alone that he risked life and fortune on a quest to locate it.

Above: Promising youth, though not a pleasant fragrance, as these visitors discover, sulphur water flows from this Fountain of Youth, St. Petersburg, 1951. Courtesy of State Archives of Florida, Florida Memory.
Background: Depiction of a popular myth. In this hand-colored woodcut from the 1500s, Juan Ponce de León's expedition searches for the Fountain of Youth in Florida. North Wind Pictures Archive/Alamy.

There is no historical evidence to suggest that Ponce was even aware of the fabled spring, let alone that he risked life and fortune on a quest to locate it.

Of course, Escalante did not invent the Fountain of Youth story, nor was he the first to associate Ponce with it. Rumors of magical rejuvenating springs had deep historical roots in medieval lore, occupying a privileged place in Eurasian mythology, along with tales of Amazon women, the Seven Cities of Cíbola, and other popular tales. Versions of these stories had long existed in many parts of Europe, the Middle East, and Asia. Thus, it is hardly surprising that not long after Columbus's initial voyages to the Caribbean, reports began to emerge that the elusive waters were to be found somewhere in the New World.

It was not until 1535, more than twenty years after Ponce's 1513 voyage to Florida and more than a decade after he died in 1521, that a historian associated him with a quest for the Fountain of Youth. It was the great Spanish chronicler Gonzalo Fernández de Oviedo y Valdés who introduced this story. In an exhaustive work of human and natural history that is widely considered the finest chronicle of the sixteenth century, Oviedo wrote about the explorers of the New World. He praised the actions of men like Christopher Columbus and to a lesser extent, Hernando Cortés; however, he vilified the greed, capriciousness, superstition, and stupidity of others. One of his targets was Juan Ponce de León.

Juan Ponce de León seeking the spring of eternal youth, 1512. The illustration is from Herbert E. Bolton, *Arredondo's Historical Proof of Spain's Title to Georgia* (Berkeley: University of California Press, 1925). Courtesy of State Archives of Florida, Florida Memory.

22 · J. Michael Francis

St. Augustine Fountain of Youth postcard. The search for eternal youth has long intrigued Florida visitors and has become an enduring part of popular culture. Courtesy of Augustine.org.

According to Oviedo, Ponce was a vain and credulous man, prone to pursue silly ventures that enhanced his own ego, no matter the cost. To illustrate this point, Oviedo claimed that a group of Indians in the Caribbean had deceived Ponce and his followers, leading them to believe that an enchanted spring was hidden somewhere in the islands of Bimini (the Bahamas) and that its waters made men young again. Convinced the rumors were true, Ponce and his men wandered aimlessly among the islands for six months, Oviedo claimed.

Continuing to mock Ponce's gullibility, Oviedo claimed that he himself had witnessed firsthand how old men could turn young, something that was achieved without the assistance of any fountain; rather, the transformation was caused simply by a weakening of the brain, which made grown men behave like boys who possessed little reason or understanding. This, Oviedo claimed, was precisely what had happened to Ponce de León.

If Oviedo initiated the link between Ponce and a search for the fabled fountain, another Spanish chronicler, Antonio de Herrera y Tordesillas, reinforced the connection. Herrera's 1601 chronicle provides the most detailed account of Ponce's 1513 voyage and appears to have been based in part on now-lost original accounts of the expedition. Often labeled as one of the great plagiarists of the early modern era (a practice that was in fact common among virtually all early modern chroniclers), Herrera borrowed liberally from previous chroniclers like Oviedo and, most likely, Escalante's captivity narrative. Since the publication of Herrera's chronicle, scores of modern writers have repeated, distorted, and often exaggerated the association between Ponce's 1513 expedition and the Fountain of Youth. Over time, what began as myth has slowly transformed into historical fact.

If he was not searching for the fountain, why then did Ponce embark on such a costly expedition? Simply put, Ponce wanted to be compensated for having been forced to surrender the governorship of Puerto Rico in 1511. With no political future in the Spanish territories of Puerto Rico or Cuba, Ponce had to seek fame and fortune elsewhere. Rumors of rich islands to the northwest of Puerto Rico led the disgruntled Ponce to negotiate with King Ferdinand for the rights and privileges of a new conquest expedition. Like so many of his contemporaries, he expected these new territories to yield wealth, titles, power, and prestige. He was never searching for a magical elixir that promised to restore his youth.

Of course, I am not the first historian to challenge the veracity of the Fountain of Youth story and its connection to Ponce de León's expeditions to Florida. Over the past century, numerous scholars have attempted to dismantle the narrative, all to little avail. In 1935, historian Frederick Davis blamed modern writers for the fable. In 1965, Luís Rafael Arana not only contested the claim about Ponce's quest but added that there was no evidence that Ponce was even aware of the story.

In 1992, Douglas T. Peck blasted previous historians for "perverting" the "factual past" in favor of the Fountain of Youth fable. And there were others. Most recently, Tony Horwitz's witty satire, *A Voyage Long and Strange on the Trail of Vikings, Conquistadors, Lost Colonists, and Other Adventurers in Early America*, presented the Fountain of Youth story as one of many contemporary historical hoaxes, aimed not to inform but rather to entertain, deceive, and relieve unsuspecting tourists of their spending money.

As Florida's most enduring popular myth, one might argue the tale has become so deeply woven into the fabric of Florida's collective identity that it has now transcended myth. It has become an integral part of Florida's past, especially over the last 150 years. I think there is some truth to that claim, and I do not advocate a campaign to dismantle it. We can learn a great deal from studying myths, how they evolve and transform, and why they persist. At the same time, the inherent danger is that myth will overshadow history. In the end, the central problem with fables such as the Fountain of Youth is that they tend to simplify and trivialize the past and hamper the opportunity to move beyond myth to share Florida's real past.

From the earliest contact in the sixteenth century, Florida's history became part of a global tale, one that extended into the vast Caribbean, across the Atlantic to the Iberian Peninsula and the rest of Europe. It became intimately connected to Africa and the slave trade. Goods from Asia circulated throughout the province.

Despite their declining numbers, Florida's disparate Indian populations always outnumbered Europeans and Africans. For more than three centuries, European, African (both free and enslaved), and Indian men and women interacted. And like all human affairs, their relationships were complex and messy. At various times, Florida's early inhabitants fought, negotiated, traded, competed, celebrated, married, raised families, exploited, and cohabited. Violent clashes occurred, but so did long periods of peace and coexistence. Tragedy blended with triumph, and events unfolded in unpredictable ways, often with surprising outcomes.

Ultimately, Florida's "real" history is far richer and, dare I say it, entertaining, than the mythical tale of an aging conquistador on a failed quest to locate a magical river whose restorative waters would bring him good health and perpetual youth.

We know the myth; it's time to share the history.

From the **Fall 2011** edition of *FORUM* magazine, "¡Viva Florida! Marking 500 Years of Spanish Heritage."

3

The Real First Thanksgiving

Half a century earlier—and 1,200 miles south—a feast of gratitude.

Michael Gannon

Michael Gannon (1927–2017) was a Distinguished Service Professor Emeritus of History at the University of Florida, where he taught for thirty-six years. He authored more than a dozen books, notably on Florida history and the history of World War II. He was named a Knight Commander of the Order of Isabella the Catholic by Spain's King Juan Carlos I. He also received Florida Humanities' inaugural Lifetime Literary Achievement Award in 2017. He grew up in St. Augustine.

The popular story promoted by Anglo-American historians holds that the first thanksgiving ceremony in what is now the United States took place as a harvest festival in 1621 at the English "Pilgrim Fathers" settlement of Plymouth in Massachusetts.

Each November, American schoolchildren dress up in black-and-white costumes meant to recall such iconic Pilgrim figures as William Bradford, Miles Standish, and Priscilla Mullins Alden. Their mothers and grandmothers prepare Thanksgiving dinners of turkey, dressing, gravy, cranberry sauce, and assorted vegetables, breads, and desserts.

But this was not the nation's first thanksgiving meal. Fifty-six years earlier, Europeans and Natives shared a thanksgiving service and a communal meal in St. Augustine, Florida. These stand as the first documented thanksgiving events in a permanent settlement anywhere in North America north of Mexico.

On September 8, 1565, Spanish admiral Pedro Menéndez de Avilés landed in St. Augustine amidst aborigines of the Seloy tribe. Accompanying him were 500 soldiers, 200 sailors, and 100 civilian farmers and craftsmen, some with wives and children. Following the admiral's claim of La Florida on behalf of his monarch Philip II, the fleet chaplain, Father Francisco López de Mendoza Grajales, celebrated a Mass of Thanksgiving for the expedition's safe arrival. Menendez's brother-in-law Gonzalo Solís de Merás recorded that, following the Mass, "the Admiral had the Indians fed and dined himself."

I have long conjectured in print that the meal laid out on that September 8 was *cocido*, a stew made from salted pork and garbanzo beans, laced with garlic seasoning, and accompanied by hard sea biscuits and red wine. This is based on information supplied by historian Eugene Lyon on what constituted the food stores of Spanish ships at the time.

There is nothing in the record to say how all that went down in Native tummies. Perhaps the Seloy people contributed food of their own, either fresh or smoked. If so, they may have limited their palates to dishes with which they were familiar. We know from archaeological remains that their diet included deer, gopher

Spanish admiral Pedro Menéndez de Avilés. The engraving by José Camarón y Boronat was published by Francisco de Paula Marti in 1791. Courtesy of Georgetown University Fine Print Collection.

tortoise, shark, drum, mullet, and sea catfish. In the plant food column we can list maize, beans, and squash, along with nuts, fruits, and miscellaneous greens. (These findings come from analyses by zooarchaeologist Elizabeth Reitz and paleoethnobotanist Margaret Scarry.)

It is very difficult to get the powdered-wig states to the north of Florida to recognize St. Augustine's priority among American cities. Even historians and journalists, particularly those of an Anglo-American bent, seem reluctant to accord any special stature to that dark-haired community, which was set in place one year following the death of Michelangelo and the birth of William Shakespeare.

On November 24, 2004, the *New York Times* ran an op-ed piece by historian Charles C. Mann, who stated, "Until the arrival of the Mayflower, continental drift had kept North America and Europe apart for hundreds of millions of years. Plymouth Colony (and its less successful predecessor in Jamestown) reunited the continents."

I sent a letter to the *Times*: "By the dates when Jamestown and Plymouth were founded, St. Augustine, Florida, was up for urban renewal. It was a city with a fort, church, marker, college seminary, six-bed hospital, and 120 shops and homes."

Writing in *Smithsonian* magazine in February 2006, Mr. Mann graciously conceded: "In September 1565, Pedro Menéndez de Avilés led about 800 Spaniards to colonize St. Augustine. The landing party celebrated their arrival, inviting the local Indians—an act of religious thanksgiving in a permanent settlement that included both Natives and newcomers. Sounds like Thanksgiving to me!"

The *Times*, meanwhile, went bounding off to even farther fields, deciding in its May 25, 2006, edition that the first permanent European settlement in the United States was none of the above. "If any place deserves to be known as the nation's birthplace," the *Times* intoned, "it is New York [City]." The evidence adduced for this preposterous assertion was that in 1609 Henry Hudson and Samuel de Champlain made exploratory voyages in nearby waters. Sometimes the reader does not know whether to laugh or cry.

But no one is beyond redemption. Just as Mr. Mann eventually looked south to Florida like a prodigal son, so too, the *Times* came home to America's birthplace. On July 9, a staff writer declared for the ages (or at least for future editors):

> The Spanish didn't just explore, they settled, creating the first permanent European settlement in the continental United States at St. Augustine, Fla., in 1565, ... Spaniards also held a thanksgiving, 56 years before the Pilgrims, when they feasted near St. Augustine with Florida Indians, probably on stewed pork and garbanzo beans.

So all's well again on that particular history front. Happy Thanksgiving meals to all. And don't forget the garbanzo beans.

Facing: The First Thanksgiving, St. Augustine, 1565, as envisioned in this painting by Michael Rosato. Courtesy of Florida Museum of Natural History.

From the **Fall 2006** edition of *FORUM* magazine, "Feast Yourself on Florida."

4

Uncovering Fort Mose

In America's first free Black town, enslaved Africans found sanctuary and liberty.

Kathleen Deagan

Kathleen Deagan is Distinguished Research Curator of Archaeology Emerita and the Emerita Lockwood Professor of Florida and Caribbean Archaeology at the University of Florida, where she is an Alumna of Outstanding Distinction. Her research focus is the archaeology of the Spanish colonial period in Florida and the Caribbean. She is author of eight books and more than seventy scientific papers, a recipient of the Society for Historical Archaeology's J. C. Harrington Award for Lifetime Distinction, and a member of the American Academy of Arts and Sciences and the Academia de História de la República Dominicana.

Image: Archaeologist Kathleen Deagan and collaborator screen Fort Mose soil for artifacts, mid-1980s. Courtesy of Florida Museum of Natural History, Historical Archaeology Collections.

FORT MOSE, Gracia Real de Santa Teresa de Mose, was the first legally sanctioned free Black town in the United States, built near St. Augustine in 1738 by once-enslaved Africans. Their fight for freedom embodied in the history of Mose highlights a facet of the African American colonial experience that is dramatically different from the more familiar story of slavery, oppression, and passivity.

Until the site of Fort Mose (pronounced Mosay) was unearthed through a controversial archaeological project that began in 1985, few Floridians, and even fewer people outside of Florida, had ever heard of the free African American colonial town. Several distinguished historians, including Luis Arana, Irene Wright, and John Tepaske, had written scholarly articles about Mose, but it remained a quaint footnote to Florida history. For most people, the story of Mose was buried as deeply as the physical remnants of the site itself.

I first became aware of Fort Mose in 1971 as a first-year graduate student at the University of Florida. That was when F. F. "Jack" Williams, a longtime resident of St. Augustine, contacted Charles Fairbanks, the late professor of archaeology, to do a test project on a piece of Williams's property that he believed to be the site of Fort Mose. Fairbanks and his students (including me) tested the site and uncovered eighteenth-century artifacts that could very likely have been left there by the residents of Fort Mose.

Like most people who first hear the story of Fort Mose, I was captivated and intrigued, returning to the site again in 1976, this time as an assistant professor at Florida State University with another group of students. The results of that project convinced us that the Williams site was, in fact, Fort Mose.

It was not until 1985 that our efforts to secure support for the excavation of Fort Mose were successful. That year, then–Florida State Representative Bill Clark of Fort Lauderdale visited the site and was moved and impressed by its importance to African American history. Clark introduced a bill in the Florida legislature to provide funds for the historical and scientific study of Fort Mose as well as for the dissemination of that information to the public.

Fort Mose, 1752. The fort was rebuilt at this slightly different site from the original, on a creek surrounded by agricultural fields. Courtesy of Florida Museum of Natural History.

The Spanish sanctuary policy, not entirely altruistic, dealt an economic and psychological blow to the English, as it enhanced the economic and defensive resources of the Spanish colony. The refugees had valuable skills and trades to offer, and many of the Africans proved to be fierce and effective fighters.

We devoted the first six months of the project to documentary research in Spanish archives. Like most historical archaeologists, we did not want to destroy any part of our site by excavation in order to learn things that could be found less destructively in documents. Historian Jane Landers, then a doctoral student in history at the University of Florida and now a professor of history at Vanderbilt University, spent countless hours in the Archive of the Indies in Seville, Spain, doing her own kind of historical "excavation."

Most researchers had assumed there would be little direct information about the people of Fort Mose in the documents since it was thought they were both non-literate and non-elite. But Landers, by combining her own skill and enthusiasm with the questions asked of her by archaeologists, unearthed an unexpectedly rich record of both the people and the site of Mose.

Fort Mose came into being as a consequence of extended Anglo-Spanish conflict over the "debatable lands" between St. Augustine and the Carolinas, provoked by the establishment of Charleston in 1670. African Americans figured in these conflicts from the beginning as they escaped from slavery on Carolina plantations, allied themselves with the Yamasee Indians, and moved, not infrequently, across the borders of Spanish- and English-claimed territories.

In 1687 a group of fugitives including eight men, two women, and a small child arrived in St. Augustine. There they were given sanctuary and protection from extradition on the basis of their religious conversion. By 1693 the Spanish Crown decreed that all such escaped fugitives would be given sanctuary and eventually freedom in Spanish Florida if they converted to Catholicism. Enslaved Africans in the English colonies moved swiftly to take advantage of this opportunity, and increasing numbers successfully made the dangerous and difficult journey to Florida through the late seventeenth and early eighteenth centuries.

The Spanish sanctuary policy, not entirely altruistic, dealt an economic and psychological blow to the English, as it enhanced the economic and defensive resources of the Spanish colony. The refugees had valuable skills and trades to offer, and many of the Africans proved to be fierce and effective fighters.

By 1738 more than 100 refugees had arrived in St. Augustine. That year the town and fort of Gracia Real de Santa Teresa de Mose was formally established about two miles north of the Castillo de San Marcos of St. Augustine. Thirty-eight men, most of them married, formed the Fort Mose militia and lived at the fort. They were expected to farm their new lands as well as man their fort.

In 1740 the English–South Carolinian forces of General James Oglethorpe laid siege to St. Augustine, largely in response to the successful Spanish-aided African resistance to enslavement. Oglethorpe's troops captured Fort Mose. African, Indian, and Spanish forces soon recaptured the fort. But Mose was so badly damaged during the battle that its residents moved to St. Augustine, where they lived as soldiers, shopkeepers, bakers, blacksmiths, sailors, cattlemen, and, in at least one case, a Spanish privateer.

In 1752, when Fort Mose was reestablished and a second, larger fort was rebuilt close to the location of the first, the Mose people returned to the site.

In 1759 there were twenty-two households and sixty-seven residents at this second site of Fort Mose, including thirty-seven men, fifteen women, and fifteen children. The community represented a diverse ethnic-linguistic group. The residents of Mose included Congos, Carabalis, Minas, Gambas, Lecumis, Sambas, Gangas, Araras, and Guineans. Many of them had lived among the English and Yamasee. Mose must have been a remarkably polyglot community, incorporating a wide variety of languages and cultural traditions.

These people lived and worked at Mose until 1763, when, by the Treaty of Paris, Florida became a British colony. The thirty-four families then at Mose joined the Spanish evacuation and left for Cuba with the rest of the Florida colonists. There they became homesteaders on another rough frontier in Matanzas.

We began our excavation of Fort Mose in 1986, armed with Landers's information and eager to uncover the details of the cultural practices of the Mose residents. Working with descriptions of the site, historical maps, and NASA multispectral imagery, we were able to demonstrate conclusively that the Williams property was, beyond a doubt, the site of the second Fort Mose. The remnants of the first fort were nearby, submerged in the marsh mud but still visible to the NASA sensors.

Today the site of the second fort and town is an isolated marsh island of about three acres surrounded by tidal-flooded mud flats. The land was not always a marsh; in 1887–1888 Henry Flagler did extensive soil dredging around Fort Mose and used the soil to fill the swampy area that became the site of his famous Hotel Ponce de León. Today it is St. Augustine's Flagler College.

The fort was located on a long-occupied Indian shell midden and escaped the dredge but is threatened both by rising sea levels and modern construction.

The site on which the people of Mose built their second settlement was occupied almost continuously from about 1000 BCE through the end of the colonial era in 1821. The eleven-year Mose occupation is represented by a thin layer of soil and shell between 5 and 15 centimeters thick embedded within a shell midden 1.5 meter deep (about 4 feet). Isolating the precious Mose deposits was thus a slow and painstaking process requiring the excavation of shell layers in individual 5-centimeter increments so as not inadvertently to mix the materials from Mose with those from earlier or later occupations.

Excavations revealed construction details of the moat, the earthwork curtain walls of the fort, and the posts from large and small interior wood-post structures. A small circular wood and thatch structure, some 12 feet in diameter, was thought to be one of Mose's domestic residences and is very similar in form and probable construction to both Florida Indian and African prototypes.

The lives of the people who lived at Mose are reflected in shards of English, Indian, and Spanish pottery; lead shot and gunflints; rum-bottle fragments, pipe stems, and nails; and a few beads, buttons, and buckles. They ate mostly fish,

Boardwalk at Fort Mose Historic State Park. The original site of Fort Mose has been transformed into the park with a museum, visitor center, hiking trails, kayak access, and more. Courtesy of TotallyStAugustine.com.

Uncovering Fort Mose · 31

The lives of the people who lived at Mose are reflected in shards of English, Indian, and Spanish pottery; lead shot and gunflints; rum-bottle fragments, pipe stems, and nails; and a few beads, buttons, and buckles.

shellfish, and locally available game, supplemented occasionally with pork or beef from St. Augustine. No plant foods have survived, but they must have been an important part of the diet.

Other items, relegated to the trash heaps, were probably thrown into the creek adjacent to the site. One of the most evocative artifacts from Mose, a small handmade silver medallion, came from the creek. It depicts St. Christopher on one side and bears a design on the other side that is reminiscent of the mariner's compass rose.

We know that conversion to Catholicism was a condition of freedom for the Mose residents, and some of the glass beads may have been used in rosaries. Although no items directly suggesting African influence have yet been recovered, it is quite likely that some of the European or Indian items could have been used in ways that combined African and Catholic traditions in the manner of so many Afro-Caribbean traditions today. We, as archaeologists, have simply not yet learned how to recognize these in the mute material record.

Only a small portion of the Mose site was excavated in the two years of fieldwork carried out there. One reason was the difficult logistical challenges posed by the site itself. Both the conditions of access and the delicacy of isolating the short Mose occupation required slower-than-usual excavation strategies. Other reasons were political. Some segments of the St. Augustine community claimed this site was not Fort Mose. They maintained the fort was located elsewhere and charged the project was misusing grant funds to create a "revisionist history."

This challenge made it imperative to demonstrate beyond a doubt that this site was, in fact, the Fort Mose shown in maps and described in documents. Because of

Replicas of artifacts found on the sites of Fort Mose in St. Johns County, dating to the mid-18th century. Photo by Kristen Grace, courtesy of the Florida Museum of Natural History at the University of Florida.

32 · Kathleen Deagan

this, our work concentrated on uncovering the structural features of the fort more intensively than we might otherwise have done; in addition, the excavations at the site were suspended sooner than expected because of local legal challenges to the purchase of the site by the state of Florida.

Recently, however, as rising coastal waters are eroding the site, archaeologists from Flagler College and the University of Florida have resumed excavations to recover information about the daily lives and practices of the Mose people. That work is ongoing.

In 1987 the Florida Museum of Natural History developed a 2,000-square-foot exhibit on Fort Mose that toured the United States from 1989 to 1999. This was the longest tour in the museum's history, and more than seven million people learned about Mose and its message. Curriculum materials, articles, and videos on Mose have been incorporated into public school lessons on Florida history.

In 1994, through vigorous lobbying by the African American community in St. Augustine and the efforts of Representative Clark, the site of Mose was purchased by the state and became part of the Florida Park System.

In 1994, through vigorous lobbying by the African American community in St. Augustine and the efforts of Representative Clark, the site of Mose was purchased by the state and became part of the Florida Park System. In 1996 it was designated a National Historic Landmark and in 2019 was named as a UNESCO Slave Trade site. Since then, fundraising efforts have enabled the construction of a site museum, with multimedia exhibits telling the story of Mose. Park visitors can view the fort site from a boardwalk that snakes through the marsh.

The consequences of these events for the St. Augustine community have been dramatic. The Fort Mose Historical Society was formed in 1995 and is a vitally active organization. It has brought Black and white residents of St. Augustine together in a common cause: protecting, promoting, and interpreting this remarkable site and its story.

Such an alliance would have been difficult to envision in St. Augustine, a community with a troubled history of race relations, even a few decades ago when knowledge of Fort Mose existed only in the pages of scholarly journals.

Most archaeologists hope that their excavations will produce new theoretical principles about culture or new insights into obscure scientific questions of change. I count myself among them, but I also feel the archaeology at Fort Mose has produced far more important results. It provides a tangible symbol of free African American history, self-determination, and active participation in colonial American life that is just as real as the story of slavery.

From the **Spring 2005** edition of *FORUM* magazine, "St. Augustine: An Ancient City in a State of Change."

5

He Persisted

Francisco Menéndez escaped slavery, became a militia leader, and then did it all again.

Darcie A. MacMahon

Rarely does such a luminary character as Francisco Menéndez emerge out of the tattered pages of history. The story of this multilingual African man who escaped slavery, led a militia, and talked his way out of trouble has been pieced together from scattered colonial documents that are nearly 300 years old. His amazing story is testimony to the bravery, perseverance, and contributions of free Black people in Spanish Florida.

Menéndez was born a Mandinga (Mandinka) in West Africa; he was enslaved and taken to English Carolina. He escaped and lived among the Yamassee Indians for several years, fighting with them against the English.

In 1724 he arrived in St. Augustine. From there his story unfolds, as pieced together through the painstaking work of historian Jane Landers, who has searched through sources as diverse as military, church, and court records in the archives of Spain, Cuba, and Florida. The fragile and disparate nature of the documents makes it even more astonishing that one person's story could possibly take shape.

Menéndez went to St. Augustine to take advantage of a Spanish policy that offered freedom to English-enslaved Africans who escaped to Florida and converted to Catholicism. He requested this religious sanctuary. But along with some other refugees from English Carolina, he was double-crossed by a Yamassee known as "Mad Dog" and sold to the Spaniards in exchange for liquor and corn.

St. Augustine's governor then sold the escapees to leading community members, convinced he should do so to compensate the British financially for losing their enslaved workers. Menéndez was enslaved to the royal accountant Don Francisco Menéndez Márquez, from whom he likely acquired his Spanish name.

The Spaniards must have quickly recognized Menéndez's leadership skills, because in 1726 they appointed him commander of a militia of enslaved Africans. (Black militia, both enslaved and free, were common throughout the Spanish colonies.) While serving as militia commander, Menéndez persisted in seeking his freedom. Finally in 1738, following a petition supported by a Yamassee leader's

---

Darcie A. MacMahon is associate director and the director of exhibits and public programs at the Florida Museum of Natural History, Gainesville, where she oversees the museum's overall public experience. She is the coauthor of *Fort Mose: Colonial America's Black Fortress of Freedom* with the museum's Distinguished Research Curator Emerita Kathleen Deagan.

Image: Plano de la ciudad y puerto de San Agustin de la Florida, by Tomás López de Vargas Machuca, Madrid 1783. WIKI.

Above left: A handwritten royal proclamation by Spain's King Charles II in 1693 on the status of enslaved people who had escaped from the English colonies and made their way to St. Augustine. He wrote, "…giving liberty to all…the men as well as the women …so that by their example and by my liberality others will do the same.…" Courtesy of the P.K. Yonge Library of Florida History, University of Florida.
Above right: Freedman and military leader Francisco Menéndez. Courtesy of Florida Museum of Natural History.

commendations and moral justifications, a new governor granted his request, along with thirty others re-enslaved.

At that point more than 100 escapees had arrived in St. Augustine. The governor decided to send these men, women, and children to establish a new fort and town in a frontier area two miles north of St. Augustine's Castillo de San Marcos. They called this new settlement Gracia Real de Santa Teresa de Mose, and it became known as Fort Mose. The men were members of the Mose militia, and all vowed to be "the most cruel enemies of the English" and to spill their "last drop of blood in defense of the Great Crown of Spain and the Holy Faith." Menéndez, who was made militia captain, was recognized as community leader, and the residents at Mose were called his "subjects."

Two years later the English attacked St. Augustine, and though Fort Mose was destroyed, the Mose militia played an important role in defeating the English. After

Somehow, against all odds, Menéndez either escaped or argued his way back to Spanish Florida. The word "determined" does not do him justice.

this victory, Menéndez directly petitioned Spain's king for a salary, sending two letters written and signed in his own hand (not with the "X" customarily signed by illiterate correspondents). He argued that he had worked with "loyalty, zeal, and love" and had "been continually at arms, and assisted in the maintenance of the bastions, without the least royal expense . . . to defend the Holy Evangel and sovereignty of the Crown." Florida's governor also recommended Menéndez to the king, recognizing him for both his military and civilian valor. But as far as we know, the king never replied.

These letters are more than evocative, written by a man who only a few years before escaped English enslavement and navigated the politics and customs of Spanish Florida well enough to write in Spanish with a flourish, achieve military and social recognition, and pursue fair treatment directly with the king.

Menéndez joined government-sanctioned corsair (privateer) efforts, which aimed to seize much-needed supplies from ships and ports of other nations.

But during a 1741 corsair mission, he was captured by the English ship *Revenge*. Upon discovering his identity, his captors tied him to a gun and threatened castration in retaliation for atrocities against the English at Mose.

Menéndez and his fellow captives countered that Indians committed the atrocities. Menéndez further explained that he enlisted as a corsair in order to reach Havana and then find a way to Spain to seek compensation for his services. But the English still gave him 200 lashes and "pickled him" (brining the wounds). Then they re-enslaved him in the Bahamas.

Back in St. Augustine, a second Fort Mose was built in 1752. The former residents moved back, along with other refugees more recently arrived. Incredibly, Menéndez shows up in the records as commander.

Somehow, against all odds, Menéndez either escaped or argued his way back to Spanish Florida. The word "determined" does not do him justice.

The only known census of the Mose community, from 1759, lists Menéndez as age forty-five and married to Ana Maria de Escovar, age thirty-nine, also from English Carolina. At that time the community had twenty-two households and a total population of sixty-seven.

In 1763 Spain ceded Florida to England, and the Florida colonists moved to Cuba. Menéndez, his wife and four dependants, and others from Mose and elsewhere were granted land in Matanzas Province, where they fashioned a new community called San Agustín de la Nueva Florida. But finding undue hardships, some of them, including Menéndez, moved to Havana. There his trail goes cold, at least for now. Historian Landers continues to comb the documents for more of his story.

From the **Fall 2011** edition of *FORUM* magazine, "¡Viva Florida! Marking 500 Years of Spanish Heritage."

6

How Seashells Saved St. Augustine

This modest mollusk displayed a secret strength.

Michael Gannon

Michael Gannon's biography is found on page 25.

Image: The mollusk species *Donax variabilis*, commonly known as coquina shells, add varied coloration to the coquina formations found along the eastern coast of Florida. Photo by Debivort, Wikimedia.

As I write these words in my study, I pass my hands over the sharp-edged chunk of shell rock that I found when, as a boy, I explored the battlements and grounds of Spain's never-conquered castle, Castillo de San Marcos, in St. Augustine. I have vivid memories of climbing about the castle's cannon and letting my imagination soar as I pictured its major battles. When I rowed my boat past the old fortress to cast a net for mullet or shrimp, I envisioned gunners, musketeers, and pikemen in its embrasures, ready to fight me off if I ventured to be as foolish as the British siege forces who attempted in vain to crack those stout defenses.

The tall walls and frowning parapets of Florida's genuine castle, though pounded by hundreds of cannonballs from English guns in the 1700s, never shattered. No amount of bombardment from the artillery of that period could breach them. Why? Because the walls and parapets were constructed from resilient seashells, tiny calcified shells forged over many millennia into shell rock that the Spaniards quarried from Anastasia Island, the long, narrow barrier island that separates St. Augustine from the sea.

To understand how this unlikely urban armor originated we have to go back roughly two million years to what geologists call the Cenozoic Era. It was then that violent ocean storms threw up banks of small shells and shell fragments on beaches at four sites: Anastasia Island; Washington Oaks State Park, below Crescent Beach; Jupiter Beach; and, outside Florida, on the west coast of Africa. The shells had been formed by a tiny mollusk known technically as donax. When the storm waters receded and sand covered the shell marl, the tightly compressed mixture of calcium carbonate and sand eventually hardened to form a compact fossiliferous limestone, on the surface of which individual, whole, or broken shells were massively visible.

The existence of this stone was not known to St. Augustine's founder, Pedro Menéndez de Avilés, whose 800 Spanish settlers in 1565 established themselves on the mainland opposite the island and christened their habitat La Ciudad de

San Agustín. Initially their homes and public buildings were of wattle and daub construction because, as the fleet chaplain complained, "stone is nowhere to be found." In 1583, however, Timucuan Natives of the district took a Spanish detail to the island and showed how, by digging through the sandy topsoil, vast quantities of shell rock were exposed.

For lack of the proper tools to quarry and move the stone, the Timucuans had not made use of it in their buildings. Neither now did the Spaniards in theirs, for the same reason. But this changed ninety-two years later when necessity lent them invention and determination. The necessity was a fortress capable of surviving both weather and British gunfire. By 1672, no fewer than nine wooden forts had stood at St. Augustine, two on the island and the remainder on the mainland. All but one had been burned or had rotted away in the water table and rains. Now, with the city a helpless victim to a British pirate raid in 1668 and newly threatened by the founding two years later of British Charles Towne (Charleston) just 250 miles to the north, Governor Manuel de Cendoya, "with spade in hand," broke ground for a durable fortress to be built entirely of Anastasia shell rock, which the Spaniards by that date called coquina.

With axes and picks, pry bars and wedges, Spanish engineers and workers cut out rectangular slabs of the calcified shells and placed them on the beds of ox-drawn wagons. The labor force consisted mainly of impressed (though paid) Florida and Georgia coastal-isle Natives, Spanish convicts and English prisoners, and enslaved Africans. When first quarried, the rock was light yellow and spongy; it gradually darkened and hardened somewhat after being in the open air and the sun. Taken to the water's edge, the rock slabs were lightered across Matanzas River to the construction

In 1583, however, Timucuan Natives of the district took a Spanish detail to the island and showed how, by digging through the sandy topsoil, vast quantities of shell rock were exposed.

Coquina is made up of seashells, typically clam and snail, ground down in seawater over time. It became an important colonial building material. Coquina's high porosity gives it a spongy appearance and a surprising ability to absorb cannonball fire. Wikimedia Commons.

St. Augustine's Castillo de San Marcos. Photo by Stacey Sather. Courtesy of FloridasHistoricCoast.com.

site, which was set high on a plateau of earth. There, other workmen operating chains and pulleys raised the slabs, one on top of another, and joined them with a quick-setting lime mortar fashioned in two nearby kilns from oyster shells.

By 1695, twenty-three years after the dedicatory spade, the castle was substantially complete. It was a square structure with jutting diamond-shaped bastions at its four corners, a design originated by the great French military engineer Sébastien le Prestre Vauban (1633–1707). Its 20-foot-high bastions and walls (curtains) were 16 feet thick at their base, narrowing to 9 feet at their tops, where the parapets bristled with cannon. To prevent the intrusion of moisture, the entire exterior was finished with off-white lime stucco. A decorative red band ran around the upper surface.

Cannonading the castillo was akin to tossing bowling balls into mud.

In November 1702, just as the Spaniards feared, St. Augustine was invaded by an 800-man force of Englishmen and Indians from Carolina. The entire population of the city, 1,500 souls, took refuge in the castle, bringing with them personal belongings and cattle; the cattle were placed in the moat from which seawater had been withdrawn. Colonel James Moore, commanding the attackers, set up an artillery battery to the south of the castillo and began a bombardment that he was confident would breach the castle walls.

But to the surprise of Englishman and Spaniard alike, the coquina possessed an entirely unanticipated property. Still relatively soft, it did not fracture when hit by a cannonball. It absorbed the ball. Cannonading the castillo was akin to tossing bowling balls into mud. One can easily imagine Moore stamping his feet in frustration. Some of the balls rolled off the coquina surface. Others stuck in the stone. At the end of a day the castle looked like a chocolate chip cookie. The Spaniards recycled the English cannonballs and sent them back with prejudice.

After fifty fruitless days of siege, Moore and his force withdrew to Carolina, thoroughly humiliated by seashells. And one would have thought that no further English attempt would be made to reduce this particular castle by artillery. But, no, another English war maker named James Oglethorpe, governor of the new colony of Georgia, a man who seems to have learned few lessons from 1702, came south thirty-eight years later to try conclusions with the same fortress, and with exactly the same results. Oglethorpe had more cannons, thirty to Moore's four, and cannonballs of heavier weight. But his battering fire had just as little effect. Wrote one of his officers, the native rock "will not splinter but will give way to cannon ball as though you would stick a knife into cheese." After twenty-seven days of siege, Oglethorpe, too, slunk home in disgrace. Once again the seashells ruled.

That 310-year-old structure still stands tall but now shows considerable wear. The years and the wind and rainfall have almost entirely eroded its original stucco finish, allowing moisture to threaten the stability of the naked coquina. To preserve the rock, the National Park Service continues to apply various preservation treatments to protect the fort and the coquina stone.

If you want to see the unshielded coquina, like the chunk I hold here in my hand, you would be well advised to visit the castillo. Touch the seashells—and imagine!

From the **Spring 2005** edition of *FORUM* magazine, "St. Augustine: An Ancient City in a State of Change."

Cache of cannonballs, Castillo de San Marco, 1880s. Courtesy of State Archives of Florida, Florida Memory.

7

On the Backs of the Enslaved

How Middle Florida and its planter class built wealth and power.

Larry Eugene Rivers

Larry Eugene Rivers is a Distinguished Professor of History at Florida A&M University, former president of Fort Valley (Georgia) State University, and the author or coauthor of eight books, including *Slavery in Florida: Territorial Days to Emancipation* and *Rebels and Runaways: Slave Resistance in Nineteenth-Century Florida*. His latest book is *Father James Page: An Enslaved Preacher's Climb to Freedom*.

Image: Plantation scene, circa 1870. Five years after the end of the Civil War, agricultural laborers pick cotton. Courtesy of State Archives of Florida, Florida Memory.

DURING THE TWENTY-FIVE YEARS leading up to the Civil War, a five-county region of north Florida grew into a virtual barony of plantations and farms that echoed the wealthiest precincts of the Old South cotton kingdom. The vast majority of Florida's enslaved Africans lived in this central part of the Panhandle along the Georgia border. Called "Middle Florida," it centered on the capital city of Tallahassee and included Gadsden, Leon, Jefferson, Madison, and Hamilton Counties and eventually expanded into central Florida's Alachua and Marion Counties.

Middle Florida holders of enslaved Africans were pioneer entrepreneurs from Old South states who migrated to Florida after it became a US territory in 1821. Many hailed from the cream of southern planter society. Coming from Kentucky, Maryland, Virginia, North Carolina, South Carolina, and Georgia, they settled on the rich, fertile land between the Apalachicola and Suwannee Rivers and established farms and plantations primarily to grow cotton. By 1860 this area, virtually unpopulated by whites before 1821, had emerged as the state's plantation belt.

Middle Florida's economy was based firmly on slavery. Nearly all of the enslaved Africans (98 percent) were involved in agricultural labor. Most of them worked on large plantations established by wealthy "planters," an elite class composed of farmers who had at least twenty enslaved workers and more than 500 acres. This planter class, 21 percent of Florida's slaveholders, held more than 75 percent of Florida's enslaved people.

The vast majority of Florida's slaveholders ran much smaller operations. They owned small or medium-size farms and enslaved fewer than ten people, often only one or two. Usually the enslaved at these farms worked alongside the white property owners on a variety of jobs and lived in small cabins near the main farmhouses.

The enslaved on the larger plantations, however, were divided up into job categories. Some worked according to a task system as carpenters, shoemakers, blacksmiths,

Left: Ambrose "Uncle Doug" Hilliard Douglass, circa 1938, postcard. Once enslaved, Douglass (1845–1940) is photographed at the Lewis Turpentine Still and Plantation in Brooksville. The still had been turned into an "Old South" tourist attraction by its proprietor, Pearce Lewis, in the 1930s. Douglass's story is among those captured in *A Folk History of Slavery in the United States from Interviews with Former Slaves*, typewritten records prepared by the Federal Writers Project, 1936–1938. *Right*: Charity Stewart, at ninety-three. This photo was taken in 1937, decades after her years in slavery. During the Civil War she was hidden in the swamps of Jefferson County to make soap for soldiers. Photos courtesy of State Archives of Florida, Florida Memory.

and so forth. But field hands (as opposed to house servants) were sorted into work "gangs." This "gang slavery" system, commonly associated with antebellum cotton culture, required each gang of slaves to routinely do one type of job, such as hoeing or plowing.

On the most fundamental level, the degree of harshness and oppression that marked an enslaved individual's life typically resulted from the nature of his or her master, his wife, and his relations. A bad master meant a bad life for slaves.

In 1860, on the eve of the Civil War, 44 percent of Florida's 140,400 residents were enslaved.

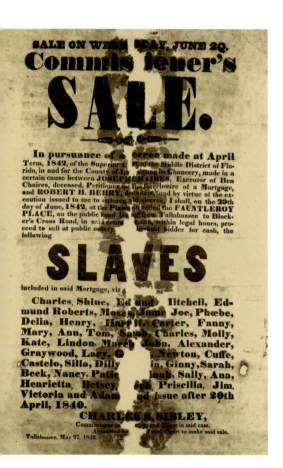

An advertisement of a slave sale in Leon County is dated May 27, 1842. Courtesy of State Archives of Florida, Florida Memory.

But there was also a common practice in the decades before the Civil War that involved leasing slaves to work on jobs outside of the owner's farm or plantation. Purchase of slaves for lease often was a part of estate planning. The state's early railroads, canals, and fortifications often owed their existence to the labor of leased bondsmen.

Cotton became the staple crop of choice in Middle Florida, just as it did in much of the lower South. Some farmers also grew other cash crops, such as tobacco and sugar; most also grew vegetables and other foods for their own use.

Some have argued that because violence rarely flared from the slave quarters of these plantations and farms, the enslaved generally were happy with their conditions. Not so. Ample evidence demonstrates slave resistance constantly plagued plantation operations, whether it involved feigned illness, sabotage, escaping, or whatever.

While Middle Florida offered the picture of a thriving and integral component of the cotton South, the other areas of east and west Florida retained some of the traditions and influences of the Spanish colonists who had controlled Florida during the previous 250 to 300 years. These areas, northeast Florida and portions of the peninsula as well as in the general area of Pensacola, tended to permit more flexibility, opportunity, and social mobility for the enslaved.

Interracial families were not uncommon. They sometimes were the result of forced relations, but recorded instances also hint at occasional romantic bonds and long-term commitments. Labor in east and west Florida varied, too, from Old South stereotypes. Enslaved people nursed, washed, and farmed, but they also engaged as stevedores, cow hunters, sailors, lumberjacks, and interpreters. Some slaves escaped and joined bands of Seminole Indians.

Most of Florida's population remained congregated in the northern part of the state until the end of the Second Seminole War in 1842. Then, to entice people to settle the lower part of the peninsula, the federal government offered an incentive plan: free 160-acre parcels of land to people who would move to the Florida frontier, south of Alachua County. The poorer Florida families, devastated by the bloody Seminole war, moved southward to take advantage of this free-land program. The property they left behind was then populated by more cotton planters, some from Middle Florida, others from southern cotton states.

Marion County and to a lesser extent Hernando County came to be dominated by South Carolinians in the 1850s. These planters brought with them a mindset that effectively extended the Middle Florida culture. Floridians moved ever closer to acceptance of Old South ideas and ideals. By the 1850s the political and economic power of Middle Florida planters in politics would grow in proportion to their landholdings and acquisition of enslaved Africans.

In 1860, on the eve of the Civil War, 44 percent of Florida's 140,400 residents were enslaved. After Abraham Lincoln was elected president in November 1860,

Tampa newspaper ad, 1860. Edmund Jones offers a reward for the return of "My Boy, NIMROD" to Jones's plantation. Courtesy of State Archives of Florida, Florida Memory.

the Florida legislature, dominated by the powerful Middle Florida planters, called for a secession convention in Tallahassee.

It came as a surprise to many in the state when delegates at that convention, most of them Middle Florida planters, voted to secede from the Union. Large numbers of Floridians proclaimed adherence to the United States, especially in east Florida.

The Civil War when it came produced a breakdown of slavery's foundations. While Middle Florida was left relatively secure during the war, Union military incursions resulted in major disruptions of the institution of slavery in east and west Florida. In the east, particularly, the proximity of Union troops held out a beacon of hope for freedom.

In time the coastal counties and the St. Johns River region, where federal gunboats patrolled, witnessed a steady stream of men, women, and children seeking freedom from bondage.

Union raiding parties also added to the toll elsewhere in the state, destroying Confederate properties, disrupting rebel operations—and liberating the enslaved. Many of those freed remained in Florida. Many also discovered that the protection of the US government did not mean a life of ease and comfort; conditions at refugee camps were tough, and white refugees always received preferential treatment.

Some slaves opted to serve in the Union Army or Navy. They participated in engagements large and small in battles both in and outside of Florida, fighting or serving as informants, guides, and river pilots. Many died fighting at places like Olustee and Natural Bridge.

The enslaved in northeast Florida and to a lesser extent in west Florida actively resisted slavery and showed their desire for a Union victory by joining the federal forces. Bond servants in Middle Florida did not have the same opportunities to escape and join Union forces. Still they tried to hinder the progress of the Confederacy in other ways.

Even on the Middle Florida plantations, which were geographically separated from the war zones, many bond servants tried to do their part from afar. In some instances they simply stopped cultivating corn and other crops for human consumption. Some slaves worked on the side of the Confederacy, but most did so as the result of impressment.

The enslaved did not rise and slay white families while the master was away at war; they refrained not from lack of opportunity but from innate decency and respect for life. Still, they began to create separate institutions such as churches and to depend upon themselves despite white expectations as they awaited the Day of Jubilee.

From the **Spring 2010** edition of FORUM magazine, "The Civil War: 'When Florida Opened Up the Gates of Hell.'"

8

Florida Gives Its All to the Civil War

Whatever their loyalties, few Floridians were spared the conflict's costs.

Robert A. Taylor

Robert A. Taylor is professor of history and dean of the College of Psychology and Liberal Arts at the Florida Institute of Technology. He served on the Florida Humanities Board of Directors for six years and is president emeritus of the Florida Historical Society. Taylor was recently co-editor of *The Governors of Florida*, which won the Florida Book Awards Gold Medal for Nonfiction.

Image: Black soldiers in the Union army, as depicted by artist John Rae. Black troops at the Battle of Olustee included the 54th Massachusetts regiment, celebrated in the 1989 movie *Glory*. Courtesy of State Archives of Florida, Florida Memory.

When Florida seceded from the Union, few doubted that the Confederate States of America would survive and prosper. Any attempts at coercion by the hated Yankees were sure to fail. If war did come it was certain to be easy, short, and of course, glorious.

The actual conflict almost began in Florida that fateful year of 1861. A tense stand-off almost came to gunfire between federals and rebels at Fort Pickens, located at the entrance of Pensacola Bay. But it was the firing on Fort Sumter near Charleston that commenced the hostilities.

Florida men of military age, and some who were not, flocked to join units bound for the greater Confederate army on the fighting fronts. Some 15,000 of the state's 140,400 inhabitants donned uniforms. This made Florida's manpower contribution to the Confederacy the largest per capita of any rebel state. Floridians soldiered in battles from Tennessee to Virginia, shedding their life's blood on fields in Chickamauga and Gettysburg. Others endured disease, poor and scanty food, and inadequate winter clothing in places far from warm Florida. Roughly 5,000 Floridians became war casualties, which was a high number for such a small state.

John Milton, a Jackson County planter, was Florida's wartime governor. Milton was devoted to the Southern cause and a firm believer in cooperation with the Confederate government in Richmond.

But he faced a dilemma. The Confederate high command called most of Florida's fighting men to serve outside the state at more strategically important rebel posts farther north, leaving Milton to figure out how to defend the state against Yankee attacks. By the late spring of 1862, the federals could claim control of much of Pensacola, St. Augustine, Fernandina, Key West, and Jacksonville (one of several Union occupations of that city). There were few men, and even fewer weapons, left anywhere in Florida. Richmond, with few exceptions, left Floridians militarily on their own for the duration.

Confederate water battery, February 1861. The Columbiad guns are arrayed at the entrance to Pensacola Bay. Courtesy of State Archives of Florida, Florida Memory.

The American cattle industry was born on Florida's piney prairies in the days of the Spanish conquistadors. By the 1850s, large herds of wild cows wandered central and southern Florida rivaling those in Texas. Cattlemen such as the legendary Jacob Summerlin sold cows to the Confederate government beginning in 1861. Summerlin eventually grew tired of being paid in Confederate scrip and, with his associates, turned to running cattle to Cuba in exchange for Spanish gold. But because beef was in such demand, the Confederates formed special cattle guard units, called the Cow Cavalry, to make sure the Florida herds got to the Georgia line. Through these efforts, vital rations were delivered to rebel troops in Tennessee and Charleston and to starving Union prisoners of war behind Andersonville's grim walls.

By 1865 Florida was an organized supply depot for the Confederate states. In fact, the system continued to function even after Lee's surrender at Appomattox Court House. Such productivity played no small role in helping Florida recover economically from the war at a faster rate than its blighted neighbor states.

A major reason Florida could be so generous with its resources during the war was the presence of many thousands of enslaved African Americans. These Floridians worked the farms, boiled the salt, and helped drive the cattle that went to the Confederacy. Their labors, mostly in the interior of the peninsula, were rarely disturbed by federal military operations. In the process, many were presented with opportunities to escape. Union soldiers and sailors offered them freedom, and many of the enslaved were forced to choose between freedom with strangers or continued bondage with family and friends.

...the Confederates formed special cattle guard units, called the Cow Cavalry, to make sure the Florida herds got to the Georgia line.

Francis Asbury Hendry (*back row, center*) was a captain of the First Florida Cow Cavalry. This photo, taken in about 1870, shows him with Seminole leaders. Hendry County is named after him. Courtesy of State Archives of Florida, Florida Memory.

Jacob Summerlin, "King of the Crackers," circa 1860s. The Florida cattle baron wearied of being paid in Confederate scrip for his cattle, so he began selling his cows to Cuba for Spanish gold. Summerlin (1820–1893) was documented as the first child born in Florida after the land was ceded to Spain. He was instrumental in founding the county seats of Orange and Polk Counties, in Orlando and Bartow. Courtesy of State Archives of Florida, Florida Memory.

The women of Florida also helped in great measure to keep the state's economy running under wartime stresses. With so many husbands and sons away fighting the war, they took up the challenge of managing farms and plantations and did heavy agricultural labor themselves when necessary. They raised families and dealt with critical shortages of consumer goods, often by improvising and "making do."

Loneliness, isolation, and fear of attack were constant companions for these women. But they endured and found strength and self-confidence they never knew they had.

All Floridians regardless of gender or race found themselves caught up in the Civil War in some fashion. This was indeed civil war, with the decidedly uncivil violence and cruelty that such conflicts generate. Pro-secession/Confederate sentiment was never monolithic in Florida, and as the war dragged on, antiwar Unionism grew. Prewar geographic and political differences did not disappear, either. By 1863 the fantasy of a short, painless war had evaporated. Confederate policies such as a military draft and impressment of private property only weakened ties. In fact, by 1865 there were two regiments of Florida Unionists in the blue-clad army, and pro-Union guerrilla bands roamed the state and clashed with their bitter rebel enemies.

On the other hand, rank-and-file Union soldiers serving in Florida found it to be very good duty. Boys from New York and Connecticut enjoyed Florida's warm weather, good rations, and exotic locales complete with palm trees. Yankees garrisoned Pensacola, Key West, and St. Augustine, which became a federal rest center. They picked fresh oranges from nearby groves, and some managed to box them up and ship them northward to families, thus beginning a Florida holiday tradition.

While Florida saw no battles on the scale of Bull Run, the state did experience combat, which tended to result from raids out of bases like Pensacola, Jacksonville, and Fort Myers. Yankee sailors sallied forth as well on the Gulf coast or from their gunboats cruising the St. Johns River.

Florida Gives Its All to the Civil War

A PROLOGUE TO SECESSION

In the years before the Civil War, thousands of enslaved people worked in the midsection of the Panhandle called "Middle Florida" on large cotton plantations owned by wealthy families from Georgia, South Carolina, and other southern states. Others toiled on smaller farms in the area.

Most of the rest of Florida was still frontier. Only three towns—Pensacola, Key West, and Jacksonville—had populations of more than 2,000. Florida's total population was 140,424 residents, and nearly 45 percent (61,745) were enslaved, according to 1860 census figures.

After Florida became a state in 1845, another wave of migrants from southern states moved down, including from South Carolina, where the "states' rights" theory was championed by leaders such as John C. Calhoun who held that states could declare null and void any federal law they deemed to be unconstitutional.

By 1860 South Carolina transplants and other plantation owners controlled much of Florida's political landscape. They denounced the Republican Party of presidential candidate Abraham Lincoln as fanatical abolitionists who threatened the economic prosperity and way of life in the South.

When the presidential election was held on November 7, 1860, Lincoln's name was not included on Florida's ballot. After Lincoln won the US presidency, protest meetings erupted in many Florida towns, and Governor Madison Starke Perry called for secession.

"YOU HAVE OPENED THE GATES OF HELL

FROM WHICH SHALL FLOW THE CURSES OF THE DAMNED WHICH SHALL SINK YOU TO PERDITION"

Florida's General Assembly held a secession convention in January 1861. Most of the appointed convention delegates were Middle Florida plantation owners and their representatives. On January 10 they voted 62-7 that Florida would secede from the Union, the third state to do so after South Carolina and Mississippi. Support for secession was far from unanimous. A large minority of Floridians was pro-Union or anti-Confederacy. Florida did not hold a popular vote on the issue even though some Unionists pushed for this.

On the day of the fateful convention vote in Tallahassee, former governor Richard Keith Call, an outspoken Unionist, told a jubilant crowd of secessionists, "You have opened the gates of Hell, from which shall flow the curses of the damned which shall sink you to perdition."

Image: A voice against secession. Richard Keith Call, Florida territorial governor during the 1830s and 1840s, spoke out against the state's plan to leave the Union. Courtesy of State Archives of Florida, Florida Memory.

Artist's depiction of Captain John Jackson Dickison and his men in a fight with Union soldiers, 1865. The Confederates won the battle near Braddock Farm in Volusia County, killing four federal soldiers and capturing fifty-one others, in addition to seizing wagons, cotton, horses, and small arms. Dickison's unit did not lose a man in the engagement. Courtesy of State Archives of Florida, Florida Memory.

The largest clashes in Florida occurred in 1864–1865 at Olustee, Fort Myers, and Natural Bridge. Only a few thousand troops fought at these places, and the battles were small compared to the titanic battles waged to the north. The bloodiest Florida fight was at Olustee, with combined losses of more than 2,800 men.

The fateful spring of 1865 saw Abraham Lincoln returned to the White House and the Confederacy teetering on the brink of collapse. Ironically, Tallahassee was the only Confederate state capital east of the Mississippi not to fall, though the Union had the military might to take it if they had truly wanted to.

By late April word of Robert E. Lee's surrender reached Florida. The Richmond government no longer existed. Florida's Confederate governor, John Milton, was dead, widely reported to have committed suicide when he heard that the Confederate cause was lost.

Rebel soldiers around the state stacked their arms, swore allegiance to the Union, and headed for home. Their war was over.

But life for returning veterans would be very different than it had been before the war. Some towns like Jacksonville suffered heavy damage; others like Apalachicola never recovered their prewar prosperity. The state's economy would have to be rebuilt minus help from the federal government. Floridians, both Union supporters and ardent Confederates, had to learn to live together in peace. Black Floridians were now free, but no one knew how the freed slaves would fit into Florida life.

Meanwhile, thousands of Union veterans recalled their duty in exotic Florida, and more than a few opted to return. They brought about Florida's first postwar population boom, along with skills and needed investment capital to help revitalize the state. Luckily, Florida still contained great natural resources not yet fully tapped. Yet the shadow of the Civil War lingered for many years as the old societal structures went the way of the past dreams of glory.

From the **Spring 2010** edition of FORUM magazine, "The Civil War: 'When Florida Opened Up the Gates of Hell.'"

PART II
Florida Comes of Age
Promise and Paradox

The young state finds itself irresistible to big dreamers and schemers—who believe anything is possible in this lush and sunlit paradise.

"Newspaper Boy on Launch Day," Titusville, 1969. The photo was taken by David Burnett, who was on assignment for *Time* magazine covering the launch of the Apollo 11 mission to the moon on July 16, 1969. Contact Press Images.

9

The Eye of the Beholder

Swampy hellhole or perfect paradise, travel writers have portrayed visions of vastly different Floridas.

Casey Blanton

Florida native **Casey Blanton** earned her PhD in literature at the University of South Florida before beginning a career in teaching at Daytona State College. She is the author of the book *Travel Writing: The Self and the World*. In 2012 she joined a group of Daytona State College faculty members to found the open access interdisciplinary *Journal of Florida Studies* (journal-offloridastudies.org). Blanton remains the journal's editor in chief.

Roughly every 100 years Florida is reinvented on the pages of the travel books that bring people to this state. Almost from the beginning, early explorers were not immune to myth making. What better way to encourage more money from financial backers in Europe than to name a barren stretch of palmetto "La Florida," then promise gold and a fountain of virility? Florida as fantasyland, complete with wild promises of health, wealth, and exotic lushness, is a theme that persists throughout the history of travel writing in Florida.

Fantasy was not unusual during the heyday of exploration in the sixteenth and seventeenth centuries. Maps and drawings of Florida include mountains in the background and comely, European-looking natives strolling through a verdant landscape. Hardy explorers like Cabeza de Vaca and Hernando de Soto, clanking around in hot, chafing armor, complained about unyielding palmettos and uncooperative Indians but still sent home glowing tales of Florida's riches they might yet find.

A century later, in 1773, under the warm sun of a late Florida spring, botanist William Bartram set out to explore the St. Johns River, Florida's earliest thruway. Bartram's book about his collecting expedition, called *The Travels of William Bartram*, describes an Edenic Florida, an ideal setting for the Pennsylvania Quaker convinced that the creative spirit resides in the natural world.

In a famous passage describing Blue Springs, near DeLand, Bartram is struck by the strange beauty of "the enchanting and amazing crystal fountain." The "cerulean" water is "absolutely diaphanous . . . transparent as ether." All is beauty and harmony along the banks of the springs, "the pendant golden Orange dancing on the surface of the pellucid waters." Fish and alligators live in a kind of Peaceable Kingdom, "with free and unsuspicious intercourse performing their evolutions."

Opening pages of William Bartram's *Travels through North and South Carolina, Georgia, East and West Florida*, published in 1791. Courtesy of BartramsGarden.org.

Later, upriver, these same peace-loving alligators attack Bartram's canoe, but even then, Florida's natural beauty remains sublime.

Travel writers who followed Bartram were less sanguine about Florida's natural attractions. James John Audubon, for one, was disenchanted with the Florida he visited. In 1831 he wrote to his wife, "I am now truly speaking in a wild and desolate part of the world—no one from the eastern United States has any true idea of this peninsula. My account of what I have or shall see of the Floridas will be far, very far from corroborating the flowery sayings of Mr. Bartram, the botanist." In fact, Audubon is singularly unimpressed with the St. Johns. After shooting "some young Eagles . . . to add to [his] store of provisions," Audubon complains that "the river did not seem to me equal in beauty to the fair Ohio: the shores were in many places low and swampy." In the end, Audubon can't escape Florida quickly enough.

Audubon is the kind of traveler that Harriet Beecher Stowe must have had in mind when she says in her book on Florida, "It is not to be doubted that fully half of the tourists and travelers that come to Florida return intensely disappointed and even disgusted." Her book *Palmetto-Leaves*, published in 1873, 100 years after Bartram's account of exactly the same landscape, is a partial corrective to the botanist's romantic hyperbole and a warning to overly idealistic travelers like Audubon who expect too much from Florida.

John James Audubon. The naturalist, ornithologist, and artist visited Florida in the early 1830s to create watercolor images of the state's birds. Courtesy of National Portrait Gallery, Smithsonian Institution.

After the Civil War, when she was already famous for *Uncle Tom's Cabin*, Stowe wintered for fifteen years on a 30-acre homestead in Mandarin on the northern banks of the St. Johns River, a place both Bartram and Audubon must have passed on their collecting expeditions. Because Stowe actually put down roots before she wrote her book, her account, although clearly favorable to Florida, attempts to reconcile the two very different Floridas presented by the famous naturalists: "Florida, like a piece of embroidery, has two sides to it—one side all tag-rag and thrum, without order or position; and the other side showing flowers and arabesques and brilliant coloring. Both these sides exist." She bluntly continues, "We caution everybody coming to Florida, Don't hope for too much."

Still, most of her book extolls the virtues of Florida, the lazy days of yellow jessamine, ripe oranges, and, of course, palmetto leaves.

But Stowe has her agenda too. She hopes her gentle, imperfect Florida will provide a model plantation for "the right treatment and education of the Negro population." Although her rationale for this employment plan—they can stand the heat, we can't—is wrongheaded, her philanthropy, a theme that runs through *Palmetto-Leaves*, is sincere.

Stowe's new myth, that Florida is not perfect but healthy and spiritually satisfying, must have appealed to northern tourists who flocked to the state in the wake of her popular book. Not coincidentally, Henry Flagler's railroad opened up the state in the years between 1885 and 1912, and the travel boom was on. As a result of this influx of tourists, Florida was never the same, and neither was travel writing about Florida.

One of the best early twentieth-century travel books is the 1939 Works Progress Administration's *WPA Guide to 1930s Florida* written and compiled as part of the Depression-era's Federal Writers' Project. In Florida, the *WPA Guide* employed Zora

Popular view of Florida. In this postcard, passengers enjoy tropical scenery of a Florida river at night. Courtesy of State Archives of Florida, Florida Memory.

Neale Hurston, Stetson Kennedy, and other less well-known out-of-work writers. Their scrupulous research and considerable writing talent resulted in more than 500 pages of the most detailed and honest guidebook to Florida ever written. One fourth of the book consists of learned introductions to Florida covering topics that range from archaeology and economics to literature and conservation.

The remainder is a more traditional guidebook, offering self-tours of Florida's cities and the rural places in between. But even here the prose is intelligent and historically and culturally accurate, often with an eye to the bizarre. A description of the same landscape we have seen earlier in Bartram, Audubon, and Stowe, the region just south of Jacksonville, shows how much the state had, by the 1930s, both changed and remained the same.

> Cabbage palms grow thickly along rivers and creeks; the undergrowth is often dense and impenetrable. . . . Thistles, ferns, and blue flag flourish in the roadside ditches. . . . Along the highway, all but lost among blatant neon lights flashing "Whiskey" and "Dance and Dine," are crudely daubed warnings erected by itinerant evangelists, announcing that "Jesus is soon coming," or exhorting the traveler to "Prepare to meet thy God."

This odd mix of pure wild, impenetrable nature, gaudy neon signs, and fly-by-night religious messages marks the beginning of the modern view of Florida that can be characterized by what some have called "the kink factor," that unreal and sometimes quirky juxtaposition of competing Floridas: an untamable landscape that could still thrill William Bartram next to a sleaziness that would shock Mrs. Stowe.

The Eye of the Beholder · 57

This odd mix of pure wild, impenetrable nature, gaudy neon signs, and fly-by-night religious messages marks the beginning of the modern view of Florida that can be characterized by what some have called "the kink factor," that unreal and sometimes quirky juxtaposition of competing Floridas.

Sign boasts Pensacola Beach as the spot with the "World's Whitest Beaches." Photo is part of Carol M. Highsmith's America Project in the Carol M. Highsmith Archive, Library of Congress.

More recent travel writing accepts these jarring contradictions and a new, more ironic Florida emerges. The contemporary writer understands the basic dilemma of Florida, that the old persistent myth of abundant nature and balmy days has, after all, caused out-of-control development. So, these are not the gaudy guidebooks promising pastel houses and endless sun to the tourist. These four books admit that Florida's beauty is complicit in its ugliness:

- *Florida Ramble.* Alex Shoumatoff, a travel writer better known for his books about Africa and the Amazon, offers an offbeat tribute to Florida. Like the writers of the *WPA Guide,* Shoumatoff incorporates history, geology, and botany into his account of a two-month ramble around Florida in a 1964 Oldsmobile convertible. And like Bartram and Stowe, Shoumatoff is amazed at Florida's abundant natural gifts. Birds, lizards, fish, and the elusive longleaf pine all fascinate and draw Shoumatoff back to the natural parts of the state. But he is repulsed by the gaudiness and sheer tentativeness of Florida's civilized places.

- *Up for Grabs.* Written by Florida resident John Rothchild, this book is a cautionary tale about Florida as a place of never-ending hucksterism. From Ponce de León's efforts to promote Florida as a land of wealth and health to the 1920s development schemes, Florida has always been "up for grabs." Like Shoumatoff, Rothchild sees Florida as an impossible extreme, home to both dogged environmentalist Marjory Stoneman Douglas and the land-dealing Mackle brothers.

58 · Casey Blanton

- **The Orchid Thief.** Susan Orlean presents the same absurd picture of a Florida too beautiful for its own good. In her book—part travel, part treatise on orchid cultivation—Orlean zeros in on a peculiar subculture of orchid growers and their role in Florida's duality. On the one hand, the orchid dealers of south Florida are obsessive about the beauty and rarity of native orchids. But even after harvesting them is deemed unlawful, some orchid hunters continue to poach as many wild species as they can from Florida's Fakahatchee swamp, stripping it almost bare. Like Rothchild's developers, the orchid thieves see Florida's bounty as their own.

- **River of Lakes.** Bill Belleville takes the reader back to Bartram country, canoeing along the St. Johns in search of "the real Florida." Belleville travels in the opposite direction from Bartram and Audubon, floating slowly downstream on the dark tannic water toward Jacksonville. Along the way he pays homage to the two earlier naturalists as well as to Stowe, whose trails he follows. But in tone and erudition, Belleville owes more to the *WPA Guide* than to Bartram and company. Like other contemporary travel writers, he is concerned with abundance and with loss, with conservation and with destruction along the river.

Mermaid Bonita Colson checking her hair in a mirror at Weeki Wachee, undated 20th century. Photo by Sparky Schumacher, courtesy of State Archives of Florida, Florida Memory.

Maybe the 1980 Florida Tourist Council had it right: "The rules are different here." In the state government's never-ending effort to lure more tourists, the council must have had in mind how life in Florida does not jibe with the rest of America's life: seasonal cold, endless work, inactive old age. But the way that Florida is different, even from itself, is much bigger than this, and for 400 years travel writers have been trying to assess the inconsistencies.

So where, amid these conflicting accounts, is the real Florida? To paraphrase Melville: It is not found in any map or travel book; true places never are.

From the **Spring 2001** edition of *FORUM* magazine, "Turning Dreams into Dollars."

10 Taking the Waters

For Victorian-era visitors, Florida held the promise of miracle cures.

Rick Kilby

Orlando-based writer and graphic designer **Rick Kilby** is the author of *Florida's Healing Waters: Gilded Age Mineral Springs, Seaside Resorts, and Health Spas*, which received the silver medal for Florida nonfiction from the Florida Book Awards and the Stetson Kennedy Award from the Florida Historical Society. His first book, *Finding the Fountain of Youth: Ponce de León and Florida's Magical Waters*, won a Florida Book Award in the Visual Arts category.

BEER BARON Charles D. Kaier had certainly prospered in America after he immigrated from Germany. He fought for his new country during the Civil War and, by 1893, owned a thriving brewery in Mahanoy City, Pennsylvania. But despite his success, Kaier lacked what philosopher Ralph Waldo Emerson called the "first wealth," his health. And so, like Emerson, Kaier would travel to Florida in an effort to recover from a lung-related illness. He arrived in St. Augustine on February 2, 1893, some sixty-six years after an ailing Emerson strolled the white sand beaches near the ancient city, occupying himself by "hitting a green orange with a stick."

Kaier and Emerson were far from unique. John Lee Williams, an influential early settler who moved to Florida in 1820 for his health, declared in 1837 that "invalids from every part of the United States" wintered in St. Augustine. The old city was especially "celebrated for restoring tone to the system" of tuberculosis patients, he added.

After the Civil War, those limited by illness in northern states learned about Florida's balmy weather and salubrious waters through a variety of travel accounts that appeared in guidebooks, newspaper travelogs, and popular illustrated magazines such as *Harper's* and *Scribner's*. Celebrated writers such as Sidney Lanier and Harriet Beecher Stowe published favorable accounts of their experiences in the state, spreading the gospel of Florida's healthfulness to an even larger audience. Readers soaked up descriptions of an exotic peninsula surrounded by saltwater and dotted with a thousand freshwater springs, many imbued with minerals.

Florida was thus well suited to become a haven for those who embraced the popular belief in the curative power of water.

Many visitors during the state's golden age of bathing, from the 1870s through the 1910s, were consumptives, sufferers of tuberculosis, who sought relief from harsh northern winters. Medical advice at the time maintained that fresh air and outdoor activity could offer a reprieve from the disease nicknamed "the white death." John Lee Williams had already observed that sea bathing restored more

Postcard labeled "Interior of Bath House, White Springs, Florida. The Spring Flows 32,400 Gallons a Minute." Courtesy of the Matheson Museum, Gainesville.

Taking the Waters in Florida

Florida visitors to health "than any other prescription" and also described the state's mineral springs as "highly medical," foreshadowing the growth in medical tourism that would follow.

THE TRADITION OF soaking in and drinking water from mineral springs has ancient origins; the Greeks erected temples around springs, and the Romans constructed enormous bath complexes throughout their expansive empire. "Balneotherapy," from the Latin word *balneum* meaning "bath," is still practiced at health spas all over the world. During the Victorian era, the practice of "taking the waters," the more commonly used term, came into vogue in this country at places including Saratoga Springs, New York, and Warm Springs, Virginia. As tourism developed in Florida in the late nineteenth century, perhaps as many as two dozen resorts were built at mineral springs, including a few that were among the grandest accommodations the state had to offer.

Florida's spa era began after the upheaval of the Civil War, when the state's warm climate lured wealthy northern visitors, both healthy and infirm, to winter in what was hailed as "the Italy of America." Many entered the state through Jacksonville, which was well positioned to serve as a hub for travel farther south into Florida. Riverboats operated from the city's docks, embarking on trips up the St. Johns, which became a critical artery for shuttling visitors to health spas at springs along

Taking the Waters · 61

Bathers at the Spring House bathhouse, White Springs, July 1919. Courtesy of State Archives of Florida, Florida Memory.

the river. Green Cove Springs, about thirty miles south of Jacksonville, was especially popular. Dubbed "the Saratoga of the South," it turns up in virtually all travel accounts about Florida written after the war. Harriet Beecher Stowe described a "peculiar feeling of refreshment and exhilaration" when taking the waters at Green Cove, while Sidney Lanier, writing a travel guide for a railroad, focused on the quality of the accommodations. The grandest hotel there, the Clarendon House, boasted broad verandas overlooking the spring, a bowling alley, and a "billiards saloon." It could accommodate 200 guests at $4 per night in the late 1870s. Today, the town that grew up around the spring remains the seat of Clay County, but little remains from Florida's era of Gilded Age bathing except one of the Clarendon's detached guest residences, now home to a bed and breakfast.

Steamboats also carried passengers to other St. Johns River resorts built near springs, including Magnolia Springs, just a short walk from Green Cove, and the Brock House at Enterprise, near the jade-hued waters of Green Springs in Volusia County. President Zachary Taylor's cousin Cornelius built an early hotel near its viridescent waters in the 1840s, one of the first erected near a mineral spring.

Other spring resorts were reliant on railroads rather than steamboats to transport guests to their locations. Railroad travel to Florida expanded in the 1880s and made large portions of the state's interior more accessible to tourists. Charles Kaier, on his quest for healing in Florida, traveled by train twice to the vast complex at Suwannee Springs on the Suwannee River. Although his wife complained of boredom and loneliness in a letter describing their journey, the spring water seemed to bring Kaier relief. Developed in 1883 by hoteliers George and Levi Scoville, the Suwannee Springs resort was fairly self-contained, but nearby White

Springs boomed as a spa town, offering a variety of recreational options, from theater to roller skating, in order to prevent pleasure-seeking tourists from suffering ennui.

White Springs' four-story spring house, constructed by Confederate widow Minnie Mosher Jackson and her physician brother, was perhaps the most significant structure developed for bathing at any Florida spring. Topped with a decorative tower, the building included a concession area, clinic, dressing rooms, and an elevator. Like Green Cove Springs, the town of White Springs developed around the spa; guest facilities included 500 rooms for rent from fourteen hotels and additional boarding houses.

Tuberculosis was just one of the ailments for which tourist-invalids sought relief, and at least two destinations offered visitors a choice of springs to help heal specific afflictions.

At Panacea Springs in Wakulla County, owner T. H. Hall produced a brochure for the 1902 season proclaiming that the site's twenty-five springs could bring relief for kidney ailments, liver disorders, and digestive issues, all while creating a "rapid improvement in general health." Safety Harbor's Espiritu Santo Springs on Old Tampa Bay also offered a spring for kidney problems as well as springs for skin diseases, liver disorders, and stomach troubles. A 1910 pamphlet claimed that this group of mineral springs, "with their most efficacious healing properties," could hardly be equaled for "quantity and quality by any other mineral waters in the United States." The pamphlet included twenty-six pages of testimonials from individuals who claimed to have been cured of everything from paralysis to "nervous prostration."

At Panacea Springs in Wakulla County, owner T. H. Hall produced a brochure for the 1902 season proclaiming that the site's twenty-five springs could bring relief for kidney ailments, liver disorders, and digestive issues, all while creating a "rapid improvement in general health."

Postcard of Pass-a-Grille on the Gulf of Mexico. Collection of Rick Kilby.

Taking the Waters · 63

Florida's Healing Waters Today

Archaeological vestiges of Florida's golden age of bathing can be found at Suwannee, White, Hampton, and Panacea Springs in north Florida, where remnants of pool structures remain more than a century after taking the waters fell out of fashion.

For a taste of what health seekers experienced during that era, Florida still offers several options. The popular spring-fed pool at Green Cove Springs is part of a remodeled city park that opened in 2017 for recreational swimming from May through October. Warm Mineral Springs in North Port, near Venice, Florida, attracts an international clientele who come to bathe in the mineral-laced waters, seven days a week. The privately owned Safety Harbor Spa and Resort in Pinellas County utilizes the waters of Espiritu Santo Springs in its swimming pools and whirlpools and has a complete menu of contemporary spa experiences.

Architectural survivors from this era include several of Flagler's properties, some of which have been lovingly restored, such as the grand Hotel Ponce de Leon, now home to Flagler College in St. Augustine. To get a glimpse into the world of hydrotherapy, one can visit the Lightner Museum in the former Hotel Alcazar across the street, where much of the original equipment used in the Alcazar baths is on display. And you can even get a drink at the bottom of the Alcazar pool, where a café now operates in the deep end.

Bathers in the Hotel Alcazar casino pool, St. Augustine, 1905. Courtesy of Library of Congress.

One of the Espiritu Santo Springs was dedicated to quenching the growing thirst for bottled mineral water from Florida. As the health-giving reputation of the state's spring waters grew, so did demand, and soon bottles were shipped nationwide, as they still are today. An advertisement for the spa in Safety Harbor credits the water's power to a "beneficent Creator" who placed in "chosen spots over this earth certain springs with healing waters to cure the ails of man and beast." A legend linked the springs' history to a US soldier who learned about the water from a Seminole imprisoned during the Second Seminole War. Similar stories flourished about other springs where promoters claimed that Native Americans had relied on the water's healing properties long before its "discovery" by people of European descent.

Sea Bathing to Sanitariums

NINETEENTH-CENTURY visitors to Florida sought healing in seawater as well as in spring water. In his 1873 travel guide for consumptives, *Going South for Winter*, Dr. Robert F. Speir wrote that "of all health-preserving exercises, sea water bathing is best." Sea or surf bathing for health purposes was an outgrowth of the age-old practice of taking the waters at mineral springs, and in the eighteenth and nineteenth centuries, seaside resorts became popular across Europe.

In Pensacola, sea bathing was as regular a habit as "supper in the evening," John Lee Williams asserted in 1837, eight years before Florida was granted statehood. In east Florida, sea bathing was not as common but was "equally beneficial to health," Williams noted. General Francis E. Spinner, former treasurer of the United States, retired to a tent on Pablo Beach near Jacksonville in 1895, claiming the water and healthful breezes kept his system in "perfect order."

The historic Hotel Alcazar pictured in an 1898 postcard. Wikimedia.

The level of elegance at seaside resorts improved significantly after Standard Oil cofounder Henry Flagler began constructing palatial hotels along the peninsula's Atlantic coast.

Like Emerson and Kaier, Flagler first came to Florida for health reasons, following doctors' advice about the best care for his consumptive wife, Mary. Ultimately Mary succumbed to her ailments, but Flagler remarried and returned to the state, honeymooning in St. Augustine. As a guest of the San Marco Hotel, he observed that the upscale resort catered to high-end guests equivalent to the "class of society one meets at the great watering places of Europe," and he soon set about creating his own empire of properties, starting with St. Augustine's magnificent Hotel Ponce de León in 1888 and its companion, the Hotel Alcazar.

Flagler's resorts, which extended from Jacksonville Beach to Key West, catered to the whims of a well-heeled clientele rather than to invalids, but they actively promoted the popularity of healthful sea bathing to visitors. "The

Taking the Waters · 65

waters of this coast are celebrated for their tonic and health-giving properties," declares a brochure for the Hotel Continental in Atlantic Beach, Flagler's northernmost hotel. In addition to sea bathing, Flagler's resorts in Palm Beach and Miami offered saltwater bathing pools for those "too timid to tempt Old Neptune's grasp" by bathing in the surf. These facilities offered swimming instruction, and eventually recreational swimming replaced the practice of sea bathing in which apprehensive bathers ventured into the surf while tightly holding a safety line.

Flagler's Hotel Alcazar in St. Augustine, built in 1889, boasted the most elaborate bathing facilities by far, including what was advertised as the world's largest indoor pool, 120 feet long by 50 feet wide, surrounded by an observation gallery and dance floors. A brochure for the hotel's Alcazar baths describes what were state-of-the-art hydrotherapy treatments in the Gilded Age. Water could be applied as a healing agent in any form, "solid, fluid, or vapor, externally or internally," through treatments that included everything from traditional Russian and Turkish baths to vapor cabinets and "hydrotherapeutic apparatus" that directed jets of water at a patient's body. Today, the hotel is the home of the Lightner Museum, and its famous former swimming pool hosts diners at the Cafe Alcazar.

For a brief time in the early twentieth century, hydrotherapy was the most commonplace form of taking the waters, and sanitariums offering water cures were established around the state. A branch of Michigan's famed Battle Creek Sanitarium opened in a former Miami Springs hotel built by famed aviator Glenn Curtiss. The facility was owned by the eccentric Dr. John Harvey Kellogg, who believed that Florida's population could be the healthiest and the "longest lived people in the world." While the state may not be the Fountain of Youth, a steady stream of visitors still flows to Florida's springs, beaches, and spas every year in search of restoration and rejuvenation. Today the tourism industry is an essential component in the state's economy, but few tourists realize that they are following in the footsteps of medical tourists who sought a different kind of magic in Florida.

From the **Spring 2021** edition of *FORUM* magazine, "Written in Water."

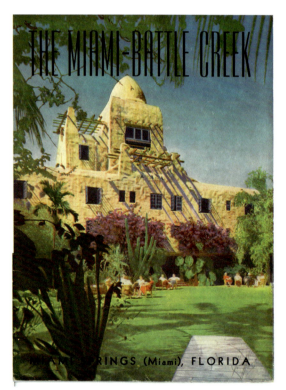

A promotional brochure for the Miami-Battle Creek Sanitarium in 1940.

11 The Florida Century

Through boom and bust, this outback became a megastate.

Gary R. Mormino

PROPELLED BY the waves of optimism following World War II, *Time* magazine mogul Henry Booth Luce coined the term "the American Century." Gauging the arc of the past 100 years, few states rival Florida's meteoric leap from the margins to the mainstream. The Florida Century is a story of improbable change with a cast of extraordinary characters.

A sense of perspective: On George Washington's birthday in 1819, the United States acquired Florida from Spain, a triumph of American diplomacy and fortune. A century later, Florida remained one of the least-populous states east of the Mississippi, with some 900,000 inhabitants. The Great War had just ended; 1919 ushered in peace but little prosperity and less optimism.

A deadly influenza pandemic killed thousands of Floridians. The price of cotton collapsed amid an infestation of boll weevils. Massive strikes paralyzed the phosphate mines, cigar factories, and shipyards.

A 1919 snapshot reveals a state on the threshold of such profound change that words such as "upheaval" seem inadequate. A majority of the state's inhabitants were Florida natives. The one constituency most likely to be native Floridians and southerners were African Americans. Florida's immigrant communities, while relatively small compared to the North, were significant by the contours of the South. Key West boasted a significant Cuban population, while Slovaks could be found in the agricultural hamlets of Slavia and Oviedo. A dynamic and colorful Greek community thrived in Tarpon Springs. Greek, Italian, and Slavic fishermen prowled the docks of Pensacola and Apalachicola. A small community of Syrian and Lebanese merchants settled in Jacksonville. Ybor City, however, dwarfed all other ethnic rivals. Thousands of Cuban, Spanish, and Sicilian immigrants bolstered Tampa's reputation as America's premier cigar-manufacturing center. Among southern cities, only New Orleans exceeded the vitality of Ybor City's immigrants.

If south Florida was sparsely populated, north Florida and the Panhandle were constituted with small towns amid the agricultural hinterlands. The so-called

Gary R. Mormino, Scholar in Residence for Florida Humanities, is the Frank E. Duckwall Professor Emeritus of History at the University of South Florida, St. Petersburg. His latest book is *Dreams in a New Century*, a study of Florida 2000–2010. He was awarded the Florida Humanities 2015 Florida Lifetime Achievement Award for Writing.

Black Belt or Middle Florida, the region between the Apalachicola and Suwannee Rivers, still dominated the state by dint of its cotton plantations, historical legacy, and malapportioned legislature. In 1916 Middle Florida boosted Sidney Johnston Catts, the self-proclaimed "Cracker Messiah," to the governor's mansion.

1919

In 1919 Floridians confronted a cold reality: demographics are destiny, and wars have consequences. The South had lost hundreds of thousands of African Americans, pushed by the cruelties of Jim Crow laws and pulled by economic opportunities in the North. Black Floridians voted with their feet in a movement known as the Great Migration.

The Great Migration also witnessed the migration to Florida of thousands of rural Georgians, South Carolinians, and Alabamans, Black and white, lured by the promise of a better life in places like Miami, Jacksonville, and Tampa.

The transition between 1919 and 1920 may be the most fraught one-year span in state history. Florida became Florida in the 1920s, an illuminating, trend-setting state. By the end of 1920, Prohibition and women's suffrage became the law of the land and the Great Florida Land Boom was under way.

The pulse beat of Florida changed. DeFuniak Springs and Bonifay, Chipley, and Marianna belonged to the agrarian ways of old Florida. New cities not even born before 1915 captured the energy and optimism of an energized south and central Florida; Miami Beach, Coral Gables, and Boca Raton defined a new Florida, incorporating architectural styles that matched a new Florida dream.

A profound population shift was under way, due to myriad factors: the importance of the railroad, the rise of the automobile, and the well-orchestrated dreams of developers such as George Merrick and Addison Mizner. But mostly, Americans were flocking to Florida having been enraptured by the tenets of the Florida dream: eternal sunshine, sandy beaches, and second chances.

Miami Beach real estate billboard, 1922. Courtesy of World Digital Library, Library of Congress.

Cuesta Rey cigar factory in Ybor City, 1930. Cigar makers listen to a *lector* read from a newspaper. Courtesy of Burgert Brothers Collection of Tampa Photographs, University of South Florida Libraries.

1929

Advertisement, "Miami's Greetings," from circa 1922. Courtesy of the Wolfsonian–FIU, the Michael Wolfson Jr. Collection of Decorative and Propaganda Arts, Promised Gift.

A BEACH CULTURE and Jazz Age emerged in the 1920s. In 1919, convention dictated that women's bathing suits should be modest, ending near if not below the knees. On Miami Beach, Jane Fisher, the irrepressible wife of land developer Carl Fisher, designed a new-age swimsuit, more fitting the times, sensuous and "form-fitting." In her autobiography, *Fabulous Hoosier*, she observed that "within a few weeks of my public pillorying, not a black cotton stocking was to be seen on the beach."

But the giddiness of the land boom collapsed in 1926, followed by a national depression in 1929. The most interesting Floridian in 1929 was not the wealthiest or most powerful and certainly not well known outside the cigar factories of Tampa. Manuel Aparicio, a Spanish immigrant, was the greatest *lector* (reader) of his generation. Like scores of other *lectores*, Aparicio read, always in Spanish, newspapers, serialized novels, and political literature to thousands of Cuban, Spanish, and Italian *tabaqueros* (cigar rollers) inside large brick factories such as Perfecto-García and Cuesta-Rey. Visitors would bring parasols and sit outside factories to listen to tales of *El Conde de Montecristo* and *Don Quixote*.

But the Great Depression threatened the world of cigar makers and readers. Consumers stopped purchasing Ybor City's handmade premium cigars. Owners, searching for a scapegoat, pointed to the readers and soon banned them. Aparicio found work as an actor and in 1936 became director of America's only federal Spanish-speaking theater. Soon the radio replaced the reader, while machines replaced the cigar makers.

The Florida Century · 69

1939

Not quite two million people lived in Florida in 1939. Floridians lived in Bagdad, Sumatra, and Sinai; Havana, Oviedo, and Boca Raton; Naples, Venice, and Italia; Masaryktown and Bohemia. Founders anointed these Florida locales with fanciful names and overarching dreams. Their exotic names notwithstanding, Bagdad, Sumatra, and Italia were best known, respectively, for their cypress, tobacco, and vegetable farms. Masaryktown, named for Czechoslovakia's first president, Tomáš Garrigue Masaryk, was founded in Hernando County by Slavic farmers who raised chickens.

Once isolated by distance and climate, Florida was becoming an international dateline. Technology—air travel, modern highways, and radio—made Florida more accessible and popular. A modern land rush brought waves of new residents, principally from the Midwest and Northeast. Ever-larger numbers of "snowbirds" spent their winter months attending baseball spring training and playing shuffleboard and horseshoes in places such as St. Petersburg and Fort Myers, Hollywood and Fort Pierce, Orlando and Ocala.

A new accent was becoming commonplace in Miami and Miami Beach: Yiddish. Foreign-born and second-generation Jewish Americans were flocking to south Florida, envisioning Miami as "the golden city." Born in Poland in 1902, the Nobel Prize–winning writer Isaac Bashevis Singer immigrated to America in 1935, spending his golden years in Miami Beach. Floridians read about the deteriorating conditions Jews faced in Europe years before World War II. Headlines such as "Jews in Germany Are Doomed under Hitler, Says Prominent Rabbi" and "Jewish Vets Ask Aid for Refugees" appeared in 1939.

As Americans nervously followed events in Europe, Floridians flocked to the cinema, escaping reality. From the balconies and mezzanines of the Athens in DeLand, the Dixie in Apalachicola, and the Paramount in Palm Beach, patrons enjoyed Hollywood's greatest year, such classics as *Gone with the Wind*, *The Wizard of Oz*, *Mr. Smith Goes to Washington*, and RKO's film adaptation of Victor Hugo's *Hunchback of Notre Dame*. In the film's heart-pounding climax, Quasimodo the bell ringer rescues Esmeralda from the gallows, spiriting her to the cathedral. Atop the bell tower, the hunchback triumphantly shouts, "Sanctuary! Sanctuary!"

In a dramatic turn, life imitated art, absent a happy ending. A newspaper headline explained, "Wandering Jewish Refugee Ship Puts into Miami Harbor." More than 900 German Jews had boarded the vessel SS *St. Louis* in Hamburg, hoping to find shelter in Cuba. The Cuban government denied their request. The captain then sailed for Miami. In Miami's Bayfront Park, pastors and rabbis pleaded with the Roosevelt administration for mercy. Washington slammed the door. The vessel returned to Germany, where many of its passengers died during the Holocaust.

Cover of Miami/Miami Beach Chambers of Commerce tourist brochure, which beckons potential visitors and transplants to sample the joys of the "Cities of the Sun," from surf bathing to polo to "economical" apartment and hotel rates, circa 1935.

70 · Gary R. Mormino

1949

Marketing photo, circa 1947. The photo was part of the promotion of Florida State College for Women's transition to the coeducational Florida State University. Courtesy of Heritage and University Archives, Florida State University.

THE YEARS BETWEEN 1939 and 1949 turned the world upside down. Florida and America would never be the same. Exemplifying the change was the transformation of higher education in Florida.

Florida's universities and colleges were overwhelmed by veterans from the state and those who had trained here during the war. Almost 8,500 men hoped to enter the all-male University of Florida in 1946; the campus could accommodate only 6,200 students. The solution was coeducation. The legislature transformed Florida State College for Women into Florida State University and allowed women to attend the University of Florida. In 1945 Florida's three public universities enrolled 7,000 students; by 1950 the number approached 20,000.

The GI bill's impact upon Florida was monumental, ushering millions of veterans into the middle classes. In 1949 the planets aligned: the war energized the economy; more importantly, millions of servicemen and women, their spouses, and new workers had been exposed to an enchanting place that one day would be home or a vacation paradise.

Florida vaulted into the ranks of the fastest-growing states in the United States. A new Florida dream began to form in 1949, emitting a powerful message that nature had endowed Florida with picturesque beaches, balmy winters, and surging natural springs. Most importantly, that dream promised second chances, renewal, and fresh hopes.

1959

Cape Coral promotional photograph, circa late 1950s/early 1960s. Brothers Leonard and Jack Rosen and partners drained, subdivided, and marketed a 103-square-mile tract of swamp land near Fort Myers in the late 1950s, which has grown into the largest city between Miami and Tampa. Courtesy of Cape Coral Historical Society/Cape Coral Museum of History.

THE 1950S TRIGGERED Florida's Big Bang. The state's population nearly doubled. Growth became creed and gospel. The decade spawned Cape Coral, Lehigh Acres, Port Charlotte, and other huge developments. A massive population shift was occurring as millions of Americans were leaving the Midwest and Northeast to come to the Sunbelt. Florida and California became the buckles of the new Sunbelt.

If there was a family that personified the optimism of 1959, it was the Mackle brothers. Frank Mackle, a British immigrant, formed the Mackle Construction Company in Jacksonville in 1908. His three sons carried on the business. They began with the construction of low-cost homes in Delray Beach and middle-class homes in Key Biscayne. Their portfolio later included Marco Island, Port Charlotte, Port St. Lucie, Spring Hill, and St. Augustine Shores.

In 1959 a reporter from *Look* magazine interviewed Frank Mackle Jr. for an irresistibly titled article, "The New Florida Land Rush: $10 Down for a Dream." Mackle encapsulated what was happening in Florida: "We've got millions of customers. Everything works toward helping us. We've got the doctors trying to get people to retire quicker. We've got a tremendous growth of pension funds; Social Security is getting stronger. There's a shorter work week."

Few Floridians fathomed the revolution that brought Fidel Castro to power in Cuba on January 1, 1959, would alter the arc of south Florida. The first plane bringing refugees to Miami was a vanguard of the Latinization of Florida.

The Florida Century · 71

One small step. On July 16, 1969, at 9:32 a.m. EDT, the swing arms move away and a plume of flame signals the liftoff of the Apollo 11 Saturn V space vehicle carrying astronauts Neil A. Armstrong, Michael Collins, and Edwin E. Aldrin Jr. from Kennedy Space Center Launch Complex 39A. Four days later, Armstrong became the first man to walk on the moon. Courtesy of NASA.

1969

Florida gained almost two million new residents during the 1960s, becoming a Sunbelt megastate. Brevard County typified the warp-speed change. In 1513, on his historic voyage of exploration, Ponce de León encountered a distinctive landmark along the east coast of La Florida. He named the promontory Cabo de las Corrientes (tip of the currents). Navigators later renamed it Cabo Cañaveral, because of the dense canebrakes. It remains one of the oldest place names in American history.

In 1897 a group of Harvard University graduates acquired 18,000 acres in Brevard County, including several miles of Cape Canaveral ocean frontage. Canaveral Club members visited the remote site to hunt and fish.

In 1949 the Cold War settled into one of the world's unlikeliest places: the lagoons, wetlands, and scrub of eastern Brevard County. The county's population was fewer than 24,000 residents. The Joint Chiefs of Staff chose 15,000 acres of land around Cape Canaveral, on a former World War II base, as the site for the Joint Long-Range Proving Ground. The paradise was soon transformed into a bulwark of the Cold War. New words—Space Age and Rocket Age—defined the era.

Each week, thousands moved to the Space Coast, to the fastest-growing county in the fastest-growing state in America. Resolved on a mission to put a man on the moon, the newcomers represented some of the brightest minds in the world, a cross-section of America.

On July 16, 1969, Apollo 11 blasted off from Kennedy Space Center. The world watched as the powerful boosters lifted the space capsule into the heavens. On July 20, the lunar module, the Eagle, carried two astronauts to the surface of the moon. Americans gasped hearing Neil Armstrong communicate with Mission Control in Texas, "The Eagle has landed." Cape Canaveral underscored an extraordinary chapter in Florida history.

The United States was inspired by faith in progress and determined to beat the Soviet Union to the moon. While the moon race summoned some of America's best qualities, faith in technology as the answer signals a dark side. The development of Florida resulted, in large part, because of a determination to tame nature.

IN THE PIVOTAL 1970s Florida added almost three million new residents. In modern Florida, Isaiah's prophecies were realized: the hot was made cool, the wet became dry, and crooked rivers were bent straight.

Florida's promise to Americans was irresistible. Here, one could have it all, prosperity amid climate control, dignity in old age, and sunsets on the beach. But a new word entered the lexicon in the go-go growth decade of the 1970s: loss.

John D. MacDonald moved to Clearwater in the 1950s. Growth in Florida both dazzled and frightened the young New York writer and his wife, Dorothy. The MacDonalds settled in Siesta Key, where they witnessed another march of progress. In 1983 he returned to Clearwater and was appalled at the price of prosperity: "It had always been especially restful and refreshing to drive back home, out across the causeway and the bridge to Clearwater Beach, to look over the rail at the broad, glassy bay. It was shocking to discover . . . that one could [now] go halfway to the beach and turn right! There was a bay-fill development down there, white roofs, tidy yards, boat docks, and flower beds."

MacDonald's gift to Florida was Travis McGee, a self-described "salvage consultant" who recovers "lost" property for desperate clients. *Condominium*, published in 1977, warns Floridians that nature bats last. The novel includes a who's who and what's what of Florida dystopia: the sleazy contractor, the crooked county commissioner, the once-beautiful Fiddler Key now home to Golden Sands condominium, and an ill-advised hurricane party.

In the 1970s an environmental movement emerged. In Washington and Tallahassee, Gainesville, Tampa, and Miami, scientists, students, poets, and concerned citizens demanded change. New and old environmental heroes emerged: Marjory Stoneman Douglas and Marjorie Harris Carr, Roger Stewart and Nat Reed.

1979

A bird's-eye view of a stretch of beach in Clearwater Beach, 1981. Photo by Mary Lou Norwood, courtesy of State Archives of Florida, Florida Memory.

The Florida Century · 73

1989

CLAUDE DENSON PEPPER, Florida icon, died in 1989. At eighty-nine, no one had represented the state longer or with more passion. The Alabama native and graduate of Harvard Law School came to Homosassa in the 1920s to make his fortune in the Florida land boom. When the boom ended, he moved to Perry and in 1928 was elected to the Florida legislature. Pepper settled in Tallahassee, a town brimming with ambitious, talented politicians in the 1930s and 1940s. He succeeded US senator Duncan Fletcher in 1936.

Pepper was a rarity in Florida and the South: a fist-pounding liberal. He idolized President Roosevelt. Perhaps no Florida politician has attracted more powerful enemies than Pepper. The darling of labor unions, defense industry, and editorial boards, Pepper was blinded by his invincibility and rapidly changing times and stumbled into the greatest race in Florida history.

In 1950 Pepper's opponents tapped a handsome young south Florida congressman, George Smathers, to challenge a legend. Anticommunism was the era's kryptonite, and Pepper had no antidote. Smathers scored a smashing victory.

F. Scott Fitzgerald said famously there are no second acts in life, but Pepper's second coming was as spectacular as it was rewarding. The defeated candidate moved to Miami, practiced law, and in 1962 ran for and won a seat in the US Congress. For almost three decades Congressman Pepper was a lion, a voice for the New Frontier, Cuban refugees, and the Great Society.

When *Time* selected Pepper for the April 25, 1983, cover, he was no longer a young gamecock but the "spokesman for the elderly." A classic Pepper quote adorns the cover: "They deserve much—and need much." When Pepper was born in 1900, about two of every hundred Floridians were sixty-five and older. When he died, almost one in five Floridians was a senior citizen.

U.S. Senator Claude Pepper campaigning in Tampa, 1938. Courtesy of State Archives of Florida, Florida Memory.

1999

THE CALENDAR ROLLOVER from New Year's Eve to New Year's Day fascinated Floridians in 1999. A centennial and millennial year, 2000 was also an election and census year. Florida mattered in 1999. Almost sixteen million residents crowded the state. Miami-Dade County alone accounted for more than two million dwellers. Not a single county lost population between 1990 and 1999.

In 1999, two of every three Floridians came from someplace else. A sense of perspective is needed to understand the whiplash of change. Consider that in 1950, Dade County numbered a half-million residents. The US Census Bureau had no category for Hispanics. Fifty years later, Miami-Dade County had exploded to 2.25 million inhabitants, of whom half were foreign-born and their children.

In the 1960s and 1970s, when one discussed immigrants in south Florida, one focused upon Cubans. But in 2000, the most arresting story was the dizzying variety of immigrants, as waves of Haitians and Brazilians, Dominicans and Mexicans, Hondurans, Jamaicans, and Nicaraguans arrived in search of the American dream. In the 1990s, Florida's Hispanic population grew by more than one million.

74 · Gary R. Mormino

Waiting for customers on Calle Ocho in Miami's historic Little Havana neighborhood. Photo by Carol M. Highsmith, Carol M. Highsmith Archive, Library of Congress, Prints and Photographs Division.

Y2K

Doomsayers warned when the clocks turned from 1999 to 2000 to prepare for chaos. Global-gloom narratives predicted nuclear missiles firing aimlessly because of cross-wired launch codes, prison doors swinging open, and computer-flawed ATM machines spewing cash to strangers. But in the end, one command saved the night: "Party like it's 1999."

The next day, newspaper headlines read, "Biggest 2000 Loser, Y2K Furor."

Shakespeare squeezed politics, culture, and drama along timeless plot lines: innocents plucked from storm-tossed seas; the odyssey of leaving the old world and encountering a wondrous new world; a citizenry furious at feckless leaders.

On November 21, 1999, Juan Miguel González expected to pick up his son at school in Cardenas, Cuba. He was told that Elián had been taken by his mother, Juan's ex-wife. Elizabet Brotons Rodríguez and her son had escaped from Cuba along with twelve other people in a tiny boat with no life preservers.

Quickly the doomed vessel was awash with saltwater, and the desperate passengers clung to rubber inner tubes. Some time later, two fishermen scanning the choppy waters off Fort Lauderdale saw what they thought was a doll strung to a float.

The "doll" was five-year-old Elián, whose mother and ten others had drowned. Elián was eligible for asylum in Miami because of America's "wet foot/dry foot" doctrine. Elián's father demanded his son's return to Cuba. Relatives in Miami's Little Havana embraced the young child as a symbol of American liberty.

Attorney General Janet Reno, a Miami native, believed law superseded politics and ordered Elián returned to his father, in June 2000. Reno died in 2016. A few days after her funeral, her sister received a call at the Reno homestead in Kendall. "This is the Cuban embassy in Washington, DC," the caller said. "The family of Elián González would like to convey their love and gratitude for sending their boy home."

2009

Venezuelan businesswomen in Miami. The women join forces to share tools and resources. Courtesy of Miami Dade College.

STILL THEY CAME. Nothing, it seemed, could derail the Florida boom.

Cassandras and Jeremiahs had long warned the Sunshine State stood on the eve of destruction. A thousand new residents had been arriving every day for several years. The newcomers represented a huge swath of society: surging numbers of retirees, Rust Belt transplants, and immigrants from across the globe. And then came the Great Recession's high tide in 2009. Articles appeared in national publications with somber titles: "Is Florida the Sunset State?" "Is Florida Over?" and "The Ponzi State."

Journalist Michael Grunwald wrote a blunt article about his adopted state in *Time*, musing, "The question is whether it will grow up." Grunwald represents a vanguard of national writers fascinated by Florida. In his best-selling study *The Swamp: The Everglades, Florida, and the Politics of Paradise* (2006), he writes about a familiar conundrum in the state: "But as the Everglades continued to wither, a few colleagues began to wonder if conservation really should mean development more than preservation. These heretics did not believe that God had created man in order to 'improve' or 'redeem' nature; they found God's grace in nature itself."

Nearly a decade after the Great Recession, Florida remains an enchanting but frustrating state. Once again we stand at a crossroads. Do we have the will to manage growth, restore ecosystems, preserve our natural springs, and inspire diverse generations of residents into a common cause? Will a new dream instill pride in our state and a resolve to leave the place better for the next generation?

Today, any discussion of state politics focuses upon two fast-growing and powerful groups: Puerto Ricans and Venezuelans. According to Fernando Rivera, director of the University of Central Florida's Puerto Rico Research Hub, Florida's Puerto Rican population grew from 480,000 in 2000 to more than 1.2 million in 2017. In 2017 Puerto Rico's utter destruction from Hurricane María resulted in a stampede to Florida.

Few soothsayers would have predicted that in 2019 the most talked-about immigrant group in Florida would be Venezuelans. In 2000, Venezuela's standard of living was the envy of its neighbors, and only about 22,000 Venezuelans resided in Miami-Dade County. Dictatorships and a plunging oil market resulted in a mass evacuation to Colombia and Florida. More than 200,000 Venezuelans lived in Florida according to a 2018 University of Miami study.

Difficult questions confront Florida today. In a state where almost everyone comes from someplace else, how do we develop a sense of unity and cohesion, where immigrants and natives, retirees and transplants think of Florida as something bigger than our own group or ourselves? Is it possible to ask Floridians to believe that we are all in this together?

From the **Fall 2019** edition of *FORUM* magazine, "What Does It Mean to Be a Floridian?"

12 Along the Backroads, 1930s

Remembering when Zora and I chased the vanishing folklife of Florida.

Stetson Kennedy

IN THE 1930s we traveled backroads the length and breadth of the Florida peninsula, toting a coffee-table-sized recording machine into turpentine camps and sawmills, into citrus groves and the Everglades, onto railroad tracks and aboard shrimp trawlers, wherever Florida folks were working, living, and singing.

"The Thing," as we called the machine, looked like a phonograph and cut with a sapphire needle directly onto a 12-inch acetate disk. Every time we shipped off another batch of disks to the Archive of American Folk Song (now the American Folklife Center) at the Library of Congress, the newspapers would report, "Canned Florida Folk Songs Sent to Washington." And now all you have to do is select a can from the website shelf, open it up, and enjoy!

The voices you hear singing, talking, laughing, joking, and telling tall tales are those of Floridians who have almost all gone to Beluthahatchee (an Afro-Seminole name for Happy Hunting Ground). As for the songs they sang and the tales they told, many are still to be heard, having been passed along as hand-me-downs from one generation to the next.

Happily, many of the folk songs recorded by the WPA have also been preserved in books . . . edited by the man who served as national director of the WPA's folklore collecting, Dr. Benjamin Botkin, [who taught us] about the interrelationship between life and culture. A bit later on, another outstanding folklorist, Zora Neale Hurston, gave us a definition that will stand for all time: "Folklore is the boiled-down juice, or potlikker, of human living."

Editor's note: Stetson Kennedy was part of the Depression-era team of "hunters" who traveled the state, employed by the Federal Writers' Project of the Works Progress Administration, to collect the stories of Florida through cultural and statistical information, songs, and folklore. The result was the *Works Progress Administration Guide to Florida*. "I urged our hunters not to overlook any of the geography, climate, flora, fauna, peoples, and occupations to be found in Florida," Kennedy said.

This piece was adapted from essays originally published on the Library of Congress website American Folklife Center.

Stetson Kennedy (1916–2011), born in Jacksonville, was known as one of the nation's pioneer folklore collectors. Kennedy's many books include *Palmetto Country*, *Southern Exposure*, *Jim Crow Guide to the U.S.A.*, and *Grits and Grunts: Folkloric Key West*.

Image: A scenic road, lined with live oaks, Largo, Florida, circa 1940. Courtesy of State Archives of Florida, Florida Memory.

Zora Neale Hurston listens to Gabriel Brown playing guitar in Eatonville, 1935. Photograph by Alan Lomax. Courtesy of Library of Congress.

Zora Neale Hurston gave us a definition that will stand for all time: "Folklore is the boiled-down juice, or potlikker, of human living."

Those were hard times back then, during the Great Depression of the 1930s. People sometimes referred to them as the "root-hog-or-die" days, meaning that if you didn't keep grubbing you were a goner. Lots of folks were "hollerin' hongry" and longing for a little gravy on their grits.

A Black preacher on the Sea Islands prayed, "Hear us, Oh Lord, we're down here gnawin' on dry bones."

And on New Year's Eve, Florida Latins intoned, "Go bad year, so we can see if the coming one is better."

All of us working on the WPA (except administrators) had to sign a Pauper's Oath that we had no job, no money, no property, and no prospect of getting any of those things. I was still a student at the University of Florida when I applied and, being eminently qualified in all of the above respects, I got the job. . . .

In 1896 the Supreme Court upheld a policy of strict racial segregation in *Plessy v. Ferguson*; this was not overturned until *Brown v. Board of Education* in 1954. Blacks and whites could not even drink out of the same water fountain in the South of the 1930s while the Jim Crow laws were in effect. It was, therefore, a rare and exciting event when one day in 1938 the director of the Florida project, Carita Doggett Corse, called the editorial staff into her office and announced,

> Zora Neale Hurston, the Florida Negro novelist, has signed onto the project and will soon be paying us a visit. Zora has been feted by New York literary circles and is given to putting on certain airs, including the smoking of cigarettes in the presence of white people. We must all make allowances for Zora.

So Zora came, and Zora smoked, and we made "allowances." Although she already had two books to her credit, Hurston had taken the Pauper's Oath with alacrity, and, like me, she had been assigned the title of "Junior Interviewer." But her pay was only $35.50 every two weeks, because according to the WPA wage scale, it cost $4 per month less to live in her all-Black hometown of Eatonville than it did for me to live in Jacksonville, where our headquarters was located.

Three years earlier, in 1935, Hurston had taken folk musicologist Alan Lomax, the son of pioneer folk song collector John Lomax, on a Florida recording expedition that began in Eatonville. Because this was a time of strict segregation in the American South, it would have been extremely dangerous for a Black woman and a white man to be seen traveling together. To avoid complications, Hurston painted Lomax's face and hands black.

"In the field, Zora was absolutely magnificent," Lomax recalled in a chat with me a half century later. Although I was nominally Hurston's boss, I didn't see much of her except on field trips. Like many of our rural fieldworkers, she worked out of her

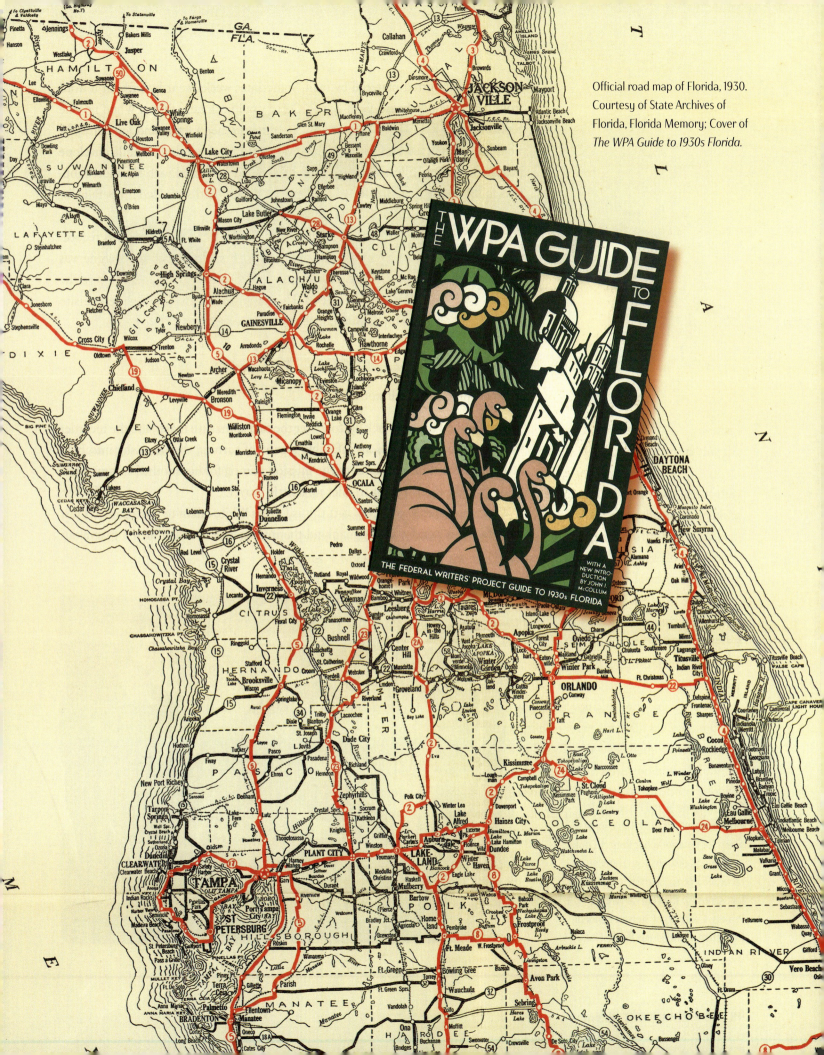

Official road map of Florida, 1930. Courtesy of State Archives of Florida, Florida Memory; Cover of *The WPA Guide to 1930s Florida*.

13

Dear Honey

*Wartime life and letters of
Marjorie Kinnan Rawlings.*

Betty Jean Steinshouer

DECEMBER 7, 1941: The elegant Castle Warden Hotel opened for business in St. Augustine. Its proprietor was Norton Baskin, known in some circles as "Mr. Marjorie Kinnan Rawlings," for he had married the Pulitzer Prize–winning author of *The Yearling* on October 27, 1941. One of the conditions of their marriage was that he would open his own business and be his own man. That day of infamy, when the Japanese bombed Pearl Harbor, the Baskins little knew how much their lives, the Castle Warden, and indeed, their beloved Florida would be affected by the war raging abroad. Nor could they know the global impact they would have, through their devotion to each other, to their country and community, and to their friends around the world.

Marjorie Kinnan Rawlings—she would continue to use her public name—knew many people already involved in the war just in the small circle of her fellow novelists published by Scribner's: the Hemingways were flying off in different directions as war correspondents, Marcia Davenport was involved in the Czech resistance, and Sigrid Undset had Nazi officers living in her house in Oslo. In Cross Creek, Rawlings wrote to her new husband in St. Augustine, "Twelve bi-motored bombers, several towing gliders, just flew so low over the house, they almost touched the pecan trees across the road. Spooky."

If there was no escaping the reality of war at the creek, Rawlings was even more aware of it when she came to Crescent Beach, where she and Norton had an ocean cottage. She wrote to Virginia novelist Ellen Glasgow on April 14, 1942, describing "big tankers sliding as close as they dare to the shore, to evade the submarines." Rawlings confided to her confidante and editor, Maxwell Perkins,

This part of the coast has become practically a military zone, and now passes are necessary to use the ocean road that leads to the cottage. I have black-out shades, and it is rather creepy alone here at night, with no traffic on beach or highway, convoys going by, bombers overhead, and the thought of saboteurs who land on isolated beach.... We hear mysterious explosions out at sea, and never know the cause.

Betty Jean Steinshouer is a writer and award-winning Chautauqua speaker, touring the United States and Canada with one-woman shows of authors including Willa Cather, Harriet Beecher Stowe, Sarah Orne Jewett, Laura Ingalls Wilder, Marjorie Kinnan Rawlings, Gertrude Stein, Flannery O'Connor, and Marjory Stoneman Douglas, based on extensive research. Her biography *Long Road from Red Cloud: Life Lessons from Willa Cather* was awarded American Book Fest's International Book Award for Biography in 2020.

Norton Baskin, Marjorie Kinnan Rawlings, and dog Pat, 1940. Fashionably attired for hunting by Abercrombie and Fitch, Baskin and Rawlings pose for a magazine photo spread. Photo courtesy of the Marjorie Kinnan Rawlings Papers, Special and Area Studies Collections, George A. Smathers Libraries, University of Florida.

The Baskins joined neighbors as enemy-plane spotters, taking shifts for two hours a day at an observation post set up not far from their beach house. The Baskins also aided the war effort in the campaigns for war bonds.

Norton hosted Hollywood starlet Veronica Lake at the Castle Warden, chivalrously carrying her fifteen pieces of luggage and reporting to his wife that Miss Lake sold $85,000 worth of bonds, "not bad for St. Augustine." Rawlings herself bought $25,000 in war bonds with her first earnings from *Cross Creek*.

The war began to dominate Marjorie's life more and more. The filming of *The Yearling* had to be abandoned because the crew was drafted and the resources for making movies were being diverted to the war effort.

No one knew fully what it meant for Marjorie Rawlings Baskin when her husband, at age forty-one, announced he had to find a way to get into the war overseas. After the breakup of her marriage to Charles Rawlings in 1931, she had waited a long time to find someone with whom to share her life. Being with Norton Baskin, she said, was like coming into harbor after a long storm.

Dear Honey · 83

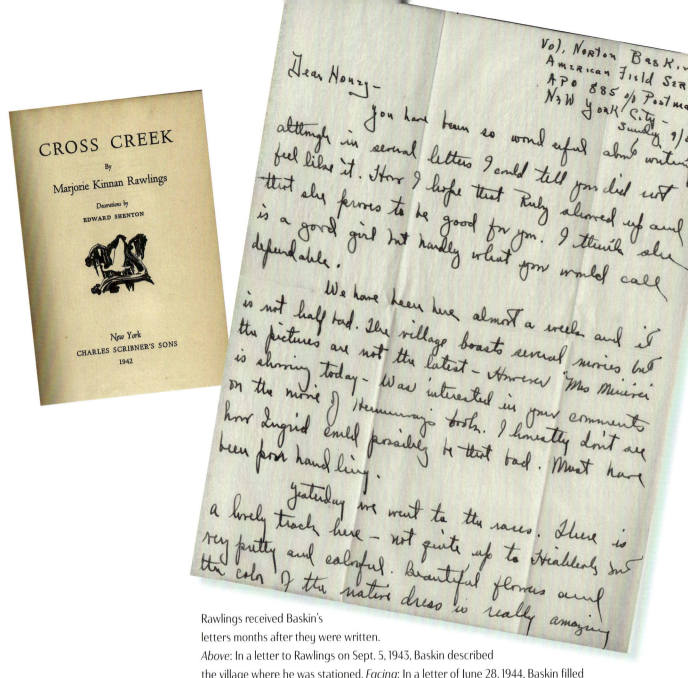

Rawlings received Baskin's letters months after they were written.
Above: In a letter to Rawlings on Sept. 5, 1943, Baskin described the village where he was stationed. *Facing*: In a letter of June 28, 1944, Baskin filled her husband in on the goings-on back home. Courtesy of Marjorie Kinnan Rawlings Papers, Special and Area Studies Collections, George A. Smathers Libraries, University of Florida.

Cross Creek, 1942 edition. Courtesy of Beth Kent.

Marjorie wrote to Norton as he was enlisting that she now understood the pride of women in male heroism and duty to country, not that she approved of it, but she understood it: "Women's pride in their men being brave is a strange thing—prehistoric, somehow—full of nobility—and as much to blame for the continuance of war as any other factor. I am terribly proud of you for what you have done, even while rebelling against it with every fibre."

Norton Baskin signed up with the American Field Service, an American volunteer ambulance service that operated under British officers. Friends rallied 'round when they heard Marjorie had a "damn hero, Hemingway-style" on her hands. Margaret Mitchell, author of *Gone with the Wind*, pointed out to Marjorie that the AFS

84 · Betty Jean Steinshouer

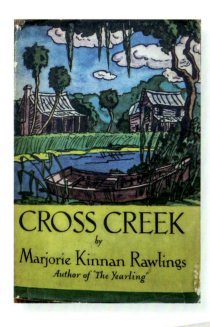

had a high calling and had done excellent work in World War I. Rawlings wrote to her close friend, publisher Norman Berg,

> They work in the front lines and in the last war their casualties were twice the ratio of regular army casualties.... But I wouldn't stop him if I could—it is what he wants to do, and a man has to make his own decisions about things like that.... Am being a good sport now, but shall quietly collapse after he goes!

Norton sailed on a troop ship out of New York Harbor on July 5, 1943. His absence was exacerbated by the fact that Marjorie had no idea where he was headed, India, the Middle East, anywhere the British army was. After weeks of uncertainty, Marjorie finally celebrated her August 8 birthday on September 3, when a telegram arrived from Norton stating he had reached his destination. She had already begun

Marjorie Kinnan Rawlings and Norton Baskin, outside her Cross Creek home. Photo courtesy of the Marjorie Kinnan Rawlings Papers, Special and Area Studies Collections, George A. Smathers Libraries, University of Florida.

Dear Honey · 85

While Marjorie was seeing after the lives of men she had never met, her husband was in India, getting ready to risk his life in the most immediate action he had seen yet, the battle for Burma.

her faithful vigil of writing daily letters to him. Their letters to each other often began "Dear Honey" and contained as much lightheartedness as they could muster.

Marjorie sent him the menus of dinners she made, news of the creek and Castle Warden, and gossip about their friend Margaret Mitchell and other celebrities:

Rita Hayworth and Orson Welles got married! With her beauty and his brains—they'll fight like hell! Your friend Veronica Lake was doing a picture, seven months pregnant, had a fall, the child, a boy, was born prematurely and died in a few days. And Bette Davis' husband fell in the street and died shortly after. Think that brings your favorites up to date.

Norton's letters, usually arriving months after they were written, bore the mark of the censors whose job it was to make sure they did not give away the Allies' location or activities. Marjorie had asked her husband to describe the flora and fauna of his surroundings. Sometimes he did this so well that the censors blacked out his descriptions for fear the enemy would distinguish the setting.

One of the last letters on file from Norton's war duty, dated November 27, 1943, shows his sense of humor was intact. He writes, "Dear Dora," addressing MKR's Jersey cow, "I feel like one of the foolish little pigs, living in huts made of mud, bamboo, and straw, but there ARE places of safety to run for if anybody comes huffing and puffing."

Christmas 1943 was hard for both Baskins. MKR was horrified to learn that Norton had not received a single one of his packages and "was in a jungle full of Japs and tigers, had been living for days on bully beef and tea, and was sleeping on the ground in a small tent without lights or a seat to sit on." She was relieved to learn that British soldiers had invited him to Christmas dinner. He was glad to know she was distracted from her loneliness by a surprise visit from novelist Zora Neale Hurston, who drove over from Daytona when she got a depressed-sounding letter from Marjorie.

Perhaps because it made her feel closer to Norton, Marjorie kept up a massive correspondence with the many soldiers who wrote to her of their appreciation for *The Yearling* and *Cross Creek*, especially for her descriptions of food. One commanding officer wrote that *Cross Creek* should be banned in the military because it made the boys so hungry for home cooking. The chapter called "Our Daily Bread" brought such a response that Max Perkins decided that Marjorie should write a cookbook, the genesis of *Cross Creek Cookery*.

Scribners had sold 52,863 copies of *Cross Creek* and 50,555 copies of *The Yearling* to the armed forces by early 1944. Marjorie was inundated with letters from soldiers. She responded to them all, and some became regular correspondents. One such letter was from a former prisoner of war who had spent three and a half years as a "guest" of the Japanese and had received copies of both *The Yearling* and *Cross Creek* from the Red Cross. He credited Rawlings's writing with greatly increasing

The Yearling, Palmetto edition.
Courtesy of Sarah Stewart.

Marjorie Kinnan Rawlings and illustrator Robert Camp at an autographing party for *Cross Creek* and *Cross Creek Cookery* at Jacksonville's Cohen's Department Store in 1942. Courtesy of the Marjorie Kinnan Rawlings Papers, Special and Area Studies Collections, George A. Smathers Libraries, University of Florida.

his determination to survive anything the Japanese military could "dish out" just to get back and enjoy the American way of life.

While Marjorie was seeing after the lives of men she had never met, her husband was in India, getting ready to risk his life in the most immediate action he had seen yet, the battle for Burma. In early April 1944 she spent two tortured weeks not knowing if Norton was dead or alive, having only sparse reports of harrowing battles. Marjorie finally heard from Norton, and he admitted to being one of the AFS men who drove an ambulance through heavy fire to an isolated British post. "He got out by the skin of his teeth," she said, "with his ambulance loaded to the roof, and lost all his personal belongings."

It seemed harder and harder for Marjorie to carry on alone, especially after a fire at the Castle Warden in late April 1944 in which two women were killed. She wrote to Ellen Glasgow on May 24, 1944, "The burden of the war is inescapable, I think, and a great pressure from it seems to weigh on one whatever else one is battling, mental or physical."

Her spirits brightened when Norton joked around in his letters, making light of the danger he was in and threatening to ask for a tourniquet if his dysentery did not stop. But no amount of humor would make Norton better, for he had contracted amoebic dysentery and grew more and more ill. The AFS notified Marjorie

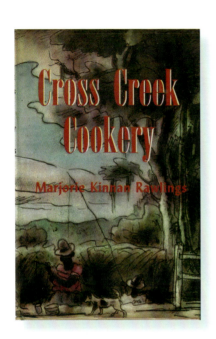

Cross Creek Cookery, 1942 edition.
Courtesy of Cynthia Barnett.

that he was critically ill in a Calcutta hospital. Finally, Marjorie's fame and connections could help her "Dear Honey." She called on her contacts in Washington, a general's wife as well as Mrs. Roosevelt, and within a few hours the commander of the China-Burma-India theater had arranged immediate transport for Norton.

Norton arrived in Miami on October 28, 1944, by hospital plane and was immediately flown to New York for advanced medical treatment. Marjorie nursed him there until nearly Christmas, when he was well enough to travel home to Florida. Dear Honey was home and well on his way to recovery, but the war endured. At least two of Marjorie's military pen pals were killed in action. She received letters from their mothers, telling her what it had meant to their sons to have Marjorie write to them so faithfully.

Marjorie's Cross Creek friend Dessie made it back safely from her tour in the Women's Army Corps (WAC) and came to visit with five other WACs in tow. Marjorie described them as "a tough bunch of pistol-packin' Mamas." She and Dessie began to plan a trip to Alaska after Dessie's discharge in 1946. They never made the trip. Marjorie had been accused of libel by a neighbor she had written about in *Cross Creek*, and the loss of the suit in 1946 was a painful blow. The very next year she lost her beloved editor and friend Maxwell Perkins. The book she had tried to write during the war, *The Sojourner*, was not published until 1952.

Marjorie Kinnan Rawlings and Cross Creek would make one final contribution to the war's survivors in 1946 when she gave her old farmhouse over for the Christmas holiday to her friend novelist-critic Marcia Davenport and the embattled Czech prime minister Jan Mazaryk. Mazaryk, who had fought long and hard for his country's freedom, found solace at the creek. He wrote of finding "a silent healing, the result of the rough and tough creation of that mysterious land called Central Florida." Tragically, Mazaryk soon became a martyr to Czech freedom.

Although their joy at the war's end was tempered by sadness, World War II was good for the Baskins in a business sense. Norton's hotel prospered long enough for him to sell it at a profit in 1946, and Marjorie's books sold exceedingly well and made her one of the decade's most popular novelists. *Cross Creek*, especially, brought balm to the wounded in body and spirit. A soldier from Marshall, Texas, Ernest Powell, expressed what the book meant in a poem he sent to its author during the war:

Beauty touches many things on earth—
A tree, a rose, a child, a limpid brook;
And she bestows on mortals hope and mirth—
Beauty's fingerprints are on this book.

From the **Fall 1999** edition of *FORUM* magazine, "War! How World War II Changed the Face of Florida."

14

When the WACs Came Marching In

How Mary McLeod Bethune—and the Women's Army Corps—rescued struggling Daytona Beach.

Gordon Patterson

Gordon Patterson is a professor of history at Florida Institute of Technology, where he began teaching in 1981. Patterson is the author of *The Mosquito Wars, The Mosquito Crusades,* and numerous articles. He is the recipient of two Fulbright Commission Awards and six grants from the National Endowment for the Humanities. In 2013 he received the Presidential Award from the American Mosquito Control Association for his contributions to the history of mosquito control. In 2021, he was named Professor of the Year by students in FIT's College of Psychology and Liberal Arts.

Image: Leaving Daytona Beach, circa 1942. The photo was part of the booklet on the WAAC Training Center. Courtesy of State Archives of Florida, Florida Memory.

IN THE FIRST YEAR of World War II, as gas rationing kept tourists at home, Daytona Beach's economy went into a swoon, and the city teetered on the edge of insolvency. Once-bustling hotels and restaurants stood empty at peak season. "It was like a water faucet being cut off," recalled Daytona Beach car dealer Saxton Lloyd. And bringing the reality of war frighteningly close to the city's famous beaches, German U-boats, like blood-thirsty sharks, prowled just offshore in the Atlantic. "It was," recalled Lloyd, "a dreadful, depressing time."

Then, in 1942, relief came from an unexpected source when the recently created Women's Auxiliary Army Corps, the WACs, established a training facility in Daytona Beach. Between October 1942 and March 1944, more than 20,000 WAC recruits passed through town, and their modest monthly paychecks helped pump nearly $5 million a month into Daytona Beach's depressed economy.

How the War Department in Washington came to choose Daytona Beach as a WAC training site is the story of political pressure from a highly unusual source being applied to the highest level of government, the White House. It began when the first WAC training facility at Fort Des Moines, Iowa, quickly proved inadequate for the growing number of recruits, and rumors circulated that Daytona Beach was being considered for a second base.

Lloyd, who ran Daytona Beach Motor Company, said a group of prominent local businessmen dispatched him to Washington to win Senator Claude Pepper's support for the training facility. Pepper arranged for Lloyd to meet with a handful of military leaders, but the meetings proved inconclusive and he returned to Daytona Beach convinced that he had failed in his mission.

Even as Lloyd found frustration in the Pentagon, another behind-the-scenes campaign was being launched that would eventually win the day. This effort involved Mary McLeod Bethune, the Black educator who established the Daytona Beach

> *Mrs. Butts made her pitch, then watched in stunned silence as the president of Bethune-Cookman "took down her telephone receiver and telephoned Franklin Delano Roosevelt as coolly as possible."…A few weeks later, Butts received a call from Bethune. "My Darling, (Mrs. Bethune always called me that)," Butts said, "you will get your wish. The WACs are coming to Daytona Beach."*

Literary and Industrial School for Training Negro Girls, which became Bethune-Cookman College and is now Bethune-Cookman University.

Eileen Butts, who served as chairman of the Bethune-Cookman Advisory Board during the war years, asked Mrs. Bethune to use her Washington contacts to win the WAC depot for Daytona Beach. "If we could get the WACs here," Mrs. Butts told her, "I do believe the tourists would come to see American women in uniform."

Mrs. Butts made her pitch, then watched in stunned silence as the president of Bethune-Cookman "took down her telephone receiver and telephoned Franklin Delano Roosevelt as coolly as possible." Apparently the president liked what he heard. "He gave her all encouragement," recalled Butts. "Mrs. Bethune thanked us for coming and told us she would keep in touch." A few weeks later Butts received a call from Bethune. "My Darling, (Mrs. Bethune always called me that)," Butts said, "you will get your wish. The WACs are coming to Daytona Beach."

The first recruits arrived in mid-October 1942, dressed in khaki uniforms with a collar insignia of Pallas Athena, Greek goddess of wisdom and the protector of heroes. Colonel Don Faith set up headquarters for the WACs at the Wingate Building on Volusia Avenue in downtown Daytona Beach. The battalion's original 400 recruits were billeted in the Osceola Hotel and Halifax Hospital. Eventually, the base spread to more than a hundred buildings.

The auxiliaries fell in love with Daytona Beach. "Gosh, I'm speechless," enthused Mildred Ayres, a member of the WAC band, on a postcard of local flora sent to her parents back in Irvington, New Jersey. "Look at the palm trees." Audrey Sewell later remembered her first impressions when she stepped off the train: "It was like heaven after leaving Pittsburgh." Then she added, "A few days later, I got one of the worst sunburns of my life."

A constant stream of servicemen poured into Daytona Beach, a residual boost to the economy of having the WACs there. "Every soldier, flyer, marine and sailor came from everywhere with their weekend passes to see the WACs," WAC recruit Doris Clarke told a Daytona Beach newspaper reporter. "They found they had more in common with us than the civilian girls." Servicemen gathered on the beach to watch the WACs exercise. Occasionally, one auxiliary remembered, "Navy air station men would fly over and throw down notes. The notes would say things like 'I want a date with the one in red.'"

Dr. Mary McLeod Bethune, in her office at Bethune-Cookman College, January 1943. Through her connections, the founder and former president and director of the NYA (National Youth Administration) Negro Relations helped bring the WACs to Daytona Beach. Courtesy of Library of Congress.

Waves of Women's Army Corps members parade down Daytona Beach's boardwalk, 1943. Their arrival proved a boon to Daytona Beach's fortunes. Courtesy of Halifax Historical Society.

Not all of their memories were positive. Some recruits were shocked by Daytona Beach's overt segregation. "The first thing I remember," recalled Clarke, "who hailed from Stamford, Connecticut, "is walking off the train and seeing 'colored' and 'for whites only' on the bathrooms. I was shocked. I had been taught that the Civil War took care of that." Among the town's segregationists, there was concern that Black auxiliaries might be assigned to Daytona Beach. That led Mary Bethune to recommend "Negro WAC troops receive their training at Negro colleges such as Atlanta, Fisk, Wilberforce, and Bennett."

At first, the press and public treated WACs as something strange and exotic. The *Daytona Beach Sunday News-Journal* published a glowing report chronicling a day in the life of a WAC recruit. One probing reporter wanted to know the color of recruits' GI underwear. Unfazed, auxiliary Lois Reistma answered they were "khaki" and "the ugliest things you ever saw." Observers praised the caliber of the recruits. "They are," wrote news reporter Liliane R. Davidson, "the women of America, these WACs. As you watch them pass you'll think 'they are not as young as I thought, averaging about 30 years old.' They have the heterogeneous physical makeup of all American groups. . . . But they all look like American women of the finest kind. They have that easy, friendly, intelligent, calm, eager look that spells American womanhood." Inevitably, though, this new and daring innovation produced a spate of myths and misunderstandings, mostly of the sexual variety. The War Department's campaign slogan for the WACs, "Release a Man for Combat," added currency to the sexual folklore. "The hardest part," recalled WAC recruit Anastasia Clyman, "was trying to convince the public and men in service that you were part of the service."

When the WACs Came Marching In • 91

Doris Clarke agreed: "A lot of people thought we were just camp followers." When the first WACs were deployed overseas in 1943, there was a public outcry, some of it undoubtedly coming from the nervous mothers, wives, and girlfriends imagining their boys meeting a WAC in some exotic land.

Newspaper columnist John O'Donnell claimed to have seen a "super-secret War Department policy" that authorized the issuance of prophylactics to "all WACs before they were sent overseas." Oveta Culp Hobby, then WACs director and later Secretary of Health, Education, and Welfare, co-owner with her husband of the *Houston Post,* and one of America's richest women, denied the allegation and challenged O'Donnell to document his claims. O'Donnell retracted his statement, but the damage was done.

Much of the public's hostility grew from the perception that the women soldiers departed from the stereotype of the stay-at-home American woman. Rumors spread about WACs who "took over" restaurants and beauty shops. Local newspaper headlines warned "Wolves Beware, WACs in Orlando Learn Judo" and "Civilians Walking with a WAC Need These Rules." But probably the most significant opposition to the WACs came from servicemen who did not want to be "released" from their office jobs for combat.

The Army, however, considered the WACs a success. By 1943 the WACs were no longer merely auxiliaries. The renamed Women's Army Corps recruits moved into a new facility at Bethune Point, named after Mary Bethune. But soon after, the WACs' days in Daytona Beach came to an end. The War Department closed the Daytona WAC training center by January 15, 1944. The WAC program was transferred to Fort Oglethorpe, Georgia, in order to accommodate the burgeoning WAC program.

On January 6, 1944, the WACs presented their final Sundown Revue, concluding with "Farewell Daytona Beach," a song written for the occasion by Captain Ruby Jane Douglas, who was a Daytona Beach WAC officer. Governor Spessard Holland hoped that the departing WACs would "spread the Good Gospel of Florida," and he predicted that "probably many of them will bring their husbands back here to live." The training center became a convalescent hospital for wounded soldiers and eventually home of Daytona Beach Community College.

More than 20,000 young women prepared for active military service in Daytona Beach and served their country with distinction. Many of the "skirted soldiers" fell in love with Florida and did indeed return to the Sunshine State to build successful careers and raise their families. And that's how the WACs saved wartime Daytona Beach—and gave the world a glimpse of things to come.

From the **Fall 1999** edition of *FORUM* magazine, "War! How World War II Changed the Face of Florida."

Booklet on the Second Women's Army Auxiliary Corps Training Center at Daytona Beach. Courtesy of State Archives of Florida, Florida Memory.

Women's Army Auxiliary Corps members in gas masks during training, Daytona Beach, November 1942. The group was photographed just prior to sailing for Europe. "Auxiliary" was dropped from the Corps' name in 1943 to better reflect its essential work. All photos on this page courtesy of National Archives.

WAAC training in Daytona Beach, circa 1942.

Postcard of the WAAC Band on Daytona Beach, circa 1942.

15

The Mighty Orange Faces Its Uncertain Future

Changing tastes, stubborn disease put the squeeze on a beloved state symbol.

Gary R. Mormino

Gary R. Mormino's biography is found on page 67.

Image: Oranges and blossoms, symbolic of Florida. Photo by Ellen Levy Finch. Wikimedia Commons.

A LONG LINE OF MUSES has chronicled the orange's journey over the centuries from China to India, Persia to Spain, and Hispaniola to Florida. The orange has stirred the imaginations of Franciscan friars, country fiddlers, and multinational conglomerates. More than anything else, Florida's signature fruit has defined the Sunshine State and its promise as the new Mediterranean.

But today the orange is in peril. An incurable disease called huanglongbing, commonly known as "citrus greening," has swept through Florida, affecting every orange-producing county. This crisis has been called "the most serious threat in [citrus] history," "a looming disaster many Floridians do not know about," and "an existential threat." The disease, also known as yellow dragon in China, where it was first detected, looms larger than any previous threat to the industry, including devastating hurricanes, the sprawl of development across agricultural land, and the expensive war of attrition to eradicate citrus canker. After marauding through orange groves in China and Brazil, the disease, a bacterium spread by a tiny flying insect called a psyllid, appeared in Florida in 2005.

Oranges become misshapen and bitter, and eventually the stricken trees die. But Florida's grove owners are resilient. They have battled the Mediterranean fruit fly and killer freezes and weathered the economic effects of wars and depressions. Still, the present challenge is so serious that scientists and state officials have debated the ethics and efficacy of genetic modification, of altering the orange's DNA in order to save it. In 2021, the US Department of Agriculture (USDA) National Institute for Food and Agriculture (NIFA) allocated $11 million in grants to combat the problem, including funding several projects at the University of Florida.

An orange crop lost. The 1895 freeze devastated groves from Jacksonville to Tampa. Courtesy of Special Collections, University of South Florida Tampa Library.

Nothing Says Florida Like the Orange

The story of the orange spans the history of Florida. In colonial St. Augustine, generations of Spanish, Minorcan, and British settlers planted orange trees in such abundance that when vessels entered the harbor in the spring, the crews identified the city's location by the fragrance of orange blossoms wafting from grove to bay.

THE ORANGE IS SO ICONIC and entwined in the Florida dream that this agricultural product is considered part of the natural landscape. After all, Florida boasts an Orange County and Citrus County and towns named Orange City, Orange Park, and Orange Springs. The orange blossom is Florida's official state flower, the orange the official state fruit, and since 1998 an orange has served as the emblem on state license plates. State law even protects oranges from defamation and bans the shipment of "green fruit."

The story of the orange spans the history of Florida. In colonial St. Augustine, successive generations of Spanish, Minorcan, and British settlers planted orange trees in such abundance that when vessels entered the harbor in the spring, the crews identified the city's location by the fragrance of orange blossoms wafting from grove to bay.

In 1835 a devastating freeze scoured Florida, destroying the beloved citrus groves of St. Augustine. "Never was a place so desolate," lamented a local judge. In the decades that followed, orange groves sprang up along the Indian and St. Johns Rivers and in the Golden Triangle area comprising the towns of Mount Dora, Eustis, and Tavares.

Mid-nineteenth-century growers faced many obstacles, most significantly distance. Steamboats ferried crates of oranges from Leesburg, Palatka, and Jacksonville, but much of the harvest spoiled before reaching eager consumers. In the late nineteenth century, revolutions in transportation helped bridge country and city, state and nation, nation and world. Florida citrus rode the rails to new heights and new markets, its cedar crates with labels advertising the Sunshine State as a winter paradise.

The Mighty Orange Faces Its Uncertain Future · 95

Fruit box labels. Colorful labels like this adorned boxes of Florida citrus headed for market in the years from 1920 to 1950. Courtesy of MacManus Citrus Label Collection, Special Collections, University of South Florida Tampa Library.

Growers helped create and popularize new markets for a product most Americans had never sampled. For generations to come, people across the country first encountered Florida by tasting an orange. If cotton was king of the Old South, the orange became the endearing and enduring symbol of Florida.

Florida was touted as a poor man's paradise. In acreage so small it seemed laughable in the Midwest, a manicured 10-acre orange grove in De Leon Springs or Dunedin imagined Jeffersonian republicanism and democratic romanticism. Beginning in the Gilded Age of the 1870s and cresting in the 1920s, orange fever brought trainloads, boatloads, and carloads of citizens eager to become gentleman grove owners. Entire cities, Temple Terrace and Howey-in-the-Hills, incorporated town and grove.

A dazzling variety of oranges took root in Florida, their names suggesting their romantic lineages: Homosassa, Hamlin, Temple, Murcott, Lue Gim Gong, Parson Brown, Sanford Bloods, Mediterranean Sweet, and Maltese Oval. To sell the fruit, roadside fruit stands and packinghouses proliferated along the orange belt, offering motorists sweet bliss and a free glass of orange juice.

Many small growers eventually quit, the victims of overproduction, freezes, and fierce competition. A handful emerged triumphant like Philip "Doc" Phillips, Antonio Rossi, and Ben Hill Griffin. But in a story all too familiar, large corporations began swallowing Florida's baronial estates as well as its family groves. Beginning in the 1940s, corporations bet wildly and successfully on Florida grove land. Just as Phillips and Griffin personified the gritty individualism of the men who built dynasties one grove at a time, Consolidated Citrus LP, Coca-Cola, and Cutrale Juices USA came to signify a new corporate presence, more multinational and multiconglomerate than personal and local.

Hard Times Hit the Groves

Historic freezes, new hybrids, and the relentless development of grove land have pushed Florida's orange belt southward over the years. In 1950 the orange belt buckled together the state's leading citrus counties that stretched across central Florida: Orange, Polk, and Lake. Orange County pointed with pride to its 80,000-plus acres of citrus. Today the belt has drooped southward: Polk, St. Lucie, Indian River, DeSoto, Hardee, Highlands, Hendry, and Collier Counties now have emerged as citrus leaders. Orange County has slipped to nineteenth place. Pinellas County, which devoted 15,000 acres of land to citrus cultivation in the 1950s, now has no commercial groves.

In January 1981 Florida shivered as the first of the decade's Alberta Clippers plunged statewide temperatures well below freezing. By the end of the decade, two more disastrous freezes had ravaged Florida's groves, killing 90 percent of Lake County's orange trees. The beneficiaries of this disaster were Florida real estate developers and Brazil. This marked a milestone in citrus history: Brazil replaced Florida as the world's leading orange producer. Astonishingly, 100,000 acres of Lake County citrus land was transformed into housing tracts, shopping centers, and nurseries. An Orlando banker summarized the opportunity: "We stopped picking oranges and started picking tourists."

From the late 1940s onward, advertising songs and jingles about the orange, fresh from the crate and frozen concentrate out of the can, captivated Americans: "Breakfast without orange juice is like a day without sunshine!" "Come to the Florida Sunshine Tree!" and "Orange juice—It's not just for breakfast anymore." Orange juice became an integral part of the standard breakfast, along with bacon and eggs and toast. But in recent years, more and more Americans are beginning their days without a glass of orange juice. OJ's greatest threat may not even be citrus greening, but rather changing tastes.

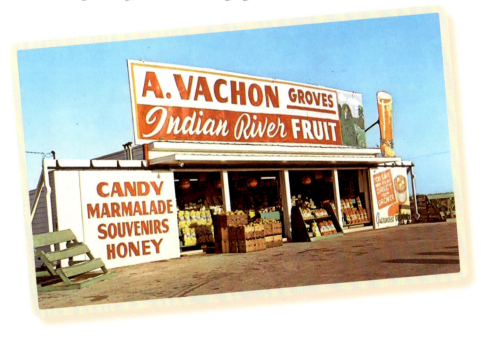

A once-familiar sight. Large signs beckon travelers to A. Vachon Groves Indian River Fruit's roadside stand at the Fort Pierce entrance to the Sunshine State Parkway. St. Lucie Historical Society.

Train passing through an orange grove, postcard. Courtesy of Florida Citrus Postcards Collection, Florida Southern College Archives.

Illustrating this point, a journalist recently posed this question: "Just when did orange juice—loaded with nutrients from vitamin C to folic acid—become the drink from hell?" In truth, OJ is brimming not only with vitamin C but carbohydrates, the arch villain of South Beach dieters and concerned pediatricians. Orange juice, moreover, holds little mystique with young Americans who typically skip breakfast, preferring a carbonated soda, vitamin-enhanced water, or espresso doppio.

By 2005, reality had wilted the blossom off the orange. The roadside citrus stand advertising a free glass of Florida sunshine was becoming as rare as small grove owners. In 1940, Polk County replaced Los Angeles as America's leading citrus county. During World War II and for succeeding decades, Florida wrested and defended the title "King of US Oranges." But California has now reclaimed the title.

Unfolding over six centuries, the story of Florida citrus is a complicated tale involving great contrasts and trajectories: old groves and new perils, small family farms and global competition, citrus barons whose names emblazon athletic fields, and the largely forgotten men and women who pruned, picked, and packed the oranges.

Threatened and squeezed by developers, foreign competition, an incurable disease, global warming, and hard freezes, the future of the orange in Florida is uncertain. But amid tumult and change, one thing remains certain: a glass of freshly squeezed Florida orange juice is pure elixir, the proper drink for a dream state.

From the **Spring 2014** edition of *FORUM* magazine, "Can Florida Save the Orange?"

16

Recollections of a Space Traveler

Former congressman and astronaut Bill Nelson shares the perils that lurked before, during, and after his historic mission.

Interview with Bill Nelson by Rick Edmonds

Bill Nelson, a former three-term US senator and six-term congressman, brings a rare perspective to his latest role as head of NASA. He grew up on the Space Coast in the 1950s and '60s, represented the area in Congress, and was chosen to fly as the first congressman-astronaut aboard the space shuttle *Columbia*. The six-day mission launched January 12, 1986. Ten days after Nelson's mission returned safely, the space shuttle *Challenger* blew up moments after liftoff, killing all onboard. He further chronicles his space flight experiences in his 1988 book (with Jamie Buckingham), *Mission: An American Congressman's Voyage to Space*.

Rick Edmonds was editor of *FORUM* from 1994 to 2000.

You were not born in Melbourne but moved there at a relatively young age, right?

Yes, my father's family had homesteaded on what is now the Kennedy Space Center. The deed for 160 acres of land came from the government, and I guess it was signed by President Wilson in 1917. I was born in Miami, but that was after the Florida land-boom bubble burst in '26. My father went to Miami and entered the first law class at the University of Miami, and when I was born they moved back to Melbourne.

Do you have memories of it, when you were a kid, as kind of a sandy, barely populated country-type place?

Absolutely. A1A I can well remember as a dirt road. I can even remember the Eau Gallie Causeway as being a wooden bridge. I can remember going north to what is now Patrick Air Force Base, and everything was just solid palmettos.

In the late 1950s once we got to Sputnik, things took off pretty fast, right?

I was in Melbourne High School, and it was quite an exciting place to be because the nation had been shocked to suddenly realize that the Russians were ahead of us. That had a tremendous impact on us even in high school.

Was there a sense of national excitement and national attention with presidential visits and parades down the street through those years?

Remember in '57 it was Sputnik and in '58 we put up Explorer. The nation had gone to Wernher von Braun, who was in Huntsville, Alabama, and he had this rocket called the Redstone. This was after the Navy had tried and tried the old Vanguard rocket, and it kept exploding on the pad. He said give me six months; in six months he had our first satellite, Explorer, in orbit. That was '58, and then we started the manned program.

I graduated in '60 and we put up in sub-orbit Alan Shepard and Gus Grissom, but the Russians surprised us again. Without us knowing it they launched Yuri Gagarin, the first human to orbit. And he orbited one orbit three weeks before we launched Alan Shepard.

Years later when I was on the floor of Congress, Tip O'Neill motioned me over and said "Billy," and this is right after I had flown in space, he said, "Billy, I want to tell you when I was a young Boston congressman, I was down at the White House with President Kennedy. I'd never seen him so nervous. He was just pacing and pacing back and forth like a cat on a hot tin roof, and I finally asked some of the staff, 'What is wrong with the president?' and they said that the count is proceeding on Alan Shepard." And Kennedy was so nervous because the entire prestige of the nation was on the line since the Soviets had surprised us and put up [Soviet cosmonaut Yuri] Gagarin successfully. And here we didn't even have a rocket powerful enough to get us into full orbit with the Mercury spacecraft.

It was ten months later that we took the Atlas rocket and put [John] Glenn up for three or four orbits. There is an interesting reason why we didn't have the throw weight. This all came out of the intercontinental ballistic missile program, and the Soviets did not have the sophistication and the miniaturization to create hydrogen

Congressman Bill Nelson and the crew of the shuttle *Columbia* in orbit, January 1986. The astronauts are (*clockwise from upper left*) Bob Cenker, Nelson, pilot Charlie Bolden, Commander Hoot Gibson, Pinky Nelson, Franklin Chang-Diaz, and Steve Hawley. Two weeks later, the *Challenger* would explode soon after takeoff, killing all aboard. Courtesy of NASA.

100 · Bill Nelson with Rick Edmonds

warheads that were the size that we had. We had it down to 1,500 pounds. So we only had to develop a rocket that could transfer intercontinentally to the Soviet Union that 1,500-pound nuclear warhead, whereas they had to create much more powerful rockets in order to transfer their payload. And so that paid off for them in that they got into space first with Sputnik and second with Gagarin.

Even though you were on your way to being a political person, not a nuclear physicist, you got a little space in your blood when you were growing up there?

Sure, all of us did. We knew the names of the astronauts. Even though we might not have had any kind of interaction with them as kids, clearly in that part of the country we were pretty excited about it.

Let's reel ahead in time to when you got to be an astronaut yourself. Am I right in remembering that you were one of three civilians including Utah senator Jake Garn and teacher Christa McAuliffe who came into the astronaut training program and then got to fly?

You can't classify Jake Garn and me in the same category as civilians with the teacher. That was a separate deal. What actually happened was, in the early '80s NASA declared the space shuttle operational, which was really a misnomer. It was never operational; it was always experimental. But they decided they were going to fly people other than the professional full-time astronauts. The first ones they reached out to were the scientists or engineers from private companies. The best illustration of that is Charlie Walker from the McDonnell Douglas Corporation, who flew on the space shuttle three times.

I'm the last one to get in, which was by design, I'm there on that launch tower looking over that darkness, and just four miles away is where my grandparents homesteaded back in 1915.

Then NASA decided it wanted to expand that. They thought of this teacher-in-space program, but concurrently they decided to give the chairmen of the two respective space committees, one in the Senate and one in the House, the opportunity. They first decided on Garn. It was a Republican administration. And once they decided on Garn, and he flew, then they said well why not fly the chairman from the House, who happens to be a Democrat. And that's when I had the opportunity. I conducted twelve medical experiments, the primary of which was protein crystal growth. It was sponsored by the Comprehensive Cancer Center at the University of Alabama at Birmingham. I had the option of selecting the experiments that I wanted to do. I did that and the first American stress test in space. I ran for forty minutes on a treadmill. So I've run halfway around the world!

We were scrubbed the first four times, and on the fifth time, almost a month later, we launched. The fact was not lost on me in that early morning darkness as all the crew had already climbed into the spacecraft and I'm the last one to get in, which was by design, I'm there on that launch tower looking over that darkness, and just four miles away is where my grandparents homesteaded back in 1915.

Recollections of a Space Traveler · 101

This was just a few weeks before the *Challenger* launch. Your space flight was delayed several times, if not for cold weather, at least on a day when it was terribly cold. Did you have a sense of great potential danger and that you were sitting on explosives? Or had it happened so many times and gone so smoothly that it was like riding on an airplane?

Well, the crew clearly understood the risk. However, it is something that you do not allow yourself to dwell on. Therefore, any fear that might arise, you just stuff it down. I remember, for example, the actual night before the day we launched we were all in the sauna trying to get relaxed so we could get to bed. Our commander was actually talking to us about what we would do if we lost our main engines. If you lose one main engine, you're going to have enough height and velocity to make the emergency landing across what they call transatlantic abort. If you lose two engines, you're in the drink. So he was telling us what we would do. Now after *Challenger*, they have completely redone their configuration, and they can actually bail out if they can get the orbiter in a controlled descent. There are no ejection seats, so they have a telescopic pole after you blow the hatch, and as you jump out it will take you out over the wing.

Back then we didn't have that, and we knew that we were in the drink. So he was going to tell us what he was going to do in case any of us survived the impact in the water, although all of us knew the reality that if you land a fully loaded space craft with a cargo payload bay full of satellites, the impact of the water is going to bring them all coming forward, crushing into the crew compartment. So we knew there was little chance. But you don't dwell on that.

Each of our four scrubs, had we launched, would have been a very bad day. Our first scrub, December 19, there was a malfunction in a sensor that said that there was a malfunction in a nozzle of one of the solid rocket boosters, and it automatically shut it down. What everybody didn't realize until after *Challenger* is that morning it was also 42 degrees as compared to the 36 degrees that *Challenger* launched in.

The second launch attempt, we were stopped with 31 seconds when an alert supervisor noticed that one of the lock's lines was too cold and took it upon himself to stop the count. When they went in, they found out what had happened was that someone had overridden the computer. As a result we had drained 18,000 pounds of liquid oxygen out of the fuel tank. Had we launched 31 seconds later, in the words of John Young, who was the daddy astronaut at the time, we wouldn't have had enough fuel to get to orbit.

The third time we had a scrub for what, I remember, was unacceptable weather in Africa or Spain, the two transatlantic abort sites. We were scrubbed on that day. Then, when they detanked, they found that a temperature probe had broken off of the ground support equipment, flowed through the liquid oxygen lock's line,

> *The crew clearly understood the risk. However, it is something that you do not allow yourself to dwell on. Therefore, any fear that might arise, you just stuff it down.*

Flying human chain in space flight training, November 1985. Two months before the successful *Columbia* and ill-fated *Challenger* launches, prime and backup payload specialists from the two missions trained together. The group shared some forty parabolas (simulations of weightlessness) in NASA's KC-135, Zero-G aircraft. They are (*left to right*) Gerard Magilton, backup payload specialist, *Columbia*; Christa McAuliffe, payload specialist/teacher citizen observer, *Challenger*; US Representative Bill Nelson, *Columbia*; Barbara R. Morgan, backup to McAuliffe; and Robert J. Cenker, payload specialist, *Columbia*. Photo by Otis Imboden, courtesy of NASA.

then stuck in a prevalve in front of one of the main engines. Had we launched on that particular day, everything would have been fine for the 8½ minutes to orbit. But on orbit, one of the three engines would not have shut off. And again, to use John Young's description at the time, it would have blown the end of the shuttle to smithereens. That was number three.

Number four: This time it's the 10th of January and we go out to the pad at four o'clock in the morning in a driving Florida rainstorm. At nine o'clock in the morning, they call off the launch because the rainstorm had now turned into a Florida lightning storm. That was the only time I saw worry on the faces of my fellow crew members, as we were sitting there waiting for them to come get us, and the lightning is flashing through the spacecraft windows, and we're sitting there on top of all that liquid hydrogen.

Two days later, on the fifth try, January 12, we launched into an almost flawless six-day mission to return January 18, and then to have *Challenger* blow up just ten days later.

And your reactions when that happened?

I had been through the debrief in Houston and had gone back to Washington because Congress was in session and voting. I gathered our congressional staff around the TV so that I could explain to them what was happening on the countdown. And, of course, it was the faraway view, not the closeup view that we saw later. So it was not immediately apparent, but it's interesting how my mind did not want to accept what my eyes were seeing. And I remember when the staff suddenly disappeared and I was in there alone. I went back in my bathroom, and I got down on my knees and I said, "Why was I spared?"

From the **Winter 1997/1998** edition of *FORUM* magazine, "Reality and Romance: The Space Program at 40."

17 Memoirs of a Child of the Space Program

Blasts from the past, in a time and place like no other.

Andrea Brunais

Poet, writer, and painter **Andrea Brunais** is the author of four books including *Hillbilly Drug Baby: The Story* and *Mercedes Wore Black*, a novel set in Florida. Her prize-winning newspaper career included work as a writer, editor, and executive with Knight-Ridder Newspapers as well as Media General. She recently retired from Virginia Tech as director of communications in the outreach and international division.

Image: Apollo 11 Astronaut Buzz Aldrin walks on the moon, July 20, 1969. In an iconic photograph taken by Astronaut Neil A. Armstrong, Buzz Aldrin treads the Moon's surface near the leg of the Lunar Module Eagle. Courtesy of NASA.

SPACE WAS EVERYTHING TO ME, my first separation from my father as a baby, my first brush with sexism as a middle-school student, my first experience as a teenager seeing a grown man cry. Mostly, space was the reason my entire life turned upside down in 1963 at the age of nine when I found myself plunked down in Florida, in a neighborhood off A1A just a mile from the beach. Here the Brunais ship had landed: a stay-at-home mom, six kids, and an engineer father who drove north along the Atlantic Ocean every day to test and prepare for launch the engines that would hurl rockets into space.

My father's fascination with machines along with his belief that science could take you anywhere resulted in makeshift devices designed to make life easier. Usually life became more strangely interesting. We kids were born when dads were banned from the delivery room. But Pop was always outside in the hallway, sticking his arm into the sterile room with a microphone at the precise moment to record our first cries. When I was a young teen, he rigged up a motor to a bicycle; then he took it apart because post-invention he found that I couldn't putt-putt down Marion Street without a license.

Dad loved his work, and so did all the other men. There was just one woman on their launch team, Linda Gainer, a twenty-four-year-old Black woman who was such a rarity that Chrysler sent out PR photos calling her "the First Lady of Space," showing her standing next to the Saturn 1B/SkyLab launch vehicle. To the engineers who commuted from Satellite Beach or Melbourne to the cape, it was never just a job. Their missions were the stuff of Tom Swift, Jules Verne, and the Wright brothers all rolled into one.

Meanwhile, my mother would put a damper on things, complaining about the Florida heat and saying nothing in the world could prompt her to sit atop a thousand tons of TNT and let it explode beneath her. That was her description of a launch. It was fun, being the daughter of a space scientist and, maternally, a long line of English teachers.

We had made one other stop along the way from Detroit to the Space Coast—Huntsville, Alabama. My father preceded us there, involved in preliminary research. Years later, I learned he was one of the elite civil service people, military personnel, and prime contractor experts working for [German-born aerospace engineer and rocket developer] Wernher von Braun. Left behind in Michigan for a time, my mother acquired less-fond memories. She mowed the lawn and tended to things in the house, fresh from the birth of the sister after me.

Back in Detroit, Pop had fervently waited for the call as he worked on the mundane militarizing of the rocket. Finally, his employer, Chrysler Corporation, embraced space. When we arrived in Florida, like the other frontier families in Brevard County, we bought a house and dug in (as much as you could dig into sand), peopling a landscape that belonged mostly to crabs, rattlesnakes, and armadillos.

For a year I wore short sleeves to the bus stop while the other kids shivered in the cold. Then my blood thinned, and I was just like the other Florida kids. Many of us had cape connections. Except for Patrick Air Force Base, the Harris plant, and a few small real estate concerns, Brevard didn't boast a whole lot of activity. The beaches were blessedly empty much of the time, and our bus driver was obliging enough to swing into one of the parking lots each afternoon so the kids could check the surf. Most days the waves were mediocre, but sometimes they were great, and when a hurricane approached they frothed to 6 feet and higher.

I'm sorry to say that, like any worldly wise kid, I soon grew so blasé about the space shots that I would rather stay in bed than get up for liftoffs that interfered with my sleep. "Get up!" my mother would call, suddenly caught up in the magic.

Ellsworth Brunais, the author's father, with his colleague Linda Gainer, one of the first women to work on a launch team, circa 1960s. Both were members of Chrysler's Saturn 1B launch crew. The Saturn 1B launched Apollo 7, the first manned Apollo flight, into orbit. Courtesy of Andrea Brunais.

Children awaiting astronaut, 1962. Students of Cocoa Beach Elementary School prepare to welcome John Glenn home from the Friendship 7 mission at a parade celebrating his return. From Nancy Yasecko's 1985 documentary *Growing Up with Rockets*, © Vanguard Productions.

"A missile's going up!" We never had to drive elsewhere for a view because our backyard was a great vantage point.

Predawn shots were a circle of light arcing skyward like the fattest, purest fireworks finale. If Pop had worked on the missile, he would be on the scene at the VAB building. The engineers slept on top of workbenches and desks throughout the night as the moment drew near.

He worked on neat-sounding projects: Redstone, Jupiter A through C, the Saturn, the Men-in-Space Mercury program.

My mom's job may have been harder. In those days, rearing happy, well-adjusted children was supposed to be the greatest accomplishment of a woman. Women who worked and whose children didn't conform were always blamed because they didn't stay home. In bad times, women who worked were chastised because they were taking work away from men.

But nothing could have prepared her for the move to Florida. Pop's long hours sometimes extended into twenty-four-hour shifts. Meanwhile, my mom never missed a week without spending hours in the doctor's office because there were six of us, and one was always sick.

Money was pretty good for the engineers, so many adults drank, overspent, and indulged in loose living. This being the '60s, kids were protesting, rebelling, and pushing the bounds of freedom. Some adults got caught up in the lifestyle themselves. Drugs were everywhere. So it was tough for Mother, trying to set some limits on freedom, influence behavior, instill values, manners, and morals, discourage extravagant spending, and stress the need for taking school seriously.

Memoirs of a Child of the Space Program · 107

Most of the men—my dreamy, laid-back Pop less so than others—had an inflated sense of their importance because of their jobs. They considered themselves above the budgeting and coping the mothers had to do. Still, my mother had to confine her reach for the stars to taking night courses and writing poetry about it.

Because You're a Girl

DURING MIDDLE SCHOOL I attended a Catholic school on the mainland. High-tech excitement rippled throughout the school when it was announced that a missile-tracking program would be designed and executed by a select group of the best students in math and science. A couple of suspenseful weeks passed while it was decided whether girls would be allowed. If so, a tiny girl named Gail Ricard (who everybody knew was the smartest kid in the school) and I were to be invited to join. Ultimately, the powers that be decreed the project to be boys-only. Just as space was something our fathers did, missile-tracking was something our male classmates did. Two boys with lower scores than Gail's and mine were let in. To have the "Right Stuff," you first had to be the Right Sex.

The eyes of the nation were on Brevard County as public schools became places where President Lyndon Johnson celebrated the grand national ambition JFK had launched. I remember most of us teenagers as myopic, caught up as we were in the identity crises of adolescence and trying to keep up with the original flower children who were our older brothers and sisters. The Vietnam War was going strong, and everyone wore black armbands on appointed days. Drugs were sweeping across high school campuses, hitting my own Satellite High School in a big way. One day, six students collapsed in various classes after ingesting something called "reds." National media picked it up, but my principal forbade me, the newspaper editor, from writing about it.

Football players and cheerleaders formed one group. Their polar opposites, "freaks," wore fringed suede and challenged authority.

I fit firmly in the second camp, engaging in mildly subversive acts such as founding the Ecology Club. So many students were sons and daughters of engineers that a member of either group could be a nerd or a geek and it would be no big deal. Satellite High School produced eight National Merit Scholars, and I attended college with Chrysler picking up my tuition.

I can't say I would have gone into rocket science if I hadn't been banned from the middle-school missile-tracking project on account of being a girl. I thought those societal messages were unimportant. I was so determined to set my own course, in newspapers. I laughed when my high school math teacher said if I were a boy he'd suggest I go into nuclear physics, but, as I wasn't, he didn't know what to say. Maybe I only thought it funny because I had already decided to go into newspapers. Maybe that slapping down, in truth, steered me away from the work of exploring the galaxy.

Local youngsters in front of the Spacarium, an early tourism attraction in Cocoa Beach, 1958. From Nancy Yasecko's 1985 documentary *Growing Up with Rockets*, © Vanguard Productions.

Triumph and Tragedy

A NANOSECOND WAS all it took to reduce my friend Max's father, another space programmer, to a bowed head and wet tears. Max and I were in her family room on July 20, 1969, watching the Armstrong-Aldrin afternoon walk on the moon.

For us it was routine. Hadn't the newscasters been predicting it for months? And writers from Jules Verne to Robert A. Heinlein had been hypothesizing the moon landing forever. So mission accomplished, already. But for Max's father, landing on the moon meant mankind had changed in some fundamental, profound way. It was the middle of the day. We didn't know whether the other men had cried at their workplaces.

If you felt bad when Princess Diana died, multiply that feeling a thousandfold and you'll know how space families of Brevard County felt when Gus Grissom, Edward White II, and Roger B. Chaffee died on the launch pad in a command module filled with fire and smoke. Years later, when the *Challenger* crew died, I was in Tampa watching the sky. I was pushing my daughter around our neighborhood

Memoirs of a Child of the Space Program · 109

Robert Edgar with his mother, Urda Edgar, holding a model of the Vanguard satellite, 1958. "One day he came home with a hardshell case," remembers Edgar of their neighbor John Neilon, later director of NASA's Unmanned Launch Operations, "and inside it was velvet lined and held the satellite." Photo by Robert Edgar Sr., then an electrical engineer with the space program. © Robert Edgar 2022.

in a stroller and composing poetry when I looked up and saw the wispy white, chaotic clouds of the explosion. Even before turning on the news I knew what must have happened.

There was no question after either disaster that the quest would go on.

My father's most exciting assignment was the SkyLab program. Only with deep regret did he leave the Space Coast, returning to Detroit midway through the third and final launch of the SkyLab crew to the orbiting SkyLab. In 1973 he was forced to again embrace work on car engines that was surer than space or lose pension benefits built up over a career.

Pop's launch team would disband after the final flight of the Apollo program, which took years of work building toward the mid-1970s launch. It was the first space flight in which different nations sent up spacecraft to dock in space. In July 1975, a US Apollo spacecraft carrying a crew of three—Thomas P. Stafford, Vance D. Brand, and Donald K. Slayton—docked with a Russian Soyuz spacecraft with its crew of two.

For us it was routine. Hadn't the newscasters been predicting it for months? … But for Max's father, landing on the moon meant mankind had changed in some fundamental, profound way. It was the middle of the day. We didn't know whether the other men had cried at their workplaces.

For Pop and his Chrysler team, this was the end of the story. Years of hopes and sweat, tears and dreams, of painstaking preparation, of building and testing parts, of returning to the drawing board, of hoping to hear the famous countdown end in the announcer's excited, "It's a go!"—all of that culminated in a mission that lasted just nine days, seven hours, and twenty-eight minutes.

I was a student at the University of South Florida when the space race lost its luster and Chrysler and the other companies began transferring or laying off their engineers.

Pop wanted to stay till the end of the SkyLab and Apollo-Soyuz programs, but his boss in Detroit would not hold the Motor City engineering position open for him. It was just as well, for by the end of that year Chrysler froze all hiring, and that lasted for several years.

Other engineers had put down roots and stayed. Even today you can go to Brevard County and find former rocket scientists running restaurants and such. I stayed in Florida, while my younger siblings moved back to Detroit to follow the breadwinner, who, with a sigh, was forced to direct his talents away from testing rocket engines and toward testing car engines.

For my father, work on the space race provided the glory years. Somehow through his passion for missiles, with their flames and vapor trails, he gave me the desire to seek out and undertake work that, at its best, can also move heaven and earth.

From the **Winter 1997/1998** edition of *FORUM* magazine, "Reality and Romance: The Space Program at 40."

18 Florida's Fields of Dreams

How sports have boosted our fortunes and, at times, healed our divides.

Steven Noll

Steven Noll is an instructional professor in the history department at the University of Florida, where he has taught since 1993. He teaches classes on Florida history, environmental history, and the history of disability. His book *Writing for the Public Good* is an edited collection of op-ed pieces written by David Colburn, the late University of Florida history professor, and former Florida governor and senator Bob Graham. Noll works closely with Florida Humanities, giving public lectures around the state on Florida history subjects.

Image: Dunedin's Crisman twins were part of the winning "Peggy's Girls" softball team in the late 1930s and '40s. Courtesy of Dunedin History Museum.

LIFE CAN BE HARD in the communities surrounding Lake Okeechobee. The towns of Pahokee and Belle Glade in western Palm Beach County are far from the glitz and glamor of Worth Avenue and Mar-a-Lago. They are among the poorest places in America. Workers, mostly Black and increasingly immigrants, harvest the sugarcane that feeds the American sweet tooth.

But something else rises in these towns in the fertile muck of the Everglades. Pahokee and Belle Glade export more football players per capita than any place in the United States. College and pro football rosters are filled with players from these communities looking for a way out of the poverty that hangs like a pall. Among them are Anquan Boldin, Reidel Anthony, Fred Taylor, Santonio Holmes, Louis Oliver, and Johnny Rutledge.

Football, in the words of a 2013 *New York Times* article, "is salvation itself, a fleeting window of escape from a place where prison or early death are real and likely outcomes."

Every year since the beginning of the 1980s, just before Thanksgiving, the Raiders of Glades Central High School, representing Belle Glade, and the Blue Devils of Pahokee High School play a game as important to those communities as the Super Bowl itself. It's called the Muck Bowl.

Complete with a glittering trophy for the school and rings for the players, the Muck Bowl is more than just a game; it represents the importance of sports to these two small towns.

Former Pahokee head coach Blaze Thompson put the game in perspective in 2014. "Selfishly, in the back of your mind, you put [beating] Glades Central ahead of a state championship," Thompson said. "It's by far the more emotional, pride-filled game. Losing that game is like losing to your brother. You have to deal with it every single day."

The Muck Bowl is a microcosm of the critical place sports has played throughout Florida history.

How Sportfishing Sparked a Florida Boom

IN THE YEARS AFTER the Civil War, Florida was a far cry from the bustling state we know today. In poor, rural, and sparsely populated Florida, wealthy northern entrepreneurs saw an opportunity to make money exploiting its untapped natural resources. Some developed the turpentine industry, some mined phosphate, and others, such as Henry Flagler and Henry Plant, built railroads to knit the state together and connect it to the rest of the nation.

Ernest Hemingway with sailfish, Key West, 1940s. Photo by Wright Langley. Courtesy of Florida Photographic Collection, State Archives of Florida.

A key to Florida's development, then and now, has been tourism. Tourism started in Florida with sportfishing, specifically for tarpon, known for their mammoth size—ranging up to 350 pounds and 8 feet long—and fighting spirit. In 1885 a wealthy New York architect named William Wood and his Florida guide, John Smith, caught a tarpon off the southwest coast of Florida. This was important because, according to University of Florida historian Jack E. Davis in his book *The Gulf*, "catching one was like going deep-sea fishing without going out to sea."

This led to Florida's first tourist boom, one centered on sportfishing for the moneyed leisure class. By 1900 Florida's Gulf coast south of the burgeoning port of Tampa was dotted with hotels catering to the sporting crowd. At a time when American masculinity was being confronted by the Industrial Age, according to Davis, "tarpon challenged you [and] renewed a faith in your physical self." The obsession with tarpon and sportfishing made Florida the focus of saltwater sportfishing in America for much of the twentieth century, catering to such iconic figures as Theodore Roosevelt, Zane Grey, Ted Williams, and "Papa" himself, Ernest Hemingway.

Here's Hemingway writing to his editor, Maxwell Perkins, in April 1928 from Key West: "Caught the biggest tarpon they've had down here so far this season—63 lbs. The really big ones are just starting to come in."

Life on the Field Reflected Society's Struggles

As FLORIDIANS MOVED into the twentieth century, the state struggled with modernity as it continued to cling to the separatist traditions of the Jim Crow South. Sports remained an integral part of that world as a growing number of high schools and colleges used sports to develop a community identity, encourage school spirit, inspire patriotism, and reinforce racial and gender norms.

The contrasting stories of Polk County natives James Van Fleet and Ken Riley, both athletic standouts, personified those ideas that still held throughout much of the twentieth century.

As a student at the all-white Summerlin Institute in Bartow, Van Fleet was captain of the 1910 football team. He then played fullback while attending the United States Military Academy, including in the iconic 1912 loss to Carlisle Indian School (led by Jim Thorpe), and as a member of the undefeated 1914 team. After serving in the Army during World War I, Van Fleet returned to Florida in 1921 to head the University of Florida's ROTC department. While at UF, he was the Fighting Gators' head football coach for two years, boasting a winning percentage of .737.

During his years growing up in Bartow and playing football for Summerlin Institute, Van Fleet would never play with or against Black players.

The Black football tradition in Bartow only began in the 1920s when Union Academy, the only Black school in Polk County, opened a high school division. Its most famous football graduate was Ken Riley, named to the Florida High School

Athletic Association (FHSAA) All-Century football team, who gained fame as a quarterback at Florida A&M and as a cornerback with the Cincinnati Bengals in the 1970s and '80s.

Because of Florida's rigid segregation laws, Riley, one of nine Union Academy players to play in the NFL, never competed in organized football against white players until he became a professional. Van Fleet and Riley represent both Florida's vibrant sports heritage and the reality of racial segregation.

Jackie Robinson's Gift

If Florida sports tourism started with tarpon fishing, it truly flourished with baseball. As early as the late 1880s, Major League Baseball teams came to Florida for spring training in what came to be known as "the Grapefruit League." But it was not until the 1910s that Florida cities actively pushed for teams to spend six weeks in February and March getting ready for the upcoming baseball season.

Led by such community boosters as Tampa mayor D. B. McKay and St. Petersburg businessman Al Lang, Floridians extolled the virtues of warm weather and inexpensive lodging to entice teams to train in the Sunshine State. By 1929, ten of the sixteen Major League teams called Florida home for spring training.

Jackie Robinson with Montreal Royals teammates, March 1946. The Brooklyn Dodgers farm team members (*from left*) Bob Fontaine, John Wright, Robinson, and Hank Behrman gathered at the Montreal Royals spring training camp at Daytona Beach. On March 17, 1946, Robinson made history when he stepped onto the field and made Daytona Beach the South's first city to allow integrated baseball. Photo by International News Photography, Sports Studio Photos, Getty Images.

Florida's Fields of Dreams · 115

That tradition continues. Many Florida towns and cities are as associated with Major League Baseball as the hometown of the team itself. Dunedin becomes a southern outpost of Canada each spring as the Toronto Blue Jays (and fans) take over the town.

In 2018 Lakeland hosted the Detroit Tigers for the eighty-second year, the longest continuous relationship between a team and a Florida locale.

When the Dodgers left their Dodgertown training facility in Vero Beach in 2009 for Arizona, it sent economic and social shock waves through the small coastal community.

"The Dodgers left more than just a simple complex behind in Vero Beach," said author Noah Frank in a March 2017 article. "Dodgertown's history runs deeper than any other such site, its traditions evoking laughter and introspection from those who lived them."

Part of Dodgertown's legacy in Florida is its place in America's civil rights history. When Jackie Robinson broke baseball's color barrier as a member of the Dodgers in 1947, it was not in Brooklyn, then home of the Dodgers, but in Daytona Beach, where the Dodgers were training. On March 17, 1946, Robinson took the field at Daytona's City Island Park (renamed after Robinson in 1989) as a member of the Montreal Royals, the Dodgers' farm team, in a game against the Dodgers. It was a game that changed both the sport and the nation.

Robinson's Florida legacy inspired a young Ed Charles, "the Glider," who played third base for the champion "Miracle Mets" in the 1969 World Series. Growing up in segregated Daytona Beach, Charles found inspiration in Robinson's breaking of the color barrier. In the words of author Ed Hoyt, seeing Robinson play as a teenager, "he knew what the moment meant—that to have aspirations, to succeed, to prosper, to merely be accepted as a human being, was suddenly a rational notion, because fulfillment of those aspirations had moved into the realm of the possible."

As Charles recalled years later, "I was just a kid, and I was awed by it all, and I prayed for him. I would say, 'Please, God, let him show the whites what we can do so that we can excel like they can.'"

Spring training still thrives in Florida; 2018 saw fifteen teams play their spring games in the Sunshine State, with an anticipated state economic impact of almost $1 billion.

If Florida sports tourism started with tarpon fishing, it truly flourished with baseball.

Golf and Tennis Meccas Sprout in the Sunshine

WHILE FLORIDA encouraged northern tourists to follow their home baseball teams to spring training, it also marketed its climate and beaches to participants in individual sports.

Today, Florida has more than 1,200 golf courses, the most of any state. Sarasota can lay claim to the title "Cradle of Golf" with the development of Scottish

Golfer on elephant caddy, 1927. Early Miami real estate developer Carl Fisher pulled out all the stops marketing his Miami Beach golf course. Photo by Claude Matlack. Courtesy of State Archives of Florida, Florida Memory.

Tennis legend Chris Evert at Lago Mar seaside resort in Fort Lauderdale, circa 1970. Photo by Roy Erikson. Courtesy of State Archives of Florida, Florida Memory.

immigrant John Gillespie's four-hole golf course in 1886. During the golden age of American golf in the 1920s and '30s, famous Americans, among them Warren Harding, Al Smith, Babe Ruth, and Babe Zaharias, played on Florida's courses, encouraged by such marketing ploys as famed Miami developer Carl Fisher's use of Rosie the Elephant as a caddy for his course in Miami Beach.

Florida's climate makes the state a mecca for tennis enthusiasts. Tennis academies, from IMG Academy in Bradenton to ProWorld Tennis Academy in Delray Beach, cater to some of the world's best junior players.

The Sunshine State is also associated with two of the most important female tennis players of all time: Althea Gibson and Chris Evert. Gibson, born in South Carolina in 1927, came to Florida A&M University in 1949 on an athletic scholarship. There she became the first Black player to participate in the US National Championships, now the US Open.

"No Negro player, man or woman, has ever set foot on one of these courts," wrote journalist Lester Rodney in 1950. "In many ways, it is even a tougher personal Jim Crow–busting assignment than was Jackie Robinson's when he first stepped out of the Brooklyn Dodgers dugout." Gibson, honored with an endowed scholarship and a historical marker at FAMU, later went on to break color barriers on the LPGA golf tour.

A generation after Gibson blazed the trail, Fort Lauderdale's Chris Evert, the daughter of a tennis pro who came to Florida after World War II, popularized the game of women's tennis in the 1970s and '80s and was ranked no. 1 in the world seven times.

Florida's Fields of Dreams · 117

The backyard pool is almost as important to a Florida home as air conditioning. In the 1920s, swimmers competed for the national championships in the indoor pool of the Hotel Alcazar in St. Augustine. Since 1965, Fort Lauderdale has been home to the International Swimming Hall of Fame, developed by Buck Dawson, who transformed his adopted hometown into a world destination for swimmers and swim teams. Today, you cannot imagine Florida without a pool, a tennis court, or a golf course. They are as much a part of the state as orange groves and Disney World.

The Most Important Man in Florida Football

FLORIDA BOASTS MANY successful college and professional football coaches. Bobby Bowden, Howard Schnellenberger, Don Shula, Jon Gruden, and Steve Spurrier are all coaches who have won national championships or the Super Bowl. Yet, arguably, none is as important to the sports world or Florida itself as Alonzo "Jake" Gaither. Gaither coached football at FAMU from 1945 to 1969, amassing a record of 204-36-4, winning six Black college national championships in the process.

In 1969 his Rattlers defeated the University of Tampa 34–28 in the first game in the South between a Black college and a white one.

It was a transformational moment for Florida sports, one that set the stage for the powerhouse teams at UF, Florida State, and Miami, all of which had only begun to integrate their football teams at the time of the game. With this game, Gaither remembered, he set out "to prove to myself that it could be done in Florida—the deepest state in the Deep South. And we did it."

To his players Gaither was, in the words of author Samuel Freedman in his book *Breaking the Line*, "coach, teacher, preacher, father. He bought them shoes when they had none, paid for the dentist when they couldn't afford it."

And forty-two of his players went on to the NFL, among them "Bullet" Bob Hayes, the only person ever to win an Olympic gold medal and a Super Bowl ring and be inducted into the Pro Football Hall of Fame. Gaither recruited Hayes from the segregated Gilbert High School in Jacksonville. At the 1964 Tokyo Olympics, Hayes won the 100-meter dash and anchored the gold-medal–winning US 4 × 100 meter relay in a performance hailed by many as the greatest race of all time.

Gaither became the face of FAMU. For him, winning a football game was about "proving Black equality, Black capacity, Black excellence." Gaither retired after that 1969 season, just as the major schools in the state began to integrate their teams.

In 1984, he was named a "Great Floridian" by the Florida Department of State in recognition of his importance to both Florida sports and Florida history.

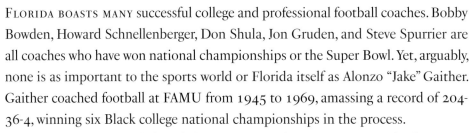

Alonzo "Jake" Gaither, head football coach at Florida A&M University from 1945 to 1969. His win-loss record was among the best of any college football coach. Courtesy of State Archives of Florida, Florida Memory.

118 · Steven Noll

Flipper and the Rise of Pro Sports

New York Jets quarterback Joe Namath surrounded by press and fans in south Florida, January 1969. The poolside photo of Namath before Super Bowl III was published in newspapers around the country and boosted the state's tourism industry as it highlighted Florida's warm winter weather. Photo by Walter Iooss Jr. for *Sports Illustrated*, Getty Images.

FLORIDA WAS LATE to catch on to the pro sports game. The AFL Miami Dolphins were Florida's first pro team, playing their inaugural season in 1966. The Dolphins put Florida pro sports on the map, going to three Super Bowls in the early 1970s, winning two of them, and capping the 1972 season with a perfect record. The Dolphins let everyone in America know they were a Florida team by having Flipper the dolphin in a tank behind the end zone when they played in the old Orange Bowl.

Today, the state has three professional football teams, two baseball teams, a basketball team, two pro soccer teams (one men's and one women's), and two pro hockey teams. Floridians often tie their identity to these franchises, although snowbirds and recent migrants often insist on loyalty to teams in their former locations—just go to The Villages and look at the accessories on all the golf carts.

Florida has also hosted America's most important civic holiday, the Super Bowl, more times than any other state. In the most important one of all, Super Bowl III, held on January 12, 1969, Joe Namath of the New York Jets boldly guaranteed a victory over the Baltimore Colts and then backed it up in a 16–7 win. For Florida, however, it was *where* Namath made that boast that was so valuable; in the middle of winter, newspapers across the nation showed images of "Broadway Joe" lounging poolside in a bathing suit in Miami.

Florida's Fields of Dreams · 119

But Florida's Super Bowls could also be problematic. In 1989, on the eve of Super Bowl XXIII, Miami boiled over in racial tension after the shooting of a Black motorcyclist by a Miami policeman. The rioting clouded Miami's image for years. Sports, even pro sports, were not just a distraction from society, but a reflection of it.

Bringing the Community Together

Pahokee takes the field to play Glades Central in "The Muck Bowl" at Anquan Boldin Stadium, Pahokee, 2016. Photo by Jim Rassol/SF Sun Sentinel/Polaris.

ATTENDANCE AT sporting events, whether small-town Friday-night football games, Saturday-afternoon university extravaganzas, or frenzied Lightning hockey matchups in Tampa, offer a sense of shared identity and common purpose.

The spirit of Florida sports is on enthusiastic display in local contests. Communities turn out to cheer for teams such as Brandon High School's wrestling squad, which won twenty-seven state championships and an incredible 458 straight dual meets, and Cedar Key's girls' and boys' basketball teams, representing a community with the smallest enrollment of any public high school in Florida.

"Sports brings the community together and gives folks a chance to cheer for their kids and neighbors," says Lenny Cimador, retired after a career as varsity baseball coach at Pasco High School.

Former University of Florida Gator football player Cornelius Ingram knows this well. He became the varsity football coach and girls' basketball coach at his alma mater, Hawthorne High School.

"The Hornets are the center of this community," Ingram says. "We are a small town, and high school sports . . . help us see the importance of working together for the benefit of everyone."

The passage in 1972 of Title IX legislation, which prohibits discrimination based on gender by any institution benefiting from federal financial assistance, opened the doors for female participation in high school and college athletics, and generations of young women are taking that opportunity.

If sports are about competition, they are also about fitness. With a growing number of Floridians of retirement age, sports and fitness are key elements in an active lifestyle. People with disabilities are also participating, as Special Olympics reaches out to provide opportunities to athletes who otherwise would not be able to compete. A flag football game between unified teams from UF and FSU, including athletes with developmental disabilities from both communities, has been a part of the UF-FSU football weekend since 2015.

Floridians take justifiable pride in their long and storied sports history. The state has produced eight Heisman Trophy winners, dozens of Olympic medalists, Super Bowl, World Series, Stanley Cup, and NBA championship winners, and NCAA championships in football, baseball, basketball, men's and women's track and field, tennis, and golf, and women's softball. Innumerable athletes, both men and women, have competed on the national and international scene.

The Story of Two All-Americans

Though they grew up in Florida at the same time, Rick Casares, *left*, and Willie Galimore never played football together until becoming Chicago Bears teammates. Here, they work out together in a photo taken in November 1958. Galimore was killed six years later in an automobile accident in Indiana. His number was retired by the Bears. Photo by the AP.

THE STORY OF Florida sports, in all its positive and negative aspects, can best be told by the account of two iconic football players who played football in Florida in the 1950s: Willie Galimore from St. Augustine and Rick Casares from Tampa.

Both players made the FHSAA All-Century football team as running backs and then attended Florida colleges. Casares went to UF and Galimore to FAMU. But because of Florida's racial policies at the time, they never played against each other, either in high school, from which Casares graduated in 1950 and Gallimore in 1952, or college.

But finally, they did. Both played pro football for the Chicago Bears and were members of Chicago's 1963 championship team. Galimore is still the all-time leading rusher in FAMU history; Casares's rushing record for the Bears was finally broken by the legendary Walter Payton.

A faded 1958 photograph shows them in the prime of their lives, two Florida superstars who lived parallel lives in the Sunshine State, working out together for an important Bears game against the then Baltimore Colts. This photo illustrates how sports can both reflect the existing social order and work as a catalyst of change to improve it.

From the **Spring 2018** edition of *FORUM* magazine, "Our Fields of Dreams: How a Love Affair with Sports Shapes Life in Florida."

Florida's Fields of Dreams · 121

19 The Mouse That Roared Quietly

*With secrecy worthy of a spy novel,
Walt Disney set his sights on Orlando.*

Richard Foglesong

Richard Foglesong is the George and Harriet Cornell Professor of Politics, Emeritus, at Rollins College and author of *Married to the Mouse: Walt Disney World and Orlando, Planning the Capitalist City*, and *Immigrant Prince: Mel Martinez and the American Dream*. He was the first recipient of Rollins's Bornstein Scholar Award honoring the faculty member whose scholarship has contributed most to the national reputation of the college. He is a frequent commentator on local and national politics and a political analyst for ABC affiliate WFTV 9 in Orlando.

Image: Walt Disney points to the location of the proposed Disney World development, a 43-square-mile land parcel sixteen miles southwest of Orlando. This 1966 photo comes from the last filmed presentation by Disney. Copyright 1966, Walt Disney Productions, courtesy of the Orange County Regional History Center.

ON NOVEMBER 22, 1963, Walt Disney and an entourage of his top executives flew from Tampa to Orlando searching for an East Coast Disneyland site. The night before they had checked into a Tampa hotel under assumed names to avoid tipping off the press and stirring up land speculation. Reports Walt had read on "Project Winter," as it was code-named, could take him only so far. Ever the artist, he needed to visualize the possibilities for himself.

Disney was close to selecting an expansion site after considering thirteen locations in the eastern United States. An early favorite, Niagara Falls, was rejected because its winter cold would prevent the park's year-round operation. Walt wanted to avoid having a seasonal workforce, fearing that carnival-type workers like those in existing amusement parks would corrupt the family atmosphere he sought to achieve. So the search turned to Florida, with its natural advantages of sunshine and water.

As the plane circled south of Orlando, Walt looked down, saw the confluence of Interstate 4, then under construction, and Florida's Turnpike and exclaimed: "That's it!" What sold Disney were the roads crisscrossing beneath him that were needed to import tourists from afar to make their business plan work. Florida had fewer residents than the Los Angeles region surrounding Disneyland, yet Walt and his executives envisioned a pleasure palace ten times the size of Disneyland. It would not be a Florida theme park so much as an East Coast tourist spa, located in Florida.

From Orlando, the entourage flew west along the Gulf coast to New Orleans, where the members disembarked for the night. During the cab ride to their hotel they learned from the radio that President Kennedy had been shot. It was a fateful

Editor's note: Excerpted from Richard Foglesong's 2001 book *Married to the Mouse: Walt Disney World and Orlando* (Yale University Press). Research for the book was supported in part by a fellowship from the National Endowment for the Humanities, of which Florida Humanities is a state affiliate.

How Disney Became a City State

"It was as though they'd put a gun to our head," recalls Harlan Hanson, the director of tri-county planning in the Orlando area. "They were offering to invest $600 million, and there was the glamor of Disney. You could hardly say no. We were all just spellbound."

The project was Walt Disney World; the year was 1967; the place was Winter Park, outside Orlando, where the poobahs of the state had gathered to hear Disney's plans for a giant theme park. Highlighting the press conference was a twenty-five-minute color film featuring the last screen appearance by Walt Disney, who had died two months previously. In the film, Walt described Epcot as the "heart" of the Florida project, a vibrant community where 20,000 people would "live and work and play."

In essence, the Disney Company sought a Vatican with mouse ears, a city-state within the larger state of Florida, controlled by the company yet enjoying regulatory powers legally reserved for popularly elected governments. Said Roy Disney, who now headed the company, "This was something that we would ask for in fairness for coming to Florida."

To secure state approval, the Disney Company ably plied the old-boy system. An example was a meeting in April 1967 between J. J. Griffin, a former state representative who became a Disney lobbyist, and Verle Pope, the powerful president of the Florida Senate. In the private meeting, Griffin tried to explain the complex Disney charter when Pope stopped him short: "J. J.," he said, "is this good for Florida?" In response, Griffin said, "Yes sir, I believe it is." Said Pope, "Well, that's good enough for me."

With Pope on board, the legislation sailed through the senate, passing unanimously and without debate in May 1967. In the house there was one dissenting vote, from Miami. Less than an hour later, the State Road Board approved emergency funding for Disney's road requests.

Cinderella's Castle is a symbol of Walt Disney World, 2018. Photo by Matt Clare, Creative Commons license, Flickr.

day for the nation and, for entirely different reasons, for central Florida. Walt's "that's it" reaction started a chain of events that would transform sleepy Orlando into the world's most popular tourist destination.

If Walt practiced gut decision making, his brother Roy and others on the Project Winter team were more methodical. Returning from the Florida flyover, they commissioned a "Central Florida Study" to compare Orlando and Ocala as potential theme park sites, dispatching William Lund to Florida from Economic Research Associates, the Disney site consultant.

Wanting complete secrecy to avoid triggering a real estate price run-up, they contacted the company's New York counsel, William Donovan, of the firm Donovan, Leisure, Newton, and Irvine. He was the same "Wild Bill" Donovan who directed the Office of Strategic Services (OSS), the predecessor of the CIA, during World War II. Donovan procured a business card, letterhead stationery, and a phone number identifying Lund as a member of the Burke and Burke law firm, located one floor beneath Donovan and Leisure at One Wall Street in New York.

Arriving in Orlando, the thirty-three-year-old Lund called on two banks and was steered to Florida Ranch Lands Inc. (FRL), a real estate agency, where he met on December 9, 1963, with salesman David Nusbickel. He introduced himself as William Lund from Burke and Burke in New York and told Nusbickel that he represented a major investment trust wanting information on large tracts of land near the crossing of I-4 and the Turnpike.

Disney representatives inspecting Lake Buena Vista property for Disney World, circa 1963. Courtesy of State Archives of Florida, Florida Memory.

The following day, Nusbickel took Lund to see three contiguous land parcels southwest of Orlando: the 12,440-acre Demetree tract, owned by Bill and Jack Demetree; the Bay Lake tract, owned by ten investors; and land east of the Demetree tract owned by Wilson and Carroll Hamrick. Lund spent a third day in Ocala before flying—through New York—back to California.

Thus, when Nusbickel called for Lund at Burke and Burke in New York on December 23, the message was forwarded to Lund in LA. Similarly, Nusbickel wrote Lund at Burke and Burke on January 13, 1964, and Lund wrote back a week later on Burke and Burke stationery, expressing continuing interest in the Demetree property. That was the last anyone at FRL heard from Lund.

Meanwhile, Project Winter was moving forward, and a decisive meeting occurred at Disney's Burbank headquarters on January 16. Hanging on the walls were 30 × 40-inch visuals created from charts that Nusbickel had given to Lund. They showed the direction of future growth in Orlando as well as drive times between major Florida cities and Orlando's many road linkages.

124 · Richard Foglesong

Walt and Roy Disney, flanking Governor Haydn Burns, at a 1965 press conference announcing the Disney Company's intention to build a theme park outside Orlando. Courtesy of State Archives of Florida, Florida Memory.

Supported by these materials, site consultant Lund made the case for Orlando. It had the state's best tourist bypass traffic. It would have a good airport once McCoy Air Force Base was converted to full civilian use. It was larger and faster-growing than Ocala, with a stronger employment base. And it had several large properties available with interesting water features and convenient access. The only negative was Orlando's heavy summer rainfall. But the rain fell in short bursts, said Lund, and "did not disrupt business to any significant extent."

Accepting Lund's recommendation, Disney dispatched general counsel Robert Foster to assemble land for the project.

Secrecy now became imperative, so Foster returned to ex-spymaster Donovan, who directed him to Paul Helliwell, Miami lawyer, former OSS associate, and money-launderer for the Bay of Pigs invasion. Helliwell in turn recruited the services of Roy Hawkins, a trusted veteran Miami real estate man who had developed much of Biscayne Boulevard for the Phipps family.

In short order, Project Winter operatives acquired an option on the Demetree property, bypassing FRL and using Hawkins as the broker. They also purchased an option on a 9,000-acre tract in Osceola owned by State Senator Irlo Bronson. They wanted land in both Orange and Osceola Counties to preserve their future options, according to Foster, who was following Walt's dictum: "Whenever you deal with government, always deal with two."

The Demetree property posed a problem, because of its many "outs," individually owned parcels within the larger tract. The land, much of it water-sogged, had been subdivided in 1912 and sold by catalog to persons across the country, complicating the task of land assembly. For help they turned once again to Florida Ranch Lands.

To confound sleuths, Disney counsel Foster, who was overseeing the project, avoided flying directly between California and Florida.

FRL's Nelson Boice remembers Roy Hawkins asking for assistance on getting the Demetree outs. Boice recalls that one thing struck him as strange: Hawkins arrived carrying FRL brochures, which had a distinctive yellow band at the bottom, under his arm. Looking back, the brochures should have tipped him off that FRL's sales work had led—through Lund—to the Demetree purchase. But he had no reason then to connect Hawkins with Lund.

The Project Winter team used dummy corporations with odd names like AyeFour Corporation to make the purchases, which led to media speculation through spring and summer of 1965 about the mystery land buyer's identity. McDonald Aircraft, Hercules Powder, Ford Motor, Hughes Tool, and even the Walt Disney Company were among the rumored purchasers. To confound sleuths, Disney counsel Foster, who was overseeing the project, avoided flying directly between California and Florida. Since his name had appeared in a Disney annual report, he also adopted a pseudonym when he came to Florida, combining his first and middle names to become "Bob Price."

In mid-October 1965, the *Orlando Sentinel* identified Disney as the mystery land buyer. Improbably, the Project Winter team had maintained secrecy for eighteen months while they assembled a 43-square-mile parcel for which they paid less than $200 an acre. As for FRL, it had uncovered Disney's identity a year earlier when an FRL salesman recognized Admiral Joe Fowler, chief engineer for Walt Disney Productions, from a photo in *National Geographic.* Recalls Boice, "We knew, and they knew we knew, but we didn't talk about it." Still, FRL hadn't connected Disney with the mysterious William Lund or realized that the FRL sales work actually had led to the Demetree purchase. That connection would become clear through a series of coincidences.

After Disney announced it was coming to Orlando, a group of local officials flew to California at Walt's invitation to view Disneyland's impact on Anaheim. Accompanying them to California was Chuck Bosserman, an FRL salesman, who recognized the pilot of the plane, Sim Speer, an avid real estate investor. During the flight Speer gave the delegation a research report on Anaheim-area real estate. The report's author was William Lund, identified as vice president of Economic Research Associates in Los Angeles.

Curious, Bosserman arranged an appointment with the ERA vice president, discovering that he was the same William Lund who had visited FRL in Orlando. Lund told him he assumed they had figured out his connection with Disney. When Bosserman reported this to Boice, the Orlando executive realized that Disney had circumvented FRL on the Demetree property acquisition, approaching the seller through Hawkins. This bit of legerdemain by Disney resulted in a loss of an estimated $242,000 in commission to FRL and raised serious legal and ethical questions.

Boice called Hawkins and asked to meet with Helliwell and him in Miami. Taking his local attorney with him, the FRL president recalls, "We went in and everyone was smiles. We said good morning and what a lovely day it was, and then

A marching band parades down Main Street USA at the Magic Kingdom grand opening celebration of Walt Disney World in October 1971. Courtesy of the Orange County Regional History Center.

Paul Helliwell says 'Gentlemen, I have been directed not to talk with you.'" Says Boice: "It was just a complete stonewall."

Boice sued both Walt Disney Productions and Economic Research Associates, alleging that FRL was denied its 10 percent commission on the Demetree property and should have received a full 10 percent commission on the Bay Lake and Hamrick properties. On the day before the trial, the Disney Company settled for what Boice termed a "significant amount." A stipulation prevents either side from revealing the exact figure.

Secrecy to facilitate a land deal was one thing, but Disney took advantage of the situation, in Boice's view. "They knew, no question about it, that they had an obligation to pay a commission, but since there was all this secrecy, they just did not bother to come up and say 'Hey fellows, we appreciate the work you did and here's your commission.'"

From the **Spring 2001** edition of *FORUM* magazine, "Turning Dreams into Dollars."

20

How They See Us

*The small screen portrays
a Florida you may not recognize.*

Eric Deggans

Eric Deggans is National Public Radio's first full-time TV critic, appearing on the network's shows such as *Morning Edition* and *All Things Considered*, along with writing for *NPR.org* and appearing on NPR podcasts. Deggans is adjunct instructor of journalism and public policy in the Sanford School of Public Policy at Duke University and chair of the Media Monitoring Committee for the National Association of Black Journalists. A journalist for more than three decades, he is the author of *Race-Baiter: How the Media Wields Dangerous Words to Divide a Nation*.

Image: Barbara Eden and Larry Hagman in *I Dream of Jeannie*. The TV series presented a vision of 1960s Space Age Florida. PictureLux, the Hollywood Archive, Alamy Stock Photo.

THE CAMERA SHOT BEGINS close in on a corpse splattered across the ground, before arching up quickly to catch automobiles zipping across an elevated freeway, holding for a moment to frame Miami's skyline in the distance, wavering in the muggy air.

This was a signature image from the second episode of Showtime's quirky drama about a serial killer who hunts murderers, *Dexter*. And it announced, with a showy flair, that this was an offbeat story set in an environment TV viewers had never quite seen in this way before.

Showtime's series debuted in the mid-2000s, featuring Michael C. Hall as a killer who worked in the Miami Police Department's forensics unit, with a setting cribbed from the books that inspired the show, Jeff Lindsay's *Dexter* novels. And Lindsay, who was living in Cape Coral when I interviewed him in 2007 for the *St. Petersburg Times* (now called the *Tampa Bay Times*), said he placed Dexter Morgan in Miami because when he lived in the city during the '80s and '90s, it needed an avenger like his killer of killers.

Chaos and unrest were rising in Miami back then, he said, in part because the city struggled to cope with thousands of immigrants from Cuba who arrived as part of the mass emigration from the Mariel boatlift in 1980. "I like the idea that there's a jaguar prowling the playground," he told me back then. "And all the nuts roll downhill to Florida."

That's what happens when creative minds tap into the true potential of Florida, a state large enough to hold Switzerland, Netherlands, Belgium, and Luxembourg combined, with just as many different cultures, social situations, and climates.

I've been a TV critic living and working in the state since 1997, and I haven't seen many projects take full advantage of the area's unique settings and people (even *Dexter* mostly filmed in California, filming the pilot and other selected scenes on location in Florida).

Too often, Florida is a lazy shortcut for storytellers, an odd place where working-class eccentrics and tropical heat come together to produce a bumper crop of bizarre "Florida Man" crime stories. NBC's *The Good Place*, an excellent series that kept flashing back to knucklehead adventures by Manny Jacinto's not-too-sharp Jason Mendoza in Jacksonville, was a prime offender.

It's tough for people in Hollywood to realize there are many different Floridas in one state, from the South Georgia feel of cities like Jacksonville and Pensacola to the theme park–filled tourist mecca of Orlando, retirees from the Northeast packed into places like West Palm Beach or Fort Lauderdale, and the multicultural melting pot of Miami.

Florida is often a place where people come to start over, a place where people with big dreams and sometimes sketchy histories can leave the past behind and reinvent themselves. And the best TV shows set in Florida have managed to capture that vibe in one way or another while showcasing the stirring, unique landscapes that only the Sunshine State can offer.

Miami Vice stars Don Johnson (*left*) and Philip Michael Thomas, 1984. When the show hit TV screens in 1984, it instantly redefined the city and revived interest in the area's Art Deco architecture and Caribbean flavors. Courtesy of NBC.

How They See Us · 129

Florida as a Home for "Blue Sky" Television

FLORIDA HAS OFFERED indelible images on TV since the medium's earliest days. And those early shows positioned the state as a place with boundless, bright skies, blue waters and endless adventure, a genre often called "blue sky" television, epitomized by action-adventure series like *Sea Hunt* and *Flipper*. *Sea Hunt* aired from 1958 to 1961, starring Lloyd Bridges as a former Navy frogman who would tackle a different diving job every week in scenes often shot in Florida locations like Silver Springs and Tarpon Springs.

Flipper was an adventure centered on a young boy and his pet dolphin, a kind of *Lassie* in the water, that began as a film and later became a TV series airing on NBC from 1964 to 1967. Set in the fictional Coral Key Park and Marine Reserve, the series was actually filmed at Greenwich Studios in Miami (then called Ivan Tors Studios) and in Key Biscayne, working with the Miami Seaquarium.

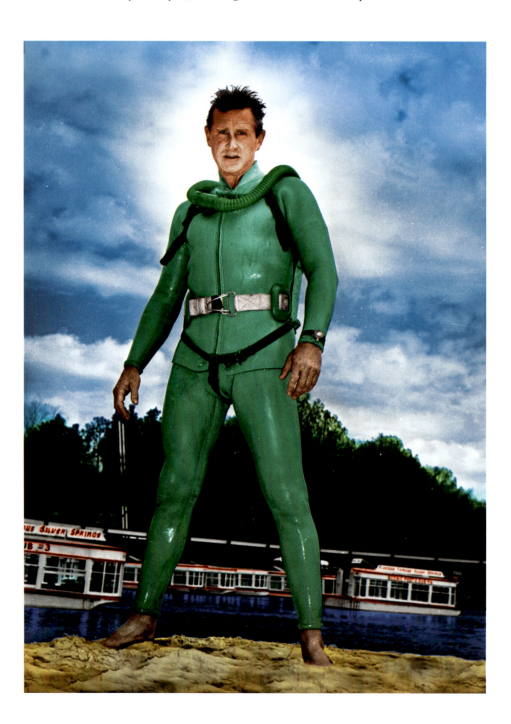

Lloyd Bridges of *Sea Hunt*, circa 1958. Bridges starred as a former Navy frogman who would tackle a different diving job every week. The series had family-friendly content and a pro-environment message. Scenes were often shot in locations like Silver Springs and Tarpon Springs. Courtesy of State Archives of Florida, Florida Memory. Colorized by David Meek.

Actor Tommy Norden, who played Bud Ricks on the TV series *Flipper* with one of the five bottlenose dolphins that portrayed the title character, 1964. The popular show, which aired for three seasons, 1964–1967, was filmed in large part in Miami, at the Ivan Tors Studios. Courtesy of MGM-TV.

Both series had family-friendly content and strong pro-environment messages, thanks to Hungarian producer and director Ivan Tors. The producer, a longtime advocate for family-friendly programming, helped develop Florida's image as a home for wholesome, often water-based adventures that Disney would supercharge with its massive theme parks, hyped by its own TV shows like *The Wonderful World of Disney*.

Flash forward sixty years or so and you reach a time when TV rediscovered the blue-sky series, and a few of them were actually set and filmed in Florida.

Perhaps the best known of those shows was USA's *Burn Notice*, a drama that mixed action, humor, and intrigue in a story about a former CIA hotshot spy trapped in Miami when his cover gets blown and he's, um, burned. The show developed a new formula for blue-sky TV that included a fun sensibility, hopeful tone, and eccentric lead character who could be a bit of an antihero.

When I visited the show's production back in 2010, hanging with chain smoking costar Sharon Gless (yes, THAT one—the *Cagney and Lacey* star), it was obvious what set the show apart. Filming inside Miami's Coconut Grove Convention Center and across the area, the show captured the white sandy beaches, rich skies, and blazing, bright visuals in Florida that were tough to reproduce anywhere else.

"One of the stars of the show is Miami," Gless told me back then for a *St. Petersburg Times* story; she had lived on nearby Fisher Island for years. "They use it so beautifully."

Back then, the state had hopes of luring Hollywood productions to take advantage of all its unique locations and environments, offering tax incentives for projects that came to Florida. But the state didn't really have the production facilities to house a lot of work; the shut-down Coconut Grove Convention Center was kind of a shabby place to house *Burn Notice*'s standing sets, and only a handful of TV projects came to play.

Once again, a few TV series revived Florida's status as a place where you could foil a master spy's plot against America and then relax with a few mai tais by the beach. But given how a certain Miami-based TV show exploded into pop culture in the 1980s, it's surprising that more series didn't follow suit.

The *Miami Vice* Period: Gritty, Glamorous Crime Drama

THE LEGEND OF *Miami Vice* and its effect on Florida's image in TV and film is well documented.

Created by *Hill Street Blues* writer Anthony Yerkovich and executive-produced by auteur-director Michael Mann, *Miami Vice* hit TV screens in 1984 and instantly redefined both the city and its genre. Drenched in a soundtrack of pop hits straight from MTV and a stylish, New Wave–inspired look that would have fit easily into any music video, *Miami Vice* captured the fear over rising crime in south Florida

How They See Us · 131

Florida is often a place where people come to start over, where people with big dreams and sometimes sketchy histories can leave the past behind and reinvent themselves. And the best TV shows set in Florida have managed to capture that vibe in one way or another while showcasing the stirring, unique landscapes that only the Sunshine State can offer.

alongside the glamor of South Beach and futility of cops trying to stop the flow of drugs at a time when cocaine flowed freely on Wall Street and in Hollywood.

Yerkovich explained to *Time* magazine, "Even when I was on *Hill Street Blues*, I was collecting information on Miami; I thought of it as a sort of a modern-day American Casablanca. It seemed to be an interesting socio-economic tide pool: the incredible number of refugees from Central America and Cuba, the already extensive Cuban-American community, and on top of all that the drug trade. There is a fascinating amount of service industries that revolve around the drug trade—money laundering, bail bondsmen, attorneys who service drug smugglers. Miami has become a sort of Barbary Coast of free enterprise gone berserk."

The look of actors Don Johnson and Philip Michael Thomas as cops Sonny Crockett and Ricardo Tubbs kicked off loads of fashion trends. Musical artists vied to land their songs on the show. And Mann's meticulous, stylized look revived interest in the area's Art Deco and Caribbean flavors.

But the show didn't produce many copycats that survived long. And the crime dramas that came after set in the state would only pick up bits of *Miami Vice*'s style, using elements to create a new signature crime style that some might call "Florida noir."

The 2005 ABC series *Karen Sisco*, inspired by characters from venerated crime novelist Elmore Leonard's work, lifted the absurdist feel of his characters and melded it with *Miami Vice*'s gritty glamor. And Ryan Murphy's 2003 drama *Nip/Tuck*, centered on a pair of outrageous plastic surgeons based in Miami, amped up the city's European-influenced styles, balmy sexuality, and darker tones with neon and pink banished from the color palette.

"When I lived (in Miami), it was a city about class . . . more than any city I've lived in, other than maybe New York," Murphy told me back then. "The colors of the city, the lightweight clothing, that sort of sexual ripeness. I've always felt Florida was an untapped resource."

Reinvention and Reaching for a Dream in the Sunshine State

AND WHEN IT COMES to class, the other face of Florida that gets lots of screen time is the world of working-class folks trying to do better.

Krystal Stubbs is a former beauty queen with a job in a rundown water park, worried that what little money her family has is being wasted by her ambitious but gullible husband, Travis, who is convinced he will succeed in an Amway-style sales organization.

She's also the lead character in Showtime's *On Becoming a God in Central Florida*, a droll drama that depicts Krystal's rise from widowed single mom—spoiler alert—to smart, savvy prime mover in that multilevel marketing sales organization. And she lives in Florida, albeit in an unnamed "Orlando adjacent" town that's more a state of mind than a spot on the map.

Kirsten Dunst plays a Floridian working to make other people's vacation dreams come true in *On Becoming a God in Central Florida*. The Florida the show depicts is hot, frustrating, and full of desperation. SHOWTIME.

"It's supposed to feel like the space between real spaces.... It's an area that's sprawling with strip malls and just this kind of everywhere between that's most of America," showrunner and executive producer Esta Spaulding told me in 2019. "There's just a mythology of Florida in a way . . . the feeling of the gators and beaches and Disney World being right there, living in the shadow of that.... It was fun to be in a place that had a feel like there was a delay before things reached there. But it also had its own really distinctive identity."

Indeed, the sliver of Florida depicted in *On Becoming* is hot, frustrating, and full of desperation. Krystal, played by Kirsten Dunst, leads a humble life, scrambling to get by while working hard to make other people's vacation dreams come true, forever stuck outside the good life looking in, like the fading water park she works in, perched on the edge of Disneyfied fabulousness.

"The show is really about consumerism and the desire to be rich," Spaulding says. "The feeling in America that anybody can be a millionaire drives people to monetize their relationships, their friendships, their family relationships in some way, that feeling that you're supposed to be working toward something more and you know at the end of your life if you're a success because you're rich. That kind of myth was the thing we wanted to explore in the show."

And what better place to explore that feeling than Florida, home to everything from a major outpost of the Church of Scientology in Clearwater, to the apex of the televised consumer hustle, the Home Shopping Network, now known as HSN, in St. Petersburg?

How They See Us · 133

On Becoming joined several Florida-set TV shows centered on working-class folks trying to succeed in an absurdly unorthodox environment. TNT's *Claws* featured Niecy Nash as a nail salon owner secretly laundering money for a local criminal outfit in Manatee County; eventually, she gets the idea she can run her own organization.

And Pop TV's short-lived *Florida Girls* centered on four girls living in a trailer park in Clearwater, living the kind of party-hearty lives that usually end as a jokey Florida Man (or Woman) segment on *The Daily Show*. They pile into a car that can only start when someone who hasn't been drinking blows into a breathalyzer—a real thing—and work in a dive bar where one of them sits in a big fish tank wearing a mermaid costume (also sort of a real thing in Weeki Wachee).

Actress, writer, creator Laura Chinn played lead character Shelby, who finds herself transformed when one of their crew finally earns her high school equivalency GED and moves away. Suddenly Shelby is wondering if she and her friends shouldn't want more out of life, a storyline based on Chinn's own childhood growing up in Clearwater.

"I feel like the Florida I see on TV a lot is, like, Miami . . . sexy girls and cars and bright beaches and stuff," Chinn said to me during a press party for *Florida Girls*. "That was not my experience. I grew up in a lower-income house. . . . All of my friends' dads were absent for various reasons, and we all were navigating different problems than you would see on, like, *Sex and the City* or *Friends*."

Shows like *Claws*, *On Becoming*, and *Florida Girls* ride the fine line of lampooning the stereotypes of eccentric, working-class Floridians while occasionally reaching for something deeper than jokes about poaching alligators and Jet Skiing under

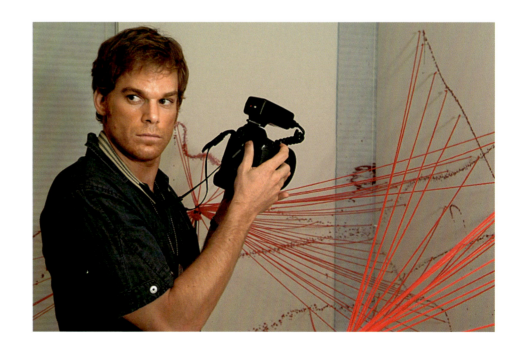

Michael C. Hall plays the title role in *Dexter*, a crime drama series set in Miami. The series, which aired from 2006 to 2013, centers on a forensic technician who leads a double life as a serial killer, hunting down murderers who have slipped through the justice system. IMBD.

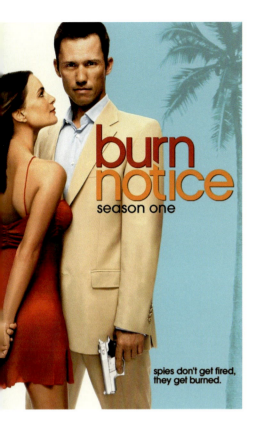

USA's *Burn Notice* mixed action, humor, and intrigue in a story built about a former CIA spy trapped in Miami when his cover gets blown. WIKI.

the influence, as compared to unscripted shows like *Siesta Key* and *Floribama Shore* that luxuriate in stereotypes about young, party-centered Floridians like Sunshine State–flavored versions of *Jersey Shore*.

Chinn insisted she wasn't trying to insult or exploit anyone on *Florida Girls*. "They're empathetic characters that at the end of the day have very light, grounded reasons for their flaws," she said. "It's definitely a fine line, and sometimes it felt like we were walking a tightrope because . . . I don't ever want it to seem like we're punching down. I think the more we show these people as human beings, the more maybe the coastal elites will have empathy for them."

Ironically, none of these shows set in Florida actually filmed the bulk of their episodes there. Since the legislature ended tax breaks that helped programs like *Burn Notice* and *Dexter* save money by filming locally, production for many shows set in Florida has moved to Savannah, Georgia (*Florida Girls*) and New Orleans (*Claws*).

Lots of TV shows set in Florida used this technique, filming most or all of their episodes in California or elsewhere and "cheating" the look to make it seem as if their characters were actually in the state. That list includes *CSI: Miami*, *Dexter*, *Nip/Tuck*, *The Golden Girls*, *Fresh off the Boat*, and the classic sitcom *I Dream of Jeannie*.

So the stories TV viewers see that are set in Florida often can't showcase what the state really looks like. The beaches aren't as dazzling. The sun doesn't look quite hot enough. The water just isn't blue enough. And audiences across the world get a watered-down version of a state that has so many distinctive environments.

It's proof that there are few locales in America that have occupied as many different spaces in our imagination as Florida, from adventure-filled natural wonderlands to gritty urban hangouts, glamorous beachified playgrounds, theme park–packed tourist traps or strip mall–dotted everylands.

And even with all the hours of television produced in and about the state, you get the sense that these shows have only scratched the surface of a place whose tangled history, wide diversity, and unique cultures offer unexplored depths that will continue to surprise us all.

From the **Summer 2020** edition of FORUM magazine, "Lights, Camera . . . Florida: How TV—and 100 Years of Filmmaking Here—Have Shaped Our Image."

NON-VIOLENCE
IS OUR
WATCHWORD

WE SHALL
WIN
BY LOVE

PART III
All Things Unequal under the Sun

While many flocked to Florida in search of opportunity, others were locked out of the dream.

Demonstrators in front of Florida Theatre in Tallahassee, circa 1963. In the background, future Florida state senator Arthenia Joyner and a man carry a sign that reads, "Non-violence is our watchword." Courtesy of State Archives of Florida, Florida Memory.

Parallel Lives

Growing up in Florida in the 1950s and '60s, two Floridians, one white and one Black, describe wildly different experiences.

THE FOLLOWING ESSAYS by Bill Maxwell and Beverly Coyle first appeared in *FORUM* in the summer issue of 1999. Evolving from a Florida Humanities' staff idea to tell stories of growing up white and Black at the same time and nearly the same place, these essays are the writers' accounts of experiencing the segregated world of 1950s Florida, including witnessing, as teenagers, the collapse of Jim Crow laws and the infancy of the civil rights movement. After the original articles appeared, Maxwell and Coyle traveled throughout the state in the Florida Humanities–sponsored program called Parallel Lives, one of the most popular of the nonprofit's programs ever. Reaching thousands of Floridians, the program encouraged those in attendance to ask questions and share their own stories. *Parallel Lives*, Coyle and Maxwell's play based on their essays, premiered in 2003 at American Stage Theatre in St. Petersburg and is still performed by groups and colleges around the country.

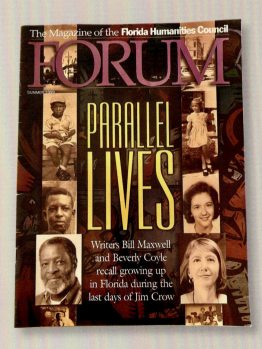

21 Raised with Love, Schooled in Cruel Realities

In childhood, he learned the harsh lessons of Jim Crow and, finally, the power of being seen.

Bill Maxwell

Bill Maxwell wrote syndicated columns and editorials for the *St. Petersburg Times* (now the *Tampa Bay Times*) from 1994 to 2019 and for the New York Times Regional Newspaper Group. The recipient of many writing awards, he is a graduate of Bethune-Cookman College and has a master's degree from the University of Chicago. He taught English and journalism at colleges in Illinois and Florida and founded the Role Models Today Foundation to support journalism students.

The early morning sun already was blazing hot as we cleared the bridge over the St. Johns River and the familiar stench of Palatka's pulpwood mills flowed through the open windows of our car as my grandfather and I neared the Putnam County Courthouse.

I was excited because I would start the paperwork for getting a restricted driver's license. I had stayed up all night, dreaming of driving my grandparents' 1949 Chevrolet, of showing off in front of the girls at all-Negro Middleton High School in Crescent City, of wearing exotic cologne and holding my wrist dangerously loose over the steering wheel as I had seen my father and other men do around women. And, of course, I dreamed of owning a fast, sporty coupe. The year was 1959, and I was a few months away from being old enough to drive legally.

My grandfather, Robert Albert Bentley, and I climbed the courthouse stairs, moving aside at the door to let three white women pass. My grandfather bowed and tipped his hat. At the counter, a clerk, an older white woman with eyes that instinctively looked through Negroes, gave me a form to fill out. My grandfather sat in the chair beneath the ceiling fan, his hat resting awkwardly on his lap. An armed sheriff's deputy, a tall white man with a ruddy face and hairy arms, stood beside me. Leaning on the counter, he chatted with the woman, studied me from head to toe, and glanced over at my grandfather.

The room was hot, and I was nervous.

When the woman asked if I had a pen, I said, "No, I don't."

I had no idea that those three simple words had violated two centuries of strict tradition and had exposed me to the absurd, unspoken oath that required white men to protect the honor of white women, especially when their honor had been trampled on by a Negro.

Editor's note: This story contains offensive and disturbing racial slurs. We included them because they accurately reflect the experience of the writer and many others at the time these events took place and are integral to understanding his story.

As I reached for the pen she was handing me, the deputy grabbed my left shoulder, spun me around to face him, shoved my back against the wall, and pressed his forearm against my chest.

"You say 'yes, ma'am,' and 'no, ma'am' to a white lady, you little nigger," he said in a low, deliberate tone, his breath smelling of tobacco.

Never will I forget the way he said "nigger" and the rage in his eyes. Over the years, I have relived this incident, assessing my reaction to it at the time and measuring its long-term effect on who I have become. Doubtless, it was a watershed in the life of a proud, happy fourteen-year-old who saw himself quickly growing into manhood.

Now, I look back and marvel that, given the racial customs of that time when white men could do almost anything they pleased to Negroes, I escaped physically unharmed.

Weighing about 190 pounds and standing nearly 6 feet, I stiff-armed the deputy in the face, as I routinely did opposing players who tried to tackle me when I ran the football. I caught him off balance, and he went back, stumbling to hold himself up.

"Keep your hands off me!" I shouted. Unaccountably, I was unafraid, only insulted and angry. He grabbed the edge of the counter and balanced himself. I looked into his eyes, sensing that he wanted to shoot me. I could feel the heat of bigotry in his eyes and the heavy burden of his being of the "superior race" guiding his actions.

As I stared at him, he looked away, turned to my grandfather and said, "Git this little trouble-making nigger out of here."

"Don't call me a nigger!" I shouted, moving toward him.

By now, my grandfather, a gentle man infused with the serenity of the deeply devout, was trembling.

Jumping to his feet, he pulled me down the hall and out of the building. Terror was in his eyes as we passed the Confederate heroes monument on the front lawn. In the car he did not look at me, nor did he speak. We drove the twenty-six miles back to Crescent City in silence.

When he died in 1995 we still had not discussed that day. I can only guess at his reason for never talking about it. But I knew even then what it had done to me: it made me feel mortal. Before then, I had felt invincible, believing that I would live forever.

On that day, though, there I stood, in that muggy courthouse, facing a man who wanted to annihilate me—who could have annihilated me with the squeeze of a finger—because my skin was black and because I momentarily had lost sight of the lay of the land and had stepped out of my "place."

Why? Because I had not said "ma'am" to a white woman. Even at that young age, I understood that my fate was in the hands of a stranger, a white adult who despised me, a mere child, for no logical reason. I clearly understood that being a Negro in northeast Florida was a high-stakes game of minimizing physical assaults.

Even more, I walked away from that courthouse with a diminished sense of self, a condition that I would spend subsequent years trying to repair.

Indeed, the courthouse encounter was a turning point for me. It also was a turning point in my growth, the point of support from which I now can appreciate the wholeness of my life. In other words, all events that occurred before that day in Palatka prepared me for surviving it.

I was born in Fort Lauderdale on October 16, 1945, in all-Negro Provident Hospital. Negroes were not permitted in the white hospitals. My parents were farmworkers who labored long and hard but could not regularly make ends meet. When I was eighteen months old, heavy rains devastated Broward County's pole bean crop, forcing my parents to "go up the road" to find work. En route to Exmore, Virginia, where they would work in potatoes, they deposited me in Crescent City with my father's mother and stepfather, Lillie Mae and Robert Bentley, where I lived most of my childhood until I went away to college in 1963.

Crescent City, between Palatka and DeLand on US Highway 17, is on the eastern rim of the Ocala National Forest, less than forty miles inland from the Atlantic Ocean. It is home to Lake Stella, tiny Lake Argenta, and Crescent Lake, fed by the St. Johns River, where bass, bream, crappie, bluegill, and several other varieties of freshwater sunfish are abundant.

Street scene, Crescent City, circa 1940. Courtesy of State Archives of Florida, Florida Memory.

Crescent City was not an Arcadia. It was, however—and I am speaking only of the Negro communities because I rarely had close contact with local whites—nature's gift to Negro children, mostly boys, who roamed the woodlands and fields "bare-feeted" without a care, where Negro girls in gingham dresses skipped rope under live oak, magnolia, and camphor trees.

And back then, for most Negroes who wanted to work, citrus, fern, and pulpwood provided jobs at least seasonally. Those incapable of holding steady jobs could eke out a living pulling deer tongue and Spanish moss and catching gopher tortoises, or "Hoover chickens," as many people called the delicious reptile.

My grandparents' house was a green-shingled, three-bedroom, shotgun-style structure with a matching two-hole outhouse across the dirt road. On three acres of sandy soil near Lake Argenta, we used a lot of fertilizer to grow all our vegetables and fruits. Our chickens laid enough eggs for five families.

Religion—the fear of a living god who, at will, intervenes in earthly matters—anchored the lives of the adults. My grandfather was a presiding elder in the House of God, Church of the Living God, the Pillar Ground of Truth without Controversy, a Black Pentecostal, or Holiness, denomination. He pastored a church in Crescent City and one in Palatka and routinely conducted or participated in tent revivals throughout the north central part of the state and the Panhandle. I accompanied him on these trips when my grandmother had to work or was "too plumb tired" to travel, as she would say.

One of the most memorable events of my early childhood involving white people occurred when I was ten years old and went with my grandfather to a three-day revival in Lake City. "Pilgrims" came from several nearby counties. On the second afternoon of the gathering, a group of boys and I walked to a store in a Negro neighborhood. I bought a frosty bottle of Nehi grape soda, a bag of salted peanuts, and a giant dill pickle. Returning to the tent, we rough-housed, "played the dozens," and fantasized about pretty girls as we approached the railroad tracks.

Out of nowhere, a green Ford pickup roared toward us. We could hear the horn blasting and the rebel yells. Three white teenage boys sat in the cab, and five or six others rode in the bed. We knew what was coming because, although we lived in different regions of the state, we had seen this game before—a potentially deadly gambit that was intended to elicit anger and instill fear in us.

We were about to be "nigger-knocked."

As the adults in our lives had taught us, we ran in different directions to confuse our attackers. I had been nigger-knocked a year earlier on my newspaper route in Crescent City. I was pedaling my bicycle along Union Avenue and was preparing to toss a copy of the *Palatka Daily News* into a yard when a car carrying three white boys approached. The passenger in the backseat hit me in the face with a balloon filled with urine.

On that day in Lake City, I knew immediately that I was doomed the second that I looked back. A boy in the truck bed held a leather belt in the air, the silver buckle twirling above his head. Suddenly, I saw the metal square descend, and just as suddenly, everything went black. Pain ripped through my face. Cupping my nose, I smelled my own blood and felt it pouring into my palms, then between my fingers. I thought that I would pass out and that I had lost both eyes.

My nose had been broken, and the gash was so deep that it exposed bone. My friends helped me back to the tent, where the standing-room-only crowd was shouting a spiritual dance to the syncopated sounds of handclapping, drums, a piano, guitars, and dozens of tambourines. My grandfather, who was on the platform with the other preachers, ran toward me. Too proud to cry, I stood in the main aisle holding the bridge of my nose. The front of my starched white shirt was covered with my blood. The wife of the local minister, with whom we were staying, took me to her house, flushed my wound with antiseptic, bandaged it, and gave me one of her husband's shirts. My grandfather drove me to a Negro doctor in Gainesville he had known for many years.

Aside from the physical harm that it caused, the social significance of nigger-knocking was its power to perpetuate the myth of the white man's dominance over us and, of course, to keep us believing in our perceived inferiority.

The Lake City incident deepened my awareness of Negro alienation. White people were a mystery to me and my peers.

They were strangers.

We would see them downtown or glimpse them driving their cars and trucks. Some of us took orders from them at work. But we rarely saw their faces up close or gave them sustained eye contact. Although his behavior appalled me, I understood why my grandfather took off his hat, lowered his eyes, and rocked back and forth when talking to white people in public places.

Race always drove a wedge between "us" and "them." But Crescent City, dubbed "The Bass Capital of the World" on the signs welcoming travelers, was not an openly brutal place. In many ways, it was better than most other towns I visited as a farmworker throughout the Southeast. Many Negroes and whites accepted the separation of the races as an act of the Almighty. Adult Negroes instinctively bowed and scraped. Whites instinctively felt superior and benevolently endured our presence. Their neglect of us—official and otherwise—was habit.

Many stores, such as Sackett's Grocery, extended credit to Negroes. Hilda's Style Shop even let us try on clothing. As far as we knew, no store in Palatka or Daytona Beach would let us do so. And the People's Bank of Crescent City never turned down qualified Negro borrowers, as far as any of us knew. The town's two doctors and one dentist, all white, had integrated waiting rooms, while many of their peers in neighboring towns had segregated waiting rooms.

Many older Negroes and older whites developed the kind of intimacy peculiar to the generations that had coexisted as master and servant.

Still, the vast differences between our two worlds were manifested almost everywhere, especially at Lake Stella, where most children, Black and white, spent their summers. We assumed that Mother Nature had drawn a line across the 308-acre lake, separating the white side from the Negro side. We swam and played on the "Babylon side"—named for the community that was home to the Negro graveyard—and whites used the "Whitesville side." It had white sand, which the town provided, on its shore. Our side was grassy and muddy and dotted with the shells of mussels that washed ashore.

Many whites had beautiful motorboats, and we envied the white children as they skimmed across the shimmering water on colorful skis. Precious few Negroes could afford a motorboat, and none of us had skis.

We enjoyed ourselves on the lake by creating games. The greatest challenge, which most of us met with ease, was swimming from our side of Stella to Billy Goat Island, owned by the Reynolds family and said to be the home of a giant, one-eyed alligator.

Bill Maxwell, age five. Courtesy of Bill Maxwell.

Raised with Love, Schooled in Cruel Realities · 143

We had the most fun, though, playing a game called "gator." We would draw lots. Whoever drew the shortest marsh reed became the gator. The game's object was to outswim the gator. After the designated gator caught someone, a great struggle would ensue as it tried to pull the captive under water and hold him there. After freeing himself or being released, the captive would become the new gator. Needless to say, we often came close to drowning the weakest swimmers. But we had fun.

Even so, we felt the racial alienation. We could not, for example, eat at Thomas Drugstore's lunch counter or at Hap's diner, which doubled as the Greyhound Bus station. When a group of us tried to integrate the drugstore counter one afternoon,

Florida migrant farmworkers, July 1940. The family was on their way to Cranberry, New Jersey, to pick potatoes. Bill Maxwell's parents also followed the crops, so he grew up with his grandparents in Crescent City. Photo by Jack Delano. Courtesy of US Farm Security Administration, Office of War Information Black and White Photographs Collection, Library of Congress.

a male clerk threatened us with jail and "ass whippings" and telephoned our principal, Harry Burney, who dutifully informed our families.

At the town's movie theater, whites sat downstairs, and Negroes sat in the tiny, hot balcony. After the theater closed and became a bowling alley, Negroes were not permitted inside except to clean up.

Nothing, however, made us feel more estranged than school busing. Until the late 1950s, Negro high school students woke between 5 and 5:30 each morning and walked more than a mile to catch the bus that took us to Central Academy High in Palatka.

The direct route, by way of US Highway 17, from Crescent City to Central Academy was about thirty miles. But we could not take the direct route. Too many kids lived in the woods. The driver picked up the first students in the southern region called Long Station.

Then she drove north to the other local Black neighborhoods—Denver, Rossville, Babylon, where I lived, and Union Avenue. Leaving Crescent City, the bus went southwest to Georgetown and Fruitland, then northwest to Welaka. From there, it traveled northeast to Pomona Park and then due north on Highway 17 to Satsuma, San Mateo, and East Palatka. The bus would arrive at Central Academy between 8:15 and 8:30, barring mechanical trouble or a boat stopping us on the Dunns Creek drawbridge.

During the shortest days of winter, we left home in darkness and returned in darkness. Many of our lasting romances began on the bus, and some who met on the bus are still married nearly forty years later. In time we realized that although we enjoyed school and our bus rides were adventures, we were victims of Jim Crow's evil, intentional cruelty.

As our innocence died and as we absorbed the reality of living as Negro children in the segregated South, play helped us escape some of the ugliness of southern Putnam County's racism.

Because we were poor and could not easily buy toys and games, we had to invent and build. A group of us performed our greatest construction feat when, after watching early episodes of *Gunsmoke*, we built our version of Dodge City. We collected scrap lumber, sheets of tin, and several pounds of nails; we chopped blackjack oaks and collected palmetto fronds. After a month of sawing, hammering, and digging, we had built six mean structures, each with its own crudely painted sign: "Long Branch Saloon," "Doc's Office," "Marshal Dillon's Office and Jail," "Dodge House Hotel," "Livery Stable," and "Church."

During the day we played Gunsmoke and waded in brown brooks teeming with crawdads and tadpoles. At night we built campfires and roasted hot dogs. Our folks let us sleep in our western town as often as we wished. During summer, only severe weather and church kept us away.

We never comprehended the incredible irony of our Dodge City experience: we

Raised with Love, Schooled in Cruel Realities · 145

were society's Black outcasts playing white characters and reenacting white situations although Negroes never appeared in the television show and although we had no sense of the universality of art and human themes. We played in our make-believe town for about three years.

One weekend, and I do not remember why, we abandoned Dodge City and never returned there to play again. In time it disappeared behind vegetation, later falling under the fern industry's bush hogs and plows.

As the decade of the '50s neared its end, we played fewer unstructured games. Varsity football and basketball, pool, cards, talking trash, playing pinball at Chuck's Barbershop, ditty bopping, flirting, and dating became our new games. We were "smelling our musk," as the men would say of teenage boys beginning to see themselves as men.

At the same time, television having entered our lives, we had begun to hear of people such as the Reverend Martin Luther King Jr., Rosa Parks, Elijah Muhammad, and Malcolm X. Times were rapidly changing.

Negroes everywhere were beginning to speak out. We children, too, were more emboldened and impatient. The civil rights movement was in full force, and we were being swept along in the tide.

I began to resent the gross unfairness of the so-called separate but equal school system that legally forced Negroes and whites to attend schools on opposite sides of town, causing us to lead parallel lives that rarely intersected. The two schools shared the town-owned football field, a situation that called for creative scheduling to prevent the mixing of the races during home games. Negroes were not permitted inside the fence during white games. If we wanted to watch the white team, we had to stand outside, away from the fence. Whites, however, had the right to sit in the bleachers during our games.

My grandparents became seriously concerned about my growing resentment of whites after I told our insurance agent to stop eating out of my grandmother's pots and pans on the stove. A friendly and talkative man, he collected our money on the same night each month. Invariably, he came while we were eating supper, knocked on the front door, and let himself in. He addressed my grandparents as Lillie Mae and Robert, even though they were his elders.

Placing his briefcase on the floor, the agent would march into the kitchen and eat whatever he wanted. My grandparents would not look at me while he banged lids and smacked his lips. All the while, he would call out things such as, "Best collards in town, Lillie Mae!" After eating, he never thanked my folks. He collected his money, belched, and drove away until the next time.

One night I told the agent that he had no right to eat our food uninvited. No Negro could do so in his house. He turned red in the face and motioned to my grandmother to follow him outside. She returned after a few minutes, her eyes reflecting the pain of a lifetime of having bowed and scraped to survive.

Bill Maxwell (*top*), age fourteen. Courtesy of Bill Maxwell.

She was the first adult, white or Negro, to suggest that I was smart enough to attend college. I believed her and began to shape my future.

"Don't never say nothing else to that white man," she said. Her expression was stern, and she held her chin high. She had salvaged dignity from her faith in her God and had begun to hum the Negro spiritual "I'll Fly Away," as she always did at such times.

"Yes, ma'am," I said, feeling sorry for her.

Fortunately for me, the insurance agent was not the last white adult to enter my life in Crescent City. My grandmother was a maid, and one of her sites was the Crescent City Women's Club. In addition to being a meeting place and a dining room, the facility served as the public library, housing at least 2,000 books. After my grandmother took me to help clean the building one Saturday morning when I was about fifteen, I saw the books for the first time. Although recognizing only a handful of titles and authors, I fell in love with the smell of old leather and parchment. After that morning I came with my grandmother often, spending more time reading than cleaning. At first she would scold me for not working. Later she encouraged me to read. Mrs. Anna Hubbard, the white lady who was often there, noticed my interest in books and began to suggest ones for me to read—*Of Mice and Men*, *The Sun Also Rises*, *Lord Jim*, *The Last of the Mohicans*, *Dracula*, and many more. Sometimes she would ask me about my reading.

One morning she sat down with me, and we discussed *Native Son*. I recall being particularly embarrassed because Richard Wright's protagonist, Bigger Thomas, murders a white woman. Sensing my discomfort, Mrs. Hubbard switched the subject to plot, character, point of view, and other literary elements of fiction.

She also introduced me to writings about A. Philip Randolph, who was born in Crescent City in 1889. He was editor of the radical Black journal *The Messenger* until 1925, when he founded the Brotherhood of Sleeping Car Porters. I read everything I could find on Randolph and wrote an essay for my civics class on the 1941 march on Washington that he organized. That march prompted President Roosevelt to issue a fair employment practices executive order that aided sleeping-car porters. I used to walk to the house, a hulking two-story structure beside the highway in the woods, where Randolph was born and marvel that such a great man had actually lived there.

Although Mrs. Hubbard and I did not become close friends, we knew that we were intellectual soulmates. And I knew back then that she, along with my English teacher, Gloria Bonaparte, had sparked my interest in classic literature. Her kindness cooled my growing hatred of white people, and she convinced me that I was a good reader, that my love of the written word would guide my life. She was the first adult, white or Negro, to suggest that I was smart enough to attend college. I believed her and began to shape my future.

One afternoon I told Mrs. Hubbard that I wished that she were one of my teachers. I will never forget her reply:

"That's nice of you," she said, "but white people can't teach in your school."

Postlude

CRESCENT CITY of nearly 2,000 residents still is not an Arcadia for anyone. But it is a far better place than it was when I lived here as a child. Although the freezes of the 1980s killed the area's thousands of acres of citrus trees, the fern industry has taken up most of the slack. The year after I graduated from all-black Middleton Junior-Senior High, Congress passed the Civil Rights Act of 1964, prohibiting discrimination in voting, employment, public facilities, and, of course, education. Unlike whites in many other small towns statewide, the overwhelming majority of whites here accepted the new legislation and built a new integrated junior-senior high school and turned the old white campus into an integrated middle school and the Black campus into an integrated elementary school.

Old Middleton is now Middleton-Burney Elementary, renamed to honor a Black man, Harry Burney Jr., my former principal. The town elected its first Black city councilman, my social studies teacher, several years ago, and Blacks now serve on civic boards and are served in all public establishments. Now, instead of merely cleaning the Women's Club, Blacks can use the facility for social events. At the adjacent library, all groups explore the world of books under the same roof. And when I come to town these days, I can sleep in either of the two motels that Negroes were barred from in the 1950s.

Perhaps my most remarkable post-1950s experience involving Crescent City occurred in 1993, when I taught English and journalism at Santa Fe Community College in Gainesville. Calling the roll on the first day of an English class, I realized that two students, both white, had the same last name: Suggs. The boy was in a wheelchair, and the girl sat next to him. After class, I told them about my childhood doctor in Crescent City whose name was Suggs. They said they were brother and sister and their father practiced in Crescent City, their hometown.

I could not believe that I, a Black man, was teaching the son and daughter of my white doctor of so many years ago, when Negroes and whites were not permitted on the same campus. The Suggs children and I had a wonderful semester, spending many hours together, talking and slaying ghosts from the past.

Although some of the vestiges of the Old South linger, I am happy to see how much the town has changed. Confederate flags that once flew in selected places were removed many years ago. The high school sports teams are no longer the "Rebels." They are now the "Raiders." Gone, too, are the police-ordered "White Only" and "Colored" signs that navigated much of our physical existence downtown. Blacks and whites even swim on the same side of Lake Stella.

My biggest regret is that my grandparents and others of their generation, especially the hardworking churchgoers, died before experiencing the new Crescent City. Their silent, dignified suffering, after all, made today's relatively tolerant town possible. One day, perhaps, the graveyards will be integrated.

From the **Summer 1999** edition of *FORUM* magazine, "Parallel Lives: Writers Bill Maxwell and Beverly Coyle Recall Growing Up in Florida during the Last Days of Jim Crow."

22 A Sheltered 1950s Childhood, Then an Awakening

All this minister's daughter knew was segregation, but slowly her eyes opened to the damage and the loss.

Beverly Coyle

Beverly Coyle is a fifth-generation Floridian whose critically acclaimed novels, published by Penguin Press, are set in Florida. Her novel *In Troubled Waters*, a story of racial conflict based on family history, was named one of the *New York Times*' Notable Books in 1993. After Florida Humanities won a grant to commission two Florida writers, one Black and one white, to write about their childhood memories of growing up under Florida's harsh Jim Crow laws, Coyle and award-winning journalist Bill Maxwell were invited to participate. The following is a short version of Coyle's experience, published side by side with Maxwell's in the Summer 1999 *FORUM*.

Image: Beverly Coyle at age five. Courtesy of Beverly Coyle.

IN MY 1950s childhood, most activities revolved around church and school. Everything seemed locked within this arena. Of course, it was not a natural one, not some undisturbed lily pond found in nature.

It was artificial, a slowly constructed pond built of laws and social custom, frequently reinforced by acts of violent repression. The result was the Jim Crow system. I grew up seeing "Whites Only" and "Coloreds Only" water fountains. I had no understanding of the hardship this system presented to Black people just in terms of daily insult, never mind those of education and work and housing and money and travel. I was illiterate when it came to these signs that underscored a law by which a whole race could be virtually removed from view. Even for my parents, the vigilante and Klan activity right after the Civil War could be said to be "before their time." We all looked at those signs without reading them. Black presence in our lives was so minimal that incidents of racial conflict did not exist in my young perspective.

My father was a Methodist clergyman and my mother a homemaker and former teacher. Their respect for differences in race and creed grew out of education and a strong belief in one God who unites us all. The folks I associated with involved themselves in the weekend devotions of church services and Sunday school. And we were proud to be Methodists. I saw us in our best dress.

Our weekends often began over at the church in our various efforts to be ready for a long Sunday of services, children, choirs, Bible study, and the occasional picnic spread, which we called "dinner on the grounds."

One day when I was about nine or ten we were visiting my mother's people in Oviedo, and I got a rude glimpse of how Methodists were perceived by some. My own grandfather, a man long convinced that church was all right for women and children, claimed that he had been reading about Methodist involvement in something called the civil rights movement. He began explaining how shocked he was to learn that the Methodists were among those Americans recently infiltrated by the Communist Party.

Mom ran from the supper table in tears; Dad, the son-in-law, sat there fuming at his plate. "What's behind this integration business?" my grandfather said. "Red Communism, that's what!"

I was born August 2, 1946, nine months to the day of my father's return from the Navy and World War II. My memories begin in Boynton Beach, where Dad had one of his early churches and where my eight-room schoolhouse is now a museum. We moved every four years within the Florida Methodist Conference: Boynton, Jacksonville, Fernandina Beach, Venice-Nokomis, and our home base in Oviedo. These are my hometowns.

Historically I hail from Lake City, where a great-great-grandparent was born. Dad was north Alabama–south Tennessee stock. His people were tenant farmers whom he essentially left behind after managing to slip away, first to college, then to Methodism, then to my mother, a graduate of Florida Southern College.

I think my father was truly liberalized at Emory University in Georgia and had a scholarly rather than literal reading of the Bible. I also think his father-in-law's antagonism and sniffing out the so-called foreign, evil influence lurking behind reform did a lot to sharpen my father's sense of who he was and how he was to behave in a changing world.

My father's "job," if you will, put tremendous burden on me as a child in terms of Christian service. I was very religious, and in my adult life I frequently recall how central to my sense of reality was the singing of such songs as "Jesus loves the little children / All the children of the world! Red and yellow, black and white / They are precious in his sight / Jesus loves the little children of the world."

And later the text "if a man hath two coats, he must give one away." I grew up in fear of our excess. I had no coats, but I had many sweaters and I knew it was wrong. I knew, even in our modest lifestyle, that we had way too much.

Sometime in the mid-'50s, the idea of the shopping center was born. One day my whole family found itself in the large parking lot of our new Jacksonville shopping center's "Grand Opening" show. A Black family pulled alongside us. The adults stood around waiting while most of us kids climbed up on the hoods. The show took forever to begin, but when it did, spotlights snapped on from all directions, and we watched while a young white girl climbed to the top of a thirty-foot ladder. Suddenly there was a drum roll. An assistant already perched on top of the ladder helped the young girl set fire to her gasoline-soaked life jacket. We held our breath

I was illiterate when it came to these signs that underscored a law by which a whole race could be virtually removed from view.

as she turned to face us, placing her hands gracefully above her head and then diving straight down into nothing more than a small tank filled with water.

We cheered at the feat and then left our cars and went into the new strip mall, set up like a new town, and we bought things. Together. Corporate America had hit upon a colorblind arena: Money.

Shopping centers gave Blacks and whites space to hang out together, after a fashion. And I think it was here that I saw my first images of Blacks in families, in units like my own. We still maintained our segregated shopping areas close to where we lived. Shopping centers were neutral ground. They sprang up out of a field that was on no particular "side of town."

If one really wanted to maintain Jim Crow, shopping centers were a big mistake. There was irony in those signs over soda fountain counters: "We reserve the right to refuse service to anyone." If two different families could walk around eating ice cream cones together in this relatively new common space, then why could one such family sit down at a counter and the other not? Shopping centers were spaces that caused me to see what I had previously been unable to see, having been born into what looked like peaceful, agreed-upon separation of Blacks and whites.

About every four years we packed up barrels of dishes, pots and pans, clothes, bedding, photographs and books, my mother's Fostoria and silver and moved. In Fernandina Beach, our new parsonage had a pink vanity table in the room that became mine in the summer of 1959. I was thirteen.

The vanity table had a set of drawers on either side of a sunken center where I kept a few toiletries. Even then I must have been aware of the table's symbolic meaning: as a girl, I was supposed to do the very best with what God had given me. Only maidens in fairy tales and novels were reported to be naturally beautiful without any help. I was to think positively, look bravely into that mirror, and work at it.

Downtown Fernandina Beach in 1965. This coastal community, north of Jacksonville, is where Beverly Coyle spent much of her girlhood. Courtesy of State Archives of Florida, Florida Memory.

It was on this vanity table that I forged my mother's name to a note. I needed her written permission to check out *Gone with the Wind* from the junior high library. One might think that back then, in Jim Crow days, a white school would require parental sign-off on a book containing racial conflict of any kind. Rumor among us kids was that the book was good and sexy. I wasn't sure if it would be okay by my mother in 1959 that I be allowed to learn, on my own, all that Scarlett O'Hara had done with what God had given *her*. I forged that note without batting an eye.

At that same time, I was resisting long looks into the vanity table's mirror. The mirror was not giving me back what I wanted to see, even when I worked hard. However, I was doing quite a bit of staring into the beautiful eyes of Johnny Mathis.

A Sheltered 1950s Childhood, Then an Awakening • 151

I was doing quite a bit of staring into the beautiful eyes of Johnny Mathis. I had all three of his albums.

I had all three of his albums. I would sit and look at his face—three versions of it, each more handsome and stunning than the other. Try as separatists' cultures will, they can only do so much to arrange a view of the world. Reality will burst right through all the wrapping that is put around white people, especially white girls. Here was a Black man on the front of the album looking right at me, permitted to eye me kindly. I had no idea that Black men couldn't do that and live. Or maybe I did have some idea. I look back now and realize Elvis scared me and, in life, would have rejected me. Pat Boone would have patted me on the head. Johnny Mathis clearly loved me. Red and yellow, black and white, I was precious in his sight. Johnny Mathis loved the children of the world.

Of course, I saw Black people: men off in the fields, men gathered alongside a sandy road waiting to go home. They worked for my farming grandparents in Oviedo. I saw the lone woman walking into white neighborhoods to cook and clean. I took separation for granted. Had the violence of a former time and the violence still occurring beyond my knowledge been explained and admitted to, I would have had a better way of interpreting my everyday images. Mostly I was left to my own devices.

For example, the times a woman was hired to help clean the parsonage, I saw my mother turn herself into a tornado, knocking herself out leaving the other woman paralyzed. I picked up a lot of "stuff" around that, two messages at least. The first was that we worked as hard as the other woman did because we truly did not set ourselves above that kind of work or the woman herself. And the second, although subtle, was still clear to me: we might have tried to prove to a white maid that we could work as hard and as fast, but with the Black woman, the effort was strained, lightly desperate—our making sure there was no tinge of race or rank. And in the strain, there it was.

I would eye with curiosity the one lone janitor, keeping to himself, quietly eating his lunch in that airless room where the school stored the red disinfectant sawdust. I would see the Black faces looking down from the balcony of my neighborhood movie theater. Here's what I believe I felt when I looked up at them: I saw the people I would one day be called upon to serve as a missionary or in some other facet of my Christian work. I developed a well-defended position: they were all patiently waiting for me to grow up and come to them.

Granted, I had fears of being a lonely, old maid missionary. But I believe I was also grasping loneliness in a social sense and that I was intuiting a bigger truth that haunts me to this day, the essential loneliness of segregation, the fact that if one can't go to people right now—people who live right across town—then to go to them later is to arrive unsuitable indeed. I was being stunted by Jim Crow.

In the spring of 1960 I came home one day and announced there would be no school on Monday afternoon. The annual Lions Club minstrel show started

Teenage girls at a Tallahassee drive-in restaurant, 1957. Beverly Coyle says she grew up in an era when segregation "had virtually removed a whole race from view" when it came to social interactions. Courtesy of State Archives of Florida, Florida Memory, *Tallahassee Democrat* Collection.

I have no trouble remembering the anger in my father's voice. In hindsight I realize that he didn't know that minstrel shows were still being staged. Nor was it yet quite the year for him to find the words to say, "That's racist."

Monday, and there was going to be a matinee version for the junior high. School was going to let out at around noon, and buses would haul us over to the recreation center after lunch. The cost of the show, one dime.

A big silence fell after I made the announcement. Dad got red in the face. Finally he said, "Well, you can't go to that. You don't have my permission to go to something like that."

I wish I could remember the conversation that followed. My guess is there wasn't much of one because there almost never was when Daddy got mad. He was furious. I was confused. Was this somehow my fault? My mother and I probably left him and went into the kitchen to pretend to be cleaning up.

That's what we did when Daddy got mad. We skedaddled. I recall complaining to her, "If I don't attend the minstrel show, I'll have to go to study hall." My mother was quick to grasp how this might embarrass me, the new girl in town, if I were the only one who didn't go.

"They'll have to keep back a teacher just because of me!"

"You don't know that," my mother reasoned. "There might be all kinds of kids who won't be allowed to go."

I have no trouble remembering the anger in my father's voice. In hindsight I realize that he didn't know that minstrel shows were still being staged. Nor was it yet quite the year for him to find the words to say, "That's racist." Perhaps it was more as if one of his children had picked up dirty talk in the street and was now repeating it without knowing what was meant. To tell her was to get into something very complicated for a child who hadn't been told much, more complicated still for a person who was not yet practiced in where to begin.

Come Monday I was the only one in study hall. For all my father's shortcomings at that particular moment in 1960, I would give a lot if he were around now to know how important his strong reaction has been to me.

My guess is that my presence in study hall was noted and its meaning understood—a boycott of one. I recall how my mortification began to dissolve and then, remarkably, how quickly it was replaced with enormous pride in myself. I took credit for Dad's burgeoning courage and action. This stealing from one's parent is what children do and in so doing forge for themselves a set of personal insights whose true origins necessarily take a lifetime to trace.

Certain horrors of the day were out in the open, even when I started elementary school. No one was denying me permission to see newsreels at the movies, the ones released some ten years after World War II ended. Here was footage from the concentration camps—bodies by the hundreds spilling out of the backs of dump trucks.

And there was the Cold War. In Jacksonville, with its proximity to a naval base, I was asked to prepare in a bizarre fashion for the bomb. We all had to bring to school a canvas bag of canned goods.

Beverly Coyle at age seventeen.
Courtesy of Beverly Coyle.

Our mothers stitched up the bags, put our names on them, and placed inside them a two-week supply of food. This contraption hung on the backs of our desks. Once in a while we would have a drill. Should the bomb be headed our way during school hours, we, taking advantage of the Early Warning System, would grab our sacks and head across our sports field. Freight cars would be waiting for us on the real doomsday, at which point we'd climb aboard, apparently, and, with luck, be shipped off to safety. To Georgia.

The civil disobedience going on and the white population's violent response to it was national news, but I don't recall knowing it at the time, the arrests, the demonstrations, and the great meaning of it, dramatically and ideologically. Banning me from going to a Lions Club minstrel show was my first real news of it all.

That would have been before the bombing of a Sunday school building and the deaths of four Black children. By 1963 the press was not cooperating in keeping such things out of my view. I could see it on TV, the photographs of those little girls and their families. I knew I had seen them before! At the Shopping Center's Grand Opening, all of them and all of us seated on the tops of our cars, our faces uplifted, our same looks of fear and pleasure as that young girl prepared to set herself on fire and jump into that tiny tank. We had all screamed together in delight and relief when she made that perfectly impossible dive.

Like all the wake-up calls of this century, it would take a bomb to put an end to minstrel shows for most decent folk. Not a bomb from the enemy we were expecting, not the Soviets. But from ourselves, a bomb planted by our fellow white citizens in a Baptist church in Birmingham.

The year the Civil Rights Act passed, I was a freshman at FSU in Tallahassee. One day that fall, we students found out a certain all-white church in town was going to put to a member vote whether they would admit Blacks into their Sunday worship service. My very first Sunday sermon at the Wesley Foundation Chapel on campus was about this kind of bigotry. "The most segregated hour is the church hour," our minister intoned, preaching to a mixed audience—Methodist students having driven over from all-Black FAMU, three miles from an all-white FSU. And when it got out that the vote went badly downtown and the congregation had voted to bar Black people from worshiping with them, we were outraged. Some of us decided to post a sign on their church door and call up the press to get a picture. The sign read, "We reserve the right to refuse Salvation to anyone!"

At college I was admitted for life into a liberal community. This gives me cause for rejoicing at my good fortune. I suppose I am perceived as outspoken, prepared to take my stand against injustice. I am proud of *In Troubled Waters*, a novel I wrote in which Black and white characters struggle to know each other across a divide that still exists. I've even got a few scars from having authored it.

Black people are now in my life as students, friends, colleagues, neighbors in my building in Manhattan; they are my lawyers, doctors, editors, and the presidents

A Sheltered 1950s Childhood, Then an Awakening · 155

of universities where I'm likely to teach; they are among the most prominent bishops of the United Methodist Church. But I am insulated to this day in ways that trouble me.

In my travels I meet people wanting loudly to affirm how far we've come. Yes, I want to say, we have come some distance. But we live in separate worlds formed long ago in more parts of this country than in the South. When, from the start, various systems remove from view certain people as a group, it is devastating to contemplate that removal in its fullest terms. How much of our collective imagination is affected; how much of our experimentation and expansiveness as creative people? I suppose I am talking about the soul of the citizen and am trying to present, to myself at least, some understanding that takes in more than merely how far we have come. In refusing to serve each other at critical points along the way, individuals and entire nations can end up unable to serve.

From the **Summer 1999** edition of *FORUM* magazine, "Parallel Lives: Writers Bill Maxwell and Beverly Coyle Recall Growing Up in Florida during the Last Days of Jim Crow."

23

That Summer of '64

Martin Luther King Jr. and the fight for racial justice in St. Augustine.

David R. Colburn

David R. Colburn (1942–2019) was a University of Florida professor of history, provost emeritus, and director of the Bob Graham Center for Public Service. He was the writer or editor of fourteen books, including *Racial Change and Community Crisis: St. Augustine, Florida, 1877–1980*, and was one of the authors of Florida's Rosewood report in 1993, an inquiry into the 1923 destruction of the town of Rosewood. Most recently, his work appeared in *Writing for the Public Good: Essays from David R. Colburn and Senator Bob Graham*, edited by Steven Noll. His many honors include the Florida Humanities Lifetime Achievement Award.

AFTER ALMOST a year of demonstrations, arrests, and violence, a large crowd of Blacks and whites gathered on a sultry evening in late June of 1964 at St. Paul's African Methodist Episcopal Church, near the center of St. Augustine. They came to hear the Reverend Dr. Martin Luther King Jr. discuss the ongoing struggle for civil rights in the nation's oldest city and celebrate the recent passage of the 1964 civil rights bill by the United States Senate and President Lyndon Johnson's announcement that he would sign the measure into law.

The meeting began as it had for the past month and a half, since the arrival of the Southern Christian Leadership Conference (SCLC) in early May, first with singing of an old slave song: "Nobody knows the trouble I've seen. Nobody knows but Jesus." Perspiring heavily from the television lights and the crowding on this summer evening, the audience, nevertheless, was oblivious to the heat. Buoyed by national developments, they were confident the St. Augustine struggle was near an end.

When King entered the church, the audience cheered and broke into "When the Saints Go Marching In." The celebration and singing continued with "Which Side Are You On, Lord" as King stepped to the pulpit. The emotionalism and excitement stunned even experienced hands. An Associated Press reporter turned to Marshall Frady, a writer for *Newsweek*, and said, "My God, Marshall, have you ever heard anything like this?" Frady, who was more accustomed to the emotion of such civil rights gatherings, replied, "Look," as he extended his arm that bristled with goose bumps.

As King stood before this enthusiastic and admiring crowd in St. Augustine, his influence had never been greater. Only thirty-five years old, he had become the spokesman for civil rights reform and human rights throughout the world. He had just been named *Time* magazine's "Man of the Year" and awarded the American Baptist Convention's first annual Edwin T. Dahlburg Peace Award. In less than a month, he would be awarded the Nobel Peace Prize. King's commitment to equal rights and human dignity had touched the soul of the nation and, indeed, much of the world. And while he had stirred up the wrath and undying enmity of some as

Nationally, SCLC's focus was on the pending civil rights bill that was under consideration by the US Senate in 1964. King wrote that the enactment of the bill was "so critical for the domestic health of our national community that we must mobilize every force and pressure available to see to it that the civil rights bill before the Senate gets through—as is."

a result of campaigns like St. Augustine's, he had also assumed a unique place in both the Black and white communities of the country.

In addressing the audience at St. Paul's, King spoke enthusiastically about civil rights developments nationally and the important role these Floridians and out-of-town demonstrators played. But he also cautioned about the difficult work that lay ahead in St. Augustine. "We are at the most difficult moment," he said. "We must remain calm and not let them provoke us into violence." As King finished his speech, 350 people, including approximately 50 whites, queued up outside the church in preparation for the evening march.

Led by the Reverend Fred Shuttlesworth, the Reverend Andrew Young, and Hosea Williams, all of SCLC, the crowd walked quietly through the night toward the center of this historic community. King did not join the marchers, taking seriously the danger of threats on his life.

The marshaling of white militants and Ku Klux Klansmen in St. Augustine and the clashes earlier that day had heightened concerns of SCLC staff coordinators. In particular, efforts by civil rights leaders to integrate St. Augustine Beach on two occasions during the day had led to the near drowning of civil rights demonstrators when militants, despite the presence of state and local police, chased them into the ocean.

Waiting for the marchers at the Old Slave Market were more than 500 white militants whose anger at King and civil rights activists had been raised to a fever pitch by J. B. Stoner, Atlanta Ku Klux Klan leader, and the Reverend Connie Lynch, a pro-segregation religious zealot who drove around the country fomenting hate and bigotry. White extremists like Stoner and Lynch were drawn to St. Augustine because of King's presence, and they came to not only defeat King but to destroy the movement.

These whites turned toward the sounds of the civil rights marchers, who sang spirituals as they neared the center of town, and with Lynch's blessing began to sprint toward Shuttlesworth and Young.

As the marchers walked past the old Hotel Alcazar and into the town square, a local resident who lived nearby commented, "Things would be quiet. Then I'd hear the shuffle of feet. . . . Then I'd hear singing, then police sirens, dogs barking, and people running." For one brief moment the singing stopped, and there was near total silence, as in the eye of a hurricane. A reporter characterized it as an "eerie silence," adding, "You could hear the clicking of stop lights."

Then the storm hit. Marchers tried vainly to hold their ranks and to continue, but whites jerked individuals from the lines and pummeled them. For nearly twenty minutes the assault continued, with most marchers fleeing to the safety of the Black community.

About fifty demonstrators suffered cuts and bruises, while another eighteen had to be taken to nearby Flagler Hospital for treatment of more serious injuries. To add insult to injury, several of the injured were subsequently arrested by police for disturbing the peace.

Martin Luther King Jr. with protesters. King gives a young picketer a pat on the back as a group of youngsters started to picket in St. Augustine, June 10, 1964. AP Photo.

The civil rights campaign in St. Augustine marked a major turning point in race relations in Florida and the nation. The Reverend Martin Luther King Jr. and the Southern Christian Leadership Conference, responding to a request from local activists, had brought their nonviolent civil rights forces to St. Augustine the early spring of 1964. By the time King and SCLC intervened in the city, there had already been a year of escalating protests and incidents and beatings of local activists.

Nationally, SCLC's focus was on the pending civil rights bill that was under consideration by the US Senate in 1964. King wrote that the enactment of the bill was "so critical for the domestic health of our national community that we must mobilize every force and pressure available to see to it that the civil rights bill before the Senate gets through—as is."

King also believed it was essential that Black Americans play a central role in securing passage of the bill. Since Blacks were nearly without representation in Congress, King felt only through a moral crusade in the streets of the South could Black Americans be politically effective. But why St. Augustine? The community was attractive to the nation's most prominent civil rights organization for several reasons. First, a local movement on which to build a major civil rights campaign already existed in St. Augustine. Dr. Robert Hayling, a dentist, Henry Twine, and many other Black residents had launched demonstrations in 1963 in an unsuccessful effort to desegregate the community.

Second, the local white leadership in St. Augustine had shown no willingness to compromise on desegregation. In contrast to Albany, Georgia, in 1962, where SCLC had encountered a politically wily sheriff who had brought SCLC its first defeat, St. Augustine had no such savvy white leaders who might derail the movement.

Third, St. Augustine was heavily dependent on tourism and thus subject to a national boycott that, if successful, might bring the community to its knees.

Fourth, in 1964 St. Augustine was one year away from celebrating its 400th birthday, and plans were well under way for a momentous celebration, and to highlight the fact that it, not Jamestown or Plymouth, was the oldest community in the nation. For SCLC, the national publicity that St. Augustine had begun to receive was an added bonus.

Such national visibility was particularly crucial to SCLC's effort to win support for the civil rights bill. In announcing SCLC's forthcoming campaign in St. Augustine, King used the community's 400th anniversary to publicize the organization's struggle against what he termed "the oldest segregated community" in the nation. It was an ironic characterization of the city, however, because historically, particularly in its Spanish period but also in the first British period, St. Augustine had been a multiracial society in which whites, enslaved and free Africans, and Native Americans interacted on a daily basis.

Despite King's characterization, St. Augustine was not a hotbed of racism before the events of 1964. Black and white citizens, in fact, often conversed pleasantly in public spaces, and there seemed to be a genuine fondness between many white and Black residents. The historian David Chalmers, himself a civil rights participant in the St. Augustine campaign, found a greater degree of racial intermingling in the community than in "hundreds of other Southern towns."

Even a local Black resident commented, "You really weren't too conscious at that time of the difference that existed." Most white citizens, however, firmly embraced the color line, and while they might regard Blacks favorably as neighbors, they were not prepared to accept them as equals.

What made St. Augustine so resistant to racial change, and why did whites ignore the concerns of Black residents? It would seem a community dependent on northern tourism in a state that had changed so significantly because of immigration would adapt to social change more readily than a Birmingham, Alabama, or Jackson, Mississippi. But St. Augustine proved as difficult as any to desegregate. As with other historic communities in the South, St. Augustine's social structure had been defined by the traditions of the past, and segregation was a central element in that heritage. One could not live in St. Augustine and escape the history that oozed from every pore of city life. The traditional nature of social and political life in the community received added reinforcement from local business leaders, the religious

Press conference in St. Augustine, 1964. During the summer 1964 civil rights actions in St. Augustine, (*left to right*) Andrew Young, Martin Luther King Jr., and Robert Hayling hold a press conference at the Elks Rest on Washington Street. Photo by Frank Murray, city of St. Augustine.

community, and Governor Farris Bryant, all of whom were committed to preserving the status quo in race relations.

Moderates in the community found themselves in an untenable position and were further isolated when fellow white residents joined forces to establish a chapter of the John Birch Society in 1963.

The Birch Society maintained an office and reading room on St. George Street in the heart of the old Spanish quarter. Led by a local physician with close ties to the political leaders of St. Augustine and with more than fifty members, the Birch Society quickly became a prominent force in the civil rights struggles.

Within the Black community of St. Augustine, few public voices had emerged to condemn the state of race relations prior to 1963. Most Black residents criticized racial conditions in the abstract but, despite their close relations with many whites in the community, knew how dangerous civil rights protests could be. In the aftermath of the *Brown* decision and following the civil rights developments in Montgomery, Little Rock, Tallahassee, and Greensboro, local Blacks eagerly awaited the end of segregation in their community, but it was not clear that there would be a local civil rights movement.

Dr. Robert Hayling, who had moved to St. Augustine in 1960 to take over a dental practice, was the catalyst for the emergence of a local movement. The son of a faculty member at Florida A&M University, Hayling had lived much of his life within the Black community, partially sheltered from the racism in the South. He received his undergraduate degree at FAMU and his dental degree at Meharry Medical College in Nashville. Hayling, who had taken part in a demonstration in Nashville, chafed under the oppression of Jim Crow in St. Augustine. Although he had many white patients, Hayling could not socialize with them or get served at local

That Summer of '64 · 161

The Summer of 1964, St. Augustine. A confrontation between integrationists and segregationists at a whites-only beach. Courtesy of State Archives of Florida, Florida Memory.

restaurants. He had joined the local NAACP shortly after arriving in St. Augustine and in 1963 took over the leadership of the organization's Youth Council. It was the Youth Council that initiated protests in front of Woolworth's in late June 1963, carrying signs that asked, "If We Spend Money Here Why Can't We Eat Here?"

A sit-in at a pharmacy in July led to the arrest of sixteen young Blacks, including seven juveniles. Their jailing became the defining moment in the local movement. Following their arrest, County Judge Charles Mathis informed parents he would release the children into their custody only if they pledged to keep them away from further demonstrations. The parents of three children promised to do so, but other parents angrily rejected the judge's deal.

Judge Mathis transferred the four remaining juveniles to the state reform school and refused to release them on bond or to set a term for their incarceration. Infuriated and realizing the extent of the commitment of local whites to the status quo, many Black residents rallied behind the children and their families and committed themselves to the community's desegregation. On Labor Day 1963, more than 125 residents participated in St. Augustine's first mass demonstration to protest the city commission's refusal to appoint a biracial commission.

Mayor Shelley and other city leaders could have settled the mounting crisis by asking Mathis to free the teenagers or by appointing a biracial commission. Instead, Shelley and other leaders, including City Attorney Robert Andreu, School Superintendent Douglas Hartley, City Police Chief Virgil Stuart, and Sheriff L. O. Davis, opposed any compromise with civil rights activists.

These five men met with Dr. Norris, head of the Birch Society, at his home in 1964, where they developed plans to undermine the efforts of Black residents and SCLC.

162 · David R. Colburn

Joining Forces

UNABLE TO TALK with local civic leaders and threatened repeatedly by Ku Klux Klan members, a civil rights group led by Dr. Hayling and Henry Twine journeyed to Orlando in March 1964, where they met with the Reverend C. T. Vivian, a member of the Board of Directors of SCLC, and asked for King's assistance. SCLC had already pledged to participate in the Mississippi Freedom Summer campaign in July but was debating whether it should conduct protest activities earlier. Several in the organization, including King, felt strongly that such a campaign was necessary if Black Americans were to maintain the pressure on the Senate to pass the civil rights bill. There was no agreement, however, on where that campaign would be. Hayling, Twine, and their fellow St. Augustinians came at a propitious moment.

The match between Hayling and the SCLC would have its bumpy moments. For one thing, he was not a total advocate of nonviolence, arguing that Black citizens should be able to arm themselves when physically threatened. But Hayling was a charismatic leader and had demonstrated great physical courage that King and his colleagues could not help but admire.

Twice Hayling's home had been shot up, and he was badly beaten one night trying to observe a Klan rally. While Hayling and his colleagues gave away some control by inviting in the SCLC, in exchange they teamed up with an organization expert at mobilizing protest and worldwide attention. SCLC's experience in campaigns in Montgomery, Albany, and Birmingham had helped the organization develop a large national following and prepared it for difficult struggles like St. Augustine. The organization had become more skillful at planning and developing strategies for such campaigns since it began them in 1962 in Albany, Georgia. SCLC did not agree to participate in St. Augustine, for example, until aides had made two trips to the community and a plan of action had been prepared.

Before entering St. Augustine, SCLC recruited participants from throughout the Northeast and in Florida. SCLC launched its first demonstrations over Easter week with Mrs. Malcolm Peabody, mother of the governor of Massachusetts, and Mrs. John Burgess, wife of the Episcopal bishop of Massachusetts, leading a sit-in at a St. Augustine restaurant.

The demonstrations conducted by SCLC were carefully planned to highlight the racism Blacks endured on a daily basis, to point out the need for the civil rights bill, and to dramatize the movement so the national media would keep the nation aware of developments in St. Augustine. A few days after her arrest, Mrs. Peabody appeared on *The Today Show* to describe the racial intolerance in St. Augustine and throughout the South. She urged Congress to pass the civil rights bill so that Black citizens could freely exercise their rights as citizens. The personal commitment of this seventy-two-year-old woman captured the attention and support of white and Black Americans.

In mid-May, SCLC returned to St. Augustine and conducted daily demonstrations for two months. During this period civil rights leaders varied their tactics

That Summer of '64 · 163

Monson Motor Lodge pool. When a group of white and Black integrationists refused to exit a segregated motel pool on June 18, 1964, in St. Augustine, owner and manager James Brock poured muriatic acid into the water, shouting "I'm cleaning the pool." The demonstrators were arrested, and photos of the incident were published in newspapers around the world. Photo by Horace Cort for Associated Press.

to maintain the attention of the press and the public. King was himself arrested following an attempted sit-in at a local motel. The evening marches remained the most dramatic and dangerous because local and state police could not guarantee the safety of demonstrators, even if they were so inclined.

The protests exposed the pervasiveness of segregation, touching on every aspect of life in St. Augustine, from schools to pools and public beaches.

To assure press coverage of its demonstrations, SCLC would often notify reporters in advance. Hosea Williams, special adviser to Martin Luther King, was adept at developing new tactics. One of his most effective was the swim-in at the Monson Motor Lodge on June 18, 1964. A group of rabbis with SCLC distracted Monson owner and manager James Brock while Black and white protesters jumped into the motel's swimming pool.

Brock yelled at two of the white demonstrators, "You're not putting these people in my pool." "These are our guests," came the reply.

Brock ran into his office and returned with a two-gallon container of muriatic acid that he dumped into the pool. A group of whites, including a police officer, gathered nearby, not knowing what to do. Finally, an off-duty policeman jumped into the pool to arrest the protesters. It was such a farcical sight that few in the media could resist it as an illustration of the foolishness of segregation. The Russian newspaper *Izvestia* ran this picture of the protesters with the officer jumping into the pool on its front page, as did many American newspapers. Few would deny segregation had been doused that day at Monson's swimming pool.

The irony of local race relations was revealed one evening when white militants conducted their own march through the Black community only to encounter Black residents who welcomed them into their neighborhood.

In mid-July, at the end of two months of demonstrations, arrests, and violence, SCLC pulled out of St. Augustine, having secured passage of the Civil Rights Act of 1964 and an agreement from Governor Farris Bryant to establish a biracial commission. The crisis appeared to have ended; in fact, race relations in the community had seldom been worse.

The Aftermath

THE WHITE LEADERSHIP not only refused to accept the governor's decision and the implications of the Civil Rights Act but blamed Black residents for the community's racial turmoil and declining economic fortunes. Throughout the course of the next year, white militants continued their harassment of Black residents and conducted their own boycotts of white businesses that complied with the Civil Rights Act. The biracial commission that had been promised by the governor to ease race relations never materialized. White residents blamed local Blacks for the failure of the 400th anniversary celebration, the community's one opportunity to revitalize its image and to recoup the economic losses of 1964. Whites remained so bitter that they resisted school integration until mandated to do so by the federal courts in 1970.

It would not be until the early 1970s that racial tensions began to ease and Black residents would experience the benefits of the civil rights movement to which they contributed so much. By then many of the former civil rights leaders, including Hayling, had been forced to leave because of economic pressure and threats of violence. Historically Black Florida Memorial College, many of whose students had participated in the demonstrations, relocated to Dade County in 1968 after nearly fifty years in St. Augustine because of ongoing tensions with the white community.

Some Black leaders, such as Henry Twine, however, would continue on, his particular job as a postal clerk protected by the federal government. In the 1980s Twine was elected to the St. Augustine city commission, served two terms, expanded opportunities for Black residents, and hosted the first statewide Martin Luther King celebration in 1986. He died in 1994, having worked for most of his life to secure the dreams that civil rights activists had prayed for with King on that warm June night at St. Paul's AME church in 1964.

From the **Winter 1994/1995** edition of *FORUM* magazine, "The Civil Rights Era: 1954–1965."

Mrs. Bicknell's Nephew Dies of the Spanish Flu

Death in the U. S. service from Spanish influenza entered another St. Petersburg home yesterday when Mr. and Mrs. W. S. Bicknell received a message that Scott Coffman, a nephew of Mrs. Bicknell, had died at the Great Lakes naval training station. The young man was 29 years old and the son of Mr. and Mrs. John S. Coffman, of Sullivan, Ind. His death was due to pneumonia resulting from an attack of the influenza. Mr. Bicknell is the head bookkeeper for Charles R. Hall in this city.

Shorthand in Chinese.

The inventor of the system of shorthand established in China, must be nothing less than a genius. The language has no written vowels and consonants, and one syllable, spoken in as many as nine different tones, has as many meanings. In spite of these difficulties, the new system permits a speed of 140 words a minute. Schools for teaching shorthand are being established in various parts of the country.

port of the entire population struggle to stave off a humi peace with Germany.

As the men who had fought sanguinary field of Marasesti, is the Gettysburg of Rumania, ed by, each bearing on his brea coveted "Michael the Brave," for gallantry, the queen brok tears and, turning to the king stood beside her, said, in a voi betrayed deep emotion:

"What a tragedy that this n cent army must lay down its But, please God, it shall not for I repeat it, it shall not be for Germany by her might and b ness may subdue, but she can crush the spirit and will of n diers. With God's help, we wi again and I pray that the day far off. My soul will never re til the honor of the country is cated before the eyes of our al

Another to Be Found.

A tracer sent to locate the old ioned man who wore a peach watch charm, reports from Clea Pa.: "Located my man. He als ries a combination pen, pencil, pick, and rubber stamp. Any in tions?" Certainly; draw for ex money and hunt for the old-fash woman who used to grease the cake griddle with a pork rind.—falo News.

PART IV

When a Deadly Pandemic Strikes

As the world shifted, we hear of one family's story navigating new realities during Covid-19.

Schoolboys Don Hoover and Joe Sistrunk, Starke, 1918. The students are masked and ready for school during the Spanish flu pandemic. Killing tens of millions around the world, it is considered one of the world's deadliest pandemics, after the Black Death bubonic plague of 1346–1353. Courtesy of State Archives of Florida, Florida Memory.

24

A Lesson in the Pandemic

Teaching our young daughter to cope when Dad was on Covid-19's frontlines.

Nila Do Simon

Nila Do Simon is a writer and editor whose work has appeared in *Conde Nast Traveler*, *Marie Claire*, the *New York Times*, *Garden and Gun*, *Philadelphia Style*, *Miami Magazine*, *Flamingo Magazine*, *Alaskan Airlines*, and *Bostonmagazine.com*, among other outlets. She is the founding editor-in-chief of *Venice* magazine and the custom publications *Botaniko*, *1926*, and *Florida Panthers' CATS*. Her work has received top honors, including for feature and headline writing by the Florida Magazine Association.

Image: Dr. Joshua Simon savors off-duty moments with daughter Fallyn and son Adrian, 2020. Courtesy of Nila Do Simon.

IF I'M LUCKY, the most exciting part of my day of the past three sheltering-at-home months happens around 7 p.m. If fortune is on my side, my husband comes home from work then. Sure, I love the shift change, when I can clock out from my work-from-home life with our three-year-old daughter and one-year-old son and hand the keys to their entertainment schedule over to Daddy. But that's not all.

Because when my husband arrives home, for about twelve seconds I get to see my kids showing borderline-animalistic joy. The moment the garage door rolls up and sends vibrations through the house, my children start squealing. My daughter usually drops her activity of the moment like it's on fire to jump and yell, "Daddy!" That yelp triggers her one-year-old hoss of a brother to break out into a staccato-y jig and ogre-walk to meet Daddy at the entryway.

When Daddy emerges, I imagine it's like the Beatles arriving in America. Pandemonium breaks. My son rhythmically shouts, "Da-Da, Da-Da" in between giggling, and my daughter can't stop shrieking with glee. I wordlessly stand witness, not interjecting, adding or taking away from the excitement because I know that as much as I enjoy watching these seconds, my husband exponentially lives for it even more.

But many days I don't get lucky. Out of those ninety-some quarantine days, I haven't seen this level of joy from my kids in about half of them. That's because Daddy isn't able to come home. As both a general and trauma surgeon who covers the ICU, he's been caring for Covid-19 patients as the number of cases in Florida steadily climbs. As in most households, Covid-19 has resulted in a severe disturbance in our lives. My husband's work hours have always been long and intense. Covid-19 has stretched them.

But he and other medical professionals have trained for these extreme hours and situations on both skill and emotional levels. It's their kids who have not.

Surgeon Joshua Simon FaceTimes from the hospital with his three-year-old daughter, Fallyn, 2020. Simon's work in Delray and West Palm Beach caring for Covid-19 patients meant separations and adjustments for the family. Courtesy of Nila Do Simon.

Every night my kids ask when Daddy will come home. For a majority of those days, I've had to tell them he won't be home to tuck them in bed or give them their nighttime baths. It devastates them, my daughter especially. Naturally dramatic (once, I ate the right side of a croissant instead of the left side, and she had a meltdown), my daughter is at an age where she feels the highs and lows of life on a different cosmic scale than I do.

Last week, when I broke it to her that Daddy wasn't coming home, she let out a pain-filled howl reminiscent of the sounds coming from the labor and delivery ward as the uteri of soon-to-be mothers contracted. As tears streamed down her face, she cried, "I miss Daddy! I want to see Daddy!" I comforted her as best I could, telling her that I understood and that I, too, miss Daddy. Nothing worked, so I grabbed my phone to FaceTime my husband, praying that he wasn't scrubbed into a case. He answered. As he video-chatted with his baby girl, he told her that he'll see her soon, that Daddy loves her so much. Suddenly the trauma alert sounded, and he abruptly hung up. And just like that, somehow I was left in an even worse situation than I started with.

Miraculously, we got through the night, though not without more crying and howling. The next morning I thought about a friend's suggestion over a year ago on how to emotionally prepare my daughter for the arrival of her baby brother by giving her a doll so that she could role-play and perhaps develop more empathy toward babies. I decided to apply this theory to our current situation, taking out my daughter's toy medical kit and having her care for her dolls. As her ivory teddy bear laid supine on its back, she patted him and asked how he was feeling. I then told her that's what Daddy does, that he and a team care for patients and their families, doing everything they can to get them healthy. Something clicked. My daughter began tending to teddy for the next several minutes, taking out her toy stethoscope and placing it on the bear.

The real test came when my husband had his next twenty-four-hour shift. As I braced for impact after telling her Daddy was working tonight, my daughter paused, looked down, and then quietly asked if she could FaceTime him. Yes, of course, I said, before dialing his number. And when she saw his face, she began jumping up and down, screaming, "Daddy!"

From the **Fall 2020** edition of *FORUM* magazine, "Alone, Together: Stories of Florida in a Time of Crisis."

PART V

We Were Strangers Here Ourselves

When so many are from somewhere else, what does it mean to be a Floridian?

New US citizens take the oath of citizenship at a naturalization ceremony in Miami Beach, November 2020. Jeffrey Isaac Greenberg, Alamy Stock Photo.

25 Finding Florida

*Out of so many puzzle pieces,
how can you create one state identity?*

Stephen J. Whitfield

Stephen J. Whitfield, raised in Jacksonville, is the Max Richter Professor Emeritus of American Civilization at Brandeis University, where he taught for forty-four years. He also served as a visiting professor at the Hebrew University of Jerusalem, the Catholic University of Leuven in Belgium, the Sorbonne, and the University of Munich. He is the author of ten books, including *A Death in the Delta: The Story of Emmett Till* (Free Press, 1988), *The Culture of the Cold War* (Johns Hopkins University Press, 1996), and *Learning on the Left: Political Profiles of Brandeis University* (Brandeis University Press, 2020).

Image: The Florida puzzle. Design by Russ Kramer.

DOES FLORIDA have its own culture, one that is separate and distinguishable from its neighboring states, its region, from the rest of the nation, or even from the state's Latin American neighbors? Can a state that has historically exhibited as much ethnic, religious, and racial diversity as Florida be said to have a sense of commonality that is authoritative enough, decisive enough, to form the identity of the state's residents? Such perplexing questions can be raised, but they cannot be tackled in any satisfactory fashion here. They can be addressed, if not resolved. The effort to locate something cohesive about Florida culture rubs up against the sheer diversity of a state so huge that a single county like Miami-Dade is bigger than Rhode Island, which is represented by two US senators.

Culture is now understood to be not just a given, not merely an inheritance, but also a process. In Florida that process has been durable; St. Augustine is the nation's oldest town. But distant origins are also entangled with a radically discontinuous past; values and images seem to change shape as the culture is examined. Is there a single, identifiable cultural thread that runs through Florida's history? Culture is not monochromatic or homogeneous, with one size fitting all. It's more like a kind of combat zone in which various visions, claims, and interpretations contend, and few states have more space for such collisions than Florida. "The complexity of historical events is such," anthropologist Franz Boas once proclaimed, "that the cultural life of any people can be understood only as an outgrowth of those unique conditions under which it has lived." But have the unique conditions in Florida sparked a distinctive cultural life?

Consider merely the variations among the urban, suburban, and rural parts of Florida. Such differences can be dramatized in two celebrated literary works. Marjorie Kinnan Rawlings's novel *The Yearling* topped the best-seller lists in 1938 and won the Pulitzer Prize for fiction. Her book is set in the shady woods of Cross Creek, a sparsely populated area south of Gainesville. Compare Cynthia Ozick's novella *Rosa*, which won first prize in the 1984 O. Henry Prize Stories collection

Postcards touted the state's sunny charm. Greetings from Florida, the Land of Sunshine, circa 1942. Courtesy of State Archives of Florida, Florida Memory.

and is partly set in urbanized Dade County. *Rosa* portrays aged ex–New Yorkers, some of whom are Holocaust survivors like the protagonist herself:

> Why Florida? Because here they were shells like herself, already fried in the sun.... It seemed to Rosa Lublin that the whole peninsula of Florida was weighed down with regret. Everyone had left behind a real life. Here they had nothing. They were all scarecrows, blown about under the murdering sunball.

Tonally, and not just geographically, this is far from Cross Creek, indeed as distant as Rosa is from the Hispanics a few blocks away who have made Miami the northernmost metropolis of Latin America.

Such diversity calls into question the appropriateness of considering a state a cultural unit. It seems either too small or too big. This point brings to mind a statement made in 1860 by one of the few foes of secession in South Carolina, a state whose political elite was notorious for its ardor for disunion. The state, he lamented, was "too small for a republic, but too large for an insane asylum."

States can be considered sites of cultural production but not necessarily because local conditions affect creativity. Although both Rudyard Kipling and Aleksandr Solzhenitsyn resided in Vermont, not even the most ingenious literary critic could ascertain the influence of that state on their books. Though the lines of latitude make Florida very much a southern state and though its history is scarred by slavery, segregation, and racism, the connection of Florida to the rest of the region has long been considered equivocal, and standard works in southern historiography tend to downplay the impact of so unrepresentative a state.

Finding Florida • 173

Florida has been sufficiently entangled in the distinctive history of the South for special attention to be paid to the role of Black Americans, who have lived until recently under especially onerous limitations. The commonality that culture is supposed to embrace was not historically intended to include Black Americans, which is why the limitations under which they were compelled to live provoked some to revolt, like James Weldon Johnson, born in Jacksonville, the secretary of the NAACP, and A. Philip Randolph, born in Crescent City, the key organizer of the Brotherhood of Sleeping Car Porters. Johnson could not remain in Jacksonville were he to cultivate his various talents, which included poetry and lyrics, though he did write "Lift Every Voice and Sing," which became known as "the Negro national hymn," for a Black schoolchildren's concert in Jacksonville. His brother J. Rosamond Johnson wrote the music.

An eccentric trajectory was taken by a protégée of anthropologist Franz Boas who even made it onto a US postage stamp. Born in 1891 and raised in Eatonville, Zora Neale Hurston had to leave central Florida to transform its African American folklore into literature. Yet she cherished her origins so intensely that she feared racial integration was an insult to the dignity of the souls of Black folk. Hence she objected to *Brown v. Board of Education* in 1954, even as the system of white supremacy helped send her career into a downward spiral. Two decades after making *Who's Who in America*, she was back in Florida working as a maid, and the honors heaped upon her work were mostly posthumous. Hurston died a pauper, in Fort Pierce, in 1960.

One apt metaphor for the ordeal of Jim Crow involved Ray Charles. Blinded by an illness at the age of six, orphaned at fifteen, addicted to narcotics by the age of sixteen, he had stayed in school for the deaf and blind in St. Augustine long enough to learn Braille. As though knowing how badly he needed to get out of Florida while also realizing that he was irrevocably an American, Charles asked someone to place his finger on a map at the farthest spot away that was still within the borders of the United States, which is why his career got started in Seattle.

But others remained and persisted, like Mary McLeod Bethune, who founded the first fully accredited four-year college in Florida for African Americans; some came to live in Florida after their most creative work was behind them, like Mississippi-born Bo Diddley, who moved to a farm near Gainesville. One of the grim paradoxes of southern history is that, had this musician moved two decades before his induction into the Rock and Roll Hall of Fame in 1987, he could not have been served a cup of coffee in most of downtown Gainesville, yet his songs radiated an ethos of liberation.

In a state that seems to encourage a sunny-side-up optimism, a faith in a better future, the somber sense of the human estate that the fiction of Ernest Hemingway and Isaac Bashevis Singer exemplified might not gain much traction, though both Nobel laureates had made their homes in Florida (not concurrently).

All aboard, circa 1880. Tourists view natural Florida from the decks of the river steamboat "Okeehumkee" in Silver Springs. Courtesy of State Archives of Florida, Florida Memory.

174 · Stephen J. Whitfield

Florida's people represent diverse cultures and ways of life: *Above*, a member of the Seminole Tribe of Florida sewing colorful Indian dress, 1954. Courtesy of State Archives of Florida, Florida Memory. *Above right*, a girl releases a dove as part of the Feast Day of the Epiphany in Tarpon Springs, a fishing village near Tampa with a strong Greek influence. From the documentary *Dancing As One*. *Right*, the Scull sisters dance with musician Facundo Rivero at Club Basque in Little Havana, Miami, 1985. Photo by Laurie Key Sommers, courtesy of State Archives of Florida, Florida Memory. *Far right*, cattle rancher Tom Everett Sr. speaks on his cell phone in Sumter County, 2006. Photo by Robert L. Stone, courtesy of State Archives of Florida, Florida Memory.

The injunction to "have a nice day" may be the first commandment of Florida, where guests in Orlando's Walt Disney World, as in Anaheim's Disneyland, can enjoy Tomorrowland; no such section exists in Disneyland Paris. Florida is therefore rather unpromising terrain for the nihilism or tragic vision associated with the European avant-garde, which was strikingly revealed in 1956 when Coral Gables became the site for the North American premiere of *Waiting for Godot*. Its author's sensibility was so glum that one summer during a cricket match in London, a companion mentioned to Samuel Beckett that the weather was so lovely it made one "glad to be alive," to which the playwright replied, "Oh, I don't think I would go quite so far as to say that."

By a set of bizarre circumstances, the American version of *En attendant Godot* was directed by the Russian-born Alan Schneider and starred the undoubtedly bemused comedy team of Tom Ewell and Bert Lahr.

The marquee of the Coconut Grove Playhouse was misleading. It billed the future Nobel laureate's unbearably bleak insistence upon the emptiness and estrangement of human existence as "the laugh sensation of two continents."

Although Tennessee Williams, a resident of Key West, applauded loudly at the curtain, most of the audience scarcely appreciated the play. "By the intermission," the director recalled, "at least a third of the house had left. Another third didn't come back afterward; they were too busy drowning their resentment in the theater

Finding Florida · 175

The symbolic life of the state has been decisively shaped by others whose roots are elsewhere, some of whom weren't even tourists.

Car and trailer crossing a bridge, Astor, 1957. Photo by Francis P. Johnson, courtesy of State Archives of Florida, Florida Memory.

bar, where the dialogue was more familiar." Schneider mordantly concluded, "We should never have gone to Miami."

Florida has hardly been inhospitable to the serious arts, however. The largest art museum in the state is now the Norton Museum of Art in West Palm Beach, which opened in 1941 and includes paintings by Monet, Matisse, Picasso, O'Keeffe, and Pollock. In Lakeland, the sixteen-unit master plan that Frank Lloyd Wright devised for Florida Southern College became the site where more of his buildings are located than anywhere else.

In Yulee a dance company was created at the White Oak Plantation, the home of the late Howard Gilman, an arts patron. The White Oak Dance Project was founded by dancer Mikhail Baryshnikov, who recalled, "Howard had an extraordinary knack for pulling together talented people from diverse fields and providing a comfortable environment where they could relax with each other. Something about the easy camaraderie without pressure was the richest atmosphere for me.... It was how I learned most of what I consider valuable."

But if none of these figures was indigenous, that only means that they are representative of Florida, where newcomers frequently jostle with natives and where there are so many tourists and visitors that more hotel and motel rooms have been built in Orlando than in New York City.

Indeed, what makes this topic so treacherous is that the culture of Florida is neither hermetic nor insular or isolated but is a product of outside stimuli. The symbolic life of the state has been decisively shaped by others whose roots are elsewhere, some of whom weren't even tourists. No voice has echoed more durably, for instance, than a Pennsylvanian's. Stephen Foster's "Old Folks at Home" (1851) became the state song, an eerie anticipation of the retirement communities of the twentieth century. Even though New Yorker George Gershwin misspelled "Suwannee" as "Swanee" in his 1919 song by that title, it became his most popular single hit. Neither he nor lyricist Irving Caesar had ever seen the Suwannee River. But so what? From the Marx Brothers' *The Cocoanuts* (1929) to NBC's *Miami Vice* (1984–1989) to John Sayles's *Sunshine State* (2002), Florida has been so alluring a subject that outsiders have been decisive in defining the images by which it is known.

Perhaps that is because media centers have been elsewhere, in New York and in Los Angeles. When the imbalance that favors outsiders is rectified, when self-definitions can be more powerfully inscribed, the elusive culture of Florida will not become more tangible, nor will its populace be less fragmented. But then the identification marks will perhaps become easier to spot, the patterns of meaning more apparent, and the sources of creativity, continuity, and vitality more accessible.

From the **Fall 2003** edition of *FORUM* magazine, "A Sunshine State of Mind: Florida's Place in American Culture."

26 We Are Here to Enlighten, Not Accuse

A Seminole historian urges accuracy as Florida commemorates the Spanish landing.

Willie Johns

Willie Johns (1951–2020) served as a Tribal Court chief justice of the Seminole Tribe of Florida, as the tribe's historian, and as outreach community specialist. His historical novel, *What We Have Endured*, is based largely on the life of his great-grandmother. He was a lifetime resident of the Brighton Seminole Reservation in Okeechobee.

Image: Chief Justice Willie Johns at the Tribal Court swearing-in event, 2015. Courtesy of *Seminole Tribune*.

I ALWAYS HAD a thirst, a hunger, for the history of my people. But when I was growing up, nobody talked much about it. There wasn't time for much besides survival. We lived in chickees on the Brighton Seminole Reservation. My family was dirt poor and spent most of our time working in the fields, working with cattle, anything we could find, even cutting palm fronds for the Catholics to use on Palm Sunday.

As a kid, I would hear my uncles talk about when the Seminoles all lived in camps across Florida and how they missed the free hunting and trapping way of life. When they came onto the reservation, it was like a death sentence to them. A lot of them became migrant workers just to keep food on the table. The struggle to survive overshadowed the memories of the shooting and guns and wars and genocide of the past.

When I was a boy, I also spent time in the world outside of the reservation. At the age of three I caught polio, and they took me away for three years to a crippled children's hospital in Orlando. I remember when I finally came back. The first night I woke up in a chickee I could smell the hog pens. I realized then that God had pity on me to put me on an Indian reservation because nothing was going to come to me; I had to get off my ass and run it down myself.

By age seven I had thrown my braces into a cabbage palm tree. I played four years of high school football at Okeechobee High, rode bulls, went out with the pretty girls. I was determined to make it. If there was ever any prejudice directed at me, I didn't know it.

Editor's note: Willie Johns was the Seminole Tribe's representative to the Viva Florida 500 project, commemorating the 500th anniversary in 2013 of Spanish explorers landing on Florida's shore. In that role, he was asked to share his perspective.

Seminole children at the Brighton Indian Reservation, 1948. Photo by Joseph Janney Steinmetz. Courtesy of State Archives of Florida, Florida Memory.

People would tell me stories passed down, but I knew there was more. The more I studied, the more I didn't understand the magnitude of what took place among my people.

As I got older, my hunger to learn about my people's history got stronger. I started doing research. I asked questions. People would tell me stories passed down, but I knew there was more. The more I studied, the more I didn't understand the magnitude of what took place among my people.

As time went on, I found out that other tribal members really wanted to know the history too. My phone would ring off the hook with others wanting me to find out historical information for them. They began calling me a tribal historian. I've got a history degree. I've amassed a large library of books written about my people, from every angle you can imagine. The past is very, very real to me. I am worried it could disappear unless we make a determined effort to preserve our history.

Last year I signed on as the Seminole Tribe's representative in the Viva Florida 500 project [commemorating the 500th anniversary in 2013 of Spanish explorers landing on Florida's shore].

I didn't do this to make a politically correct statement that will render everybody happy. I did it to make sure the history of my people is represented. We are here to educate, not forgive. We are here to enlighten, not accuse. We want to keep alive the memories of those days when the Europeans first came. We want to tell who the Spanish people were who came to our shores, and we want to educate people about exactly what they did.

People may not realize how many tribes and Native peoples existed before being decimated by the disease and warfare brought on by the conquistadors. With the priests looking on, Spanish explorers took out the aboriginal Floridians with massacres in the name of God. And they sent the good news back to the king!

But we can only speak for ourselves. The Florida Indians of long ago could illustrate what happened, but they didn't write books and journals. Indians all across America shared stories that were kept alive and passed down through the generations about what the European invaders did. That's how it was told to me: the truth of those days was kill the Indian or give him a blanket, invite him to supper, sneeze on his blanket, then send him away.

Yet we survived all this atrocity. We actually learned from our attackers. We learned to practice slavery from them, and we even learned the behavior to sell out our own people. Creek warriors did real well in that regard; they would come down here and hunt down the other Indians the same way the white man did. They would sell Indians as slaves, just like the white man did.

The Spanish brought in their culture and tried to make us a part of it. . . . Our cultures clashed, and the Spanish had the upper hand.

When I think of the past, I feel like we were always running. For hundreds of years, we were on the run. We ran here from all over. Some of us ran here earlier than others. We Seminoles believe we are descended from the indigenous tribes of Florida, running and hiding like all the others. You had the Calusa, the Apalachicola, the Mayaimi along Lake Okeechobee, the Ais people of the Indian River

Lagoon, the Tocobaga in Tampa, Arawak in the Caribbean, Timucua up in the northeast, and the Tequesta in the southeast. The individual tribes were too small to engage in effective warfare with the Spanish and their allies. So they ran.

The Seminole Tribe of Florida has a Tribal Historic Preservation Department that is concerned with the accurate interpretation and preservation of our history all the way back to the first peoples who occupied this land. Both the state of Florida and the United States, under the 1990 Native American Graves Protection and Repatriation Act, recognize the Seminole Tribe as the guardian of the ancient southeastern tribes who were eliminated from their homelands. It's our official duty to handle repatriations, which can include reburials of human remains and the return of funerary objects, sacred objects, and objects of cultural patrimony. We have been involved in many, many of these cases.

While all Seminole people have respect for our culture and our ancestors, not all Seminoles agree on how we should relate with our neighbors. Some who have been quite active and vocal about these issues are Independent Seminoles who choose not to be enrolled members of the organized Seminole Tribe of Florida.

They frequently speak at public meetings when issues arise where they perceive traditional Seminole culture is being wronged. Some of the Independents want to regain Paradise by loading every person in the state on a boat and then shipping 'em all out.

Addie Billie, Seminole woman, Ochopee, 1989. Photo by Jill Guttman. Courtesy of State Archives of Florida, Florida Memory.

But that ain't gonna happen. I think education is the answer. Some Independents argue that the City of St. Augustine should tear down the old fort (Castillo de San Marcos) because of the atrocities that occurred to Indians there 400 years ago. I look at it differently. I would rather it remain standing so the memories of those days would not fade away. Those who don't remember the past are doomed to repeat it.

For St. Augustine's 450th anniversary commemoration, I made a suggestion that it would be cool if we could invite representatives of all the Native tribes who were incarcerated there during and after the Seminole Wars, get them all together, and do a healing ceremony. But some tribe members refused to endorse the idea.

Many Seminoles would say, "Leave it all alone." They argue we shouldn't spend a whole lot of time, money, and effort on worrying about the Spanish conquistadors, that today there are much bigger things we need to be worried about. Maybe the best place to focus on the history is in the schools. I don't think the European invasion is discussed a lot in the classrooms. The conquistadors came over here 300 years before Andrew Jackson started chasing us. Students are taught more about the three Seminole Wars than the genocide performed by the Europeans and the Americans.

While all Seminole people have respect for our culture and our ancestors, not all Seminoles agree on how we should relate with our neighbors.

In my home of Brighton, our charter school spends a lot of time on language, which is very important to us, and on taking the kids on cultural outings. The Spanish are part of the curriculum, but I don't believe there is much said about it. We have to change that, in all Florida schools.

It's too bad we all haven't been talking about all this history all along. Maybe it would not have been so glorified. In the end, I don't believe the Spanish were ever that happy with Florida. We just didn't have what they were looking for so desperately. They were basically gone by the Revolutionary War. Then along came the American settlers.

Wouldn't you know it, they wanted the Indians' land. They held their meetings. "How are we gonna get the land? What are we gonna do with the Indians?" Somewhere, someone had an idea: "Let's hire Andy Jackson. He knows what to do: write up failing treaties, spank 'em in a few wars, go after 'em, keep 'em on the run, put 'em out West somewhere."

When the US Supreme Court ruled the Indian Removal Act was unconstitutional, ol' Andy Jackson just said, "Stop me" and rode off after the Indians anyway. If he defied the law like that today, the federal marshals would be all over him. To tell you the truth, Seminoles today despise Andrew Jackson more than the conquistadors.

But you know how they say, "Out of bad things, good things come"? When the Spanish sailed away, they left their horses and cattle here, and we used them to start the Seminole cattle industry. In fact, for most of the past 100 years in Florida, the Seminoles have thrived in the cattle industry. We once sold the meat and hides to the Cubans, even loaded up cattle on the St. Johns River. People called us the "Cow Creeks." Today, we are the fourth-largest calf producers in the country. After we stopped running, those abandoned cattle pulled us through. That was our first casino: the Spanish cow.

If it was Paradise before the Europeans came, Florida was an absolutely horrible place to live after they left. Post–Civil War, you had outlaws, bandits, deserters, every sort of bad individual, all the problems of poverty, everyone hit hard. Before we got reservations, we were surviving in little camps all over the Everglades and Big Cypress Swamp where only the mosquitoes and gators were supposed to be. Our homeland had shrunk.

But we weren't running anymore. Our communities began to grow and we began to organize. The Indians who settled in the 'Glades became the Miccosukee and Big Cypress Seminoles. Those who lived to the north were Creek speakers whose descendants are the Brighton Seminoles of today. We survived nearly 500 years of genocide and atrocity with our culture and languages still intact. That is who we are. The conquistador is a distant ghost. But we will not forget.

From the **Fall 2012** edition of *FORUM* magazine, "The View from the Shore: Florida before the Conquest."

27

Observations of a Native Son

Former governor and US senator Bob Graham on the "Cincinnati Factor" and why Florida remains the "State of Imagination."

Ron Cunningham

Ron Cunningham was a reporter at the *Fort Lauderdale Sun-Sentinel*, higher education reporter at the *Gainesville Sun*, and Tallahassee bureau chief for the *New York Times* Florida newspapers, before serving as editorial-page editor at the *Gainesville Sun* until 2013. He is a University of Florida graduate and former editor-in-chief of the *Independent Florida Alligator*.

Image: Senator Bob Graham in 2019 on the University of Florida campus, home of the Graham Center for Public Service. Photo by Lyon Duong, University of Florida.

How "Florida" is Bob Graham?

The only home he ever knew, from his birth in 1936 until he went off to get married in 1959, was a coral rock house perched on the edge of the Everglades.

His family vacationed in DeFuniak Springs because "my childhood was during World War II, and it was hard to travel. So we didn't miss many summers in the Florida Panhandle."

He graduated from Miami High School (the *Miami Herald* once named him "Best All Around Boy") and then went to the University of Florida, where he met his future wife, Adele, and got himself inducted into Florida Blue Key, before leaving the state temporarily to earn a law degree at Harvard University.

How Florida is Bob Graham?

When he ran for governor, his campaign theme song was "I'm a Florida Cracker, I'm a Graham cracker." And he has been known to burst into spontaneous renditions of that little ditty with very little prompting.

"I am sitting in my office in Miami Lakes, approximately five miles from the house where I was brought to from the hospital a few days after my birth," Graham says in a recent telephone conversation. "I have lived in other places, Washington DC, for eighteen years [while serving as a Democrat in the US Senate], but I have always maintained my legal residence in Dade County."

So, yes, it is fair to say that Bob Graham knows Florida. And having served in public office almost continuously from 1966 through 2005 (he never lost an election), Graham also knows a thing or two about trying to govern in a state in which so many "Floridians" are from somewhere else.

Which is why he often talked about the "Cincinnati Factor" during his years in politics. Graham would begin by reading a fictional but stereotypical Florida obituary: *Mr. Smith, a Miami resident for twenty-five years, has passed away.* The obituary

One of the beliefs which I still strongly hold is that many Floridians don't appreciate the diversity of Florida.... One of my personal campaigns is to try to encourage residents of Florida to make an effort to see as much of the state as they can if they want to appreciate the diversity, vitality, and strength that is Florida.

would go on to mention his Florida-based fraternal organizations, business activities, civic involvements, and so on.

And invariably it would end with *Mr. Smith's body is being flown back to Cincinnati for burial.*

"So many people who have lived here a substantial part of their life on Earth never made the full transition to being a Floridian," Graham says.

That lack of a Florida group identity has definite cultural and political ramifications. The Cincinnati Factor meant you probably rooted for the Bengals rather than the Dolphins. It meant that you spent your early years paying taxes somewhere else and didn't really care to support new spending initiatives in your adopted state.

It meant that your final resting ground was likely to be a family burial plot some distance north of the Florida/Georgia border.

"In a way, Florida has been a victim of its own success," Graham muses. "In the beginning, Florida was thought of as being little more than a swamp to be avoided at all costs."

Still, in many ways, Graham says, Florida is a "state of the imagination." And he believes it is no coincidence that "many of the people who made the greatest impact on Florida were recent arrivals."

"Henry Flagler came from New York at the end of the nineteenth century and saw St. Augustine as a French Riviera. He thought the United States was yearning for a French Riviera, and by God he was going to give it to them and give them a railroad to get there."

And then there was Chicago native turned California cartoonist-entrepreneur Walt Disney. "He started thinking about the possibility of building a grand theme park to commercialize his creativity and decided Florida was the place to do it."

"Disney's [Orlando] property used to belong to the Bronson family. My dad was a very good friend of the Bronsons, and we often went to visit them. As a born-in-Florida person I would never have conceived of something like Disney World in my backyard."

Now in his eighty-second year, Bob Graham, thirty-eighth governor of Florida and three-term US senator, mostly divides his time between Miami Lakes and Gainesville, where he and Adele have an apartment. His official papers, including his celebrated wire-bound notebooks, are archived at the University of Florida.

As a candidate and during his years in public office, Graham was never without one of his small notebooks, into which he jotted down meticulous observations about the people he encountered and the events of his day.

Drawing on his papers, notebooks, and other source materials, Graham intends to write a biography of his father—engineer, cattle rancher, and state senator Ernest "Cap" Graham—while also working on his own autobiography.

UF is also the home of the Bob Graham Center for Public Service, an institute founded by Graham to help develop leadership skills and promote citizenship values among young people.

Young Robert "Bob" Graham in 1952 at a 4-H competition in Orlando with his Holstein heifer, Tiny Two. Courtesy of Bob Graham.

Graham has given a lot of thought to what it means to be a Floridian in a state so dramatically shaped by in-migration from all points of the compass.

"One of the beliefs which I still strongly hold is that many Floridians don't appreciate the diversity of Florida," he says. "If they live in Miami, they think that's what the rest of the state is like. One of my personal campaigns is to try to encourage residents of Florida to make an effort to see as much of the state as they can if they want to appreciate the diversity, vitality, and strength that is Florida."

As governor, Graham signed landmark measures intended to preserve Florida's rivers, seashores, and undeveloped lands. And in retirement he cofounded the Florida Conservation Coalition to continue to focus attention on the plight of the Everglades, Lake Okeechobee, and other Florida natural treasures, urging greater environmental stewardship in one of the fastest-growing states in the nation.

Bob Graham, then a Florida state senator, at the 50th Anniversary of Pan Am Celebration in East Martello, Key West, 1977. Pictured (*left to right*) are Jack Church (then-president of the Key West Art and Historical Society), band member Harry "Chip" Chase, Graham, an unidentified band member, and band member Lofton "Coffee" Butler. The Ida Woodward Barron Collection, Florida Keys Public Libraries.

"As a public official I have tried to protect as much of natural Florida as possible," Graham says. "There's no such thing, really, as the original Florida. It's changed so much. But I think we are doing a better job now."

"Florida used to be thought of as a commodity," he continues. "There were no constraints about bringing out the bulldozers and creating something new."

But with red tide now threatening beaches and green algae infesting Florida rivers and lakes, "we have begun more and more to think about natural Florida as a treasure to be protected and preserved."

As for the Cincinnati Factor, Graham believes even that phenomenon has begun to fade, especially in recent decades, when waves of newcomers have been as likely to arrive from Cuba, Haiti, or Puerto Rico as Ohio, New York, and Michigan.

"Obviously the millions of people who have come to Florida in the last fifteen to twenty years have a wide range of views about their decisions to come here and to stay here," he says. "I think for most people, the longer they live here, the looser the ties become to their previous residencies, and there is a commensurate increase in their affection for Florida."

Those deepening Florida ties, Graham hopes, will help strengthen public resolve behind the imperative that Florida "be protected for the future so that generations to come will have the same opportunities to enjoy and share this beautiful part of the planet."

From the **Fall 2019** edition of *FORUM* magazine, "What Does It Mean to Be a Floridian?"

Cuban children arriving at Miami airport, 1961. Courtesy of Operation Pedro Pan Cuban Children's Program Records, Barry University Archives and Special Collections, Miami Shores, Florida.

been Pedro Pan children. Sabina figured it out in 1990 when a Sunday newspaper headline caught his eye: "Airlift Carried Cubans to Freedom." "As I began to read the first few lines of the article, I got goosebumps, and the hair on my arm stood out," Sabina wrote in *Cuban Born, American Forever*, an unpublished manuscript produced with St. Petersburg Beach resident Allen Polon.

"Of course! That had to be it! It had all been so smooth. There had to have been some sort of master plan like this. I just never knew it," Sabina wrote.

The operation began in December 1960 as fearful Cuban parents looked for ways to protect their sons and daughters, even when it meant breaking up families.

Recalled Sabina, "When Castro's men found out that my father was speaking out against the new government, they figured out that my father might be dangerous to their cause.... My mother insisted on staying with my father in spite of the danger she was in. She would never have left Cuba without him. Therefore, William and I had to make the ninety-mile trip to freedom without them, not knowing what would happen to them or if we would ever see them again."

The Sabina brothers were among those fortunate enough to get placed in a home in Florida, where the weather was similar to what they had known in Cuba and where established Cuban enclaves existed in Miami and Tampa.

Some others wound up being sent to communities in other states, including Nebraska, Montana, and Indiana, where they learned to cope with harsher climates and what, to them, were alien cultures.

This extraordinary episode in Cold War history was the largest children's refugee effort ever recorded in the Western Hemisphere. It involved smuggling visas into Cuba and keeping everything hush-hush through an underground system of communication.

Journalist Yvonne Conde, author of *Operation Pedro Pan: The Untold Exodus of 14,048 Cuban Children*, tells of Maria Cristina Romero, a twelve-year-old sent to Colorado. The child was certain that Indians lived there and that she would be scalped: "I was petrified. When we landed I expected the Indians to come. Going from the airport to the orphanage you went by a stockyard. And it smelled."

Another girl, Ana Gema Lopo, who was thirteen when she arrived with her younger sister, told Conde about staying in a Pedro Pan processing center in Kendall, near Miami. "I was terrified of that place. They were old barracks. We lived in bunk beds," Lopo told Conde. "I remember it was Mother's Day, and we all went to bed and someone started crying and I started crying, since it was the first Mother's Day away from our mothers. Before you knew it, the whole entire floor was crying. Oh, it was so awful! Some little girls came over and held other little girls; it was the saddest thing."

Conde reports that some children wound up in homes or orphanages where they were abused or treated like criminals. But in a poll she conducted with 442 former Pedro Pan children, 69.6 percent described their experience as positive. Many of the youngsters were placed with families with whom they formed lifelong relationships.

The Sabina brothers were among those fortunate ones. After a short, unpleasant stay in one foster home, they were placed in another, the home of Earle and Peggy Day in St. Petersburg. It proved to be a good fit. The boys were from a close-knit, middle-class family in Cuba, where their father worked in a cigarette factory. After the Castro revolution, all such middle-class families were labeled *gusanos* and *burgéses*—worms and bourgeoisie.

Cuban brothers Osvaldo and William Sabina (*left to right*) with foster brother Jack Day in St. Petersburg. Courtesy of Day family.

The Days ran a successful insurance business and lived in a comfortable home with their three children, who were close in age to the Sabina brothers. "All of them did whatever it took to be sure we felt like part of their family and not just a couple of boys visiting or boarding with them," Sabina wrote.

The brothers lived with the Days for more than three years. In 1966, after four unsuccessful attempts, their parents eventually made it out of Cuba. By then, Sabina had enlisted in an Army Reserve unit based in St. Petersburg. The unit eventually was activated to serve in Vietnam. To this day, Sabina, now a successful businessman, flies the US Army flag from the top story of his house.

Pedro Pan stories, like that of Sabina, are finally being told in newspapers, magazines, books, and at least one play. A website, PedroPan.org, encourages a continuing search for children who were part of this historic Cuban exodus. Thousands of stories remain to be told about the children who flew away.

From the **Fall 2008** edition of *FORUM* magazine, "Florida's Caribbean Connection."

29

When Life Takes Flight

Thirty years after fleeing Cuba, Ileana Ros-Lehtinen made history in the US Congress.

Dalia Colón

Dalia Colón is a multimedia journalist who serves as cohost and associate producer of WEDU Arts Plus and as host and executive producer of *The Zest*, a Florida food podcast from Tampa Bay's NPR affiliate. A former entertainment reporter for the *Tampa Bay Times*, Colón has interviewed everyone from the late Maya Angelou to Pauly Shore. Her work has appeared on NPR and in the *New York Times Magazine*, *Miami Herald*, and *Los Angeles Times*, on the Visit Florida website, and more. She lives with her family in Riverview.

Image: State Representative Ileana Ros-Lehtinen. Photo used with permission of Ileana Ros-Lehtinen.

For eight-year-old Ileana Ros, her first plane ride brought one emotion: excitement.

"My brother and I were thrilled because we were on an airplane, but my mom cried the whole flight," Ileana Ros-Lehtinen recalls. "It was an unsettling time, to say the least."

Unsettling because this was no ordinary airplane ride. In 1960, the Ros family left their home in Havana, Cuba, and boarded a Pan American World Airways flight for Miami, joining an estimated 1.4 million Cubans who would flee Fidel Castro's regime for the United States, according to the Migration Policy Institute in Washington, DC.

"We purchased a roundtrip ticket—that's how optimistic we were that everything was going to blow over," Ros-Lehtinen says. "I still have the return ticket. It was $25. It has an open return date. Unfortunately, Pan Am is no longer in business, but the regime is still in business."

So the Ros family settled into their new life in Miami. They made their home in Little Havana, spent about two years in York, Pennsylvania, as part of a government relocation program ("We got to see snow," she says), then returned to the south Florida suburbs.

In some ways, Florida wasn't so different from Cuba. There were mango and avocado trees in the yard, just as there had been in Havana. Ileana and her older brother, Henry, lived comfortably enough, thanks to the American jobs their parents had secured. Their father, Enrique, worked for a laundry pickup and delivery service, and their mother, Amanda, would bring home leftover food from her job in the kitchen of a Miami Beach hotel.

"We always had clean clothes, and we always had something good to eat," Ros-Lehtinen remembers with a laugh.

But not everything about Florida resembled her birthplace of Havana. For starters, there was the language barrier. These were the days before bilingual education, so young Ileana had to learn English as she fumbled through her days at the public Southside Elementary School.

> *For many generations of refugees, no matter from where they come, we see Florida as a place of refuge, a safe haven.*

"It was sink or swim," she says.

At home, Spanish was still the dominant language, with her anti-Castro parents keeping tabs on the dictator via the radio. They also welcomed a steady stream of newly arrived Cuban refugees into their home.

Their rented house "was more of a refugee center than anything else," Ros-Lehtinen says with a laugh. "There were people coming and going."

This, in fact, is what Florida means to her.

"For many generations of refugees, no matter from where they come, we see Florida as a place of refuge, a safe haven," Ros-Lehtinen says. "It's a welcoming state. It's a place that's adapted to changes. We've had mass migrations [of Latin Americans], and our community has always welcomed new people."

Ros-Lehtinen returned Florida's embrace, earning her bachelor's and master's degrees from Florida International University and a doctorate in education from the University of Miami.

It turns out that little Ileana, so excited for her first airplane ride, would grow up to be Republican Congresswoman Ileana Ros-Lehtinen, who traveled the world representing Florida's 27th Congressional District from 1989 to 2019. She was the first Latina elected to the US Congress.

"I really had to pinch myself every day that I was in Congress that I was given this opportunity," she says. "We love Miami. We love every inch of it, and what a thrill to have represented this area in Congress."

Now a senior adviser for the Washington, DC, law firm Akin Gump, she and her husband, Dexter Lehtinen, split their time between the District of Columbia and the upscale Miami suburb of Pinecrest, where she reflects on what Florida means to her now.

Florida, Ros-Lehtinen says, is mellow. It's Margaritaville. It's picking mangoes from a tree in her yard. It's caring about climate change. It's bumping into her friend former Florida governor Bob Graham when she's in town or sitting down to a plate of *vaca frita* at Miami's CasaCuba Restaurant. It's speaking her native tongue to her adult children and grinning when her gringo husband is mistaken for a Spanish speaker.

Florida means all of these things because Ros-Lehtinen is all of these things.

"Being a Floridian also means that you're accepting of other cultures and other lands and understanding what the refugee experience is all about," whether you've lived through it or not, she says.

For Ros-Lehtinen, her Floridian experience is her American experience. During her time in Congress, she chaired the House Foreign Affairs Committee with a California Democratic Congressman and Holocaust survivor, the late Tom Lantos.

"We were both naturalized Americans," Ros-Lehtinen notes, "and we always made it a point to say, 'Wow, is this a great country or what?'"

From the **Fall 2019** edition of *FORUM* magazine, "What Does It Mean to Be a Floridian?"

Ileana and her older brother, Henry, as young children in Cuba. Courtesy of Ileana Ros-Lehtinen.

When Life Takes Flight · 191

30 Sweetness of Memory

Photographer Andy Sweet poignantly captured the waning days of South Beach's elderly Jewish community before his own life was cut short.

Bill DeYoung

Bill DeYoung worked at newspapers around Florida for more than thirty-five years. He is the author of five books, including *Skyway: The True Story of Tampa Bay's Signature Bridge and the Man Who Brought It Down* and two *Vintage St. Pete* historical volumes. He is a senior writer and editor at the *St. Pete Catalyst*.

Image: Andy Sweet, circa 1970s. Sweet's smile endeared him to his photo subjects. Used with permission of Andy Sweet Photo Legacy.

There's a moment in *The Last Resort*, the 2018 documentary about the late Miami Beach photographer Andy Sweet, that all but explains the unlikely chemistry between the cherubic, shaggy-haired twenty-something and his subjects, the elderly Jewish residents of South Beach in the late 1970s.

In the film, Sweet's fellow partner-in-pictures, Gary Monroe, is remembering a night the two spent photographing a packed dance floor at the 21st Street Community Center. As they weaved in and out between the swaying couples, snapping away, Sweet told his friend, "I feel like I'm dancing with them."

Looking at Andy Sweet's voluminous body of work, photo after photo of old people smiling, laughing, relaxed, and looking directly into the lens of his camera, it becomes obvious that they felt like he was dancing with them too. Somehow, he belonged.

"Andy always went for the joy," says *The Last Resort* producer-director Dennis Scholl. "And you see that over and over again." Sweet's color photos contrast sharply with those of Monroe, who shot "studies" of South Beach residents in solemn black and white.

"You particularly feel it when you look at them against Gary's photographs, which were absolutely, technically spectacular," says Scholl. "And he was willing to take a more broad emotional range. Andy went for the joy in his photographs and boy, do we respond to that."

At first, Andy's sun-drenched photographs seem informal, like snapshots. But the composition—the combination of light, shadow, color, and subject—reveals a much deeper artistic sensibility.

Couple in Matching Bathing Suits, 1977. Photo by Andy Sweet. Used with permission of Andy Sweet Photo Legacy.

Capturing a Kind of Paradise

BY THE MID-1970s, South Beach's roughly two square miles at the southern end of Miami Beach were alive and thriving with fixed-income retirees who dined, swam, played mahjong and canasta, and kibitzed under the glorious Florida sun. Many were Holocaust survivors, just learning to smile again after one last exodus.

They'd abandoned New York, New Jersey, or the Midwest, weary of the bitter winters and drawn by the promise of warm winds, gentle surf, and day-to-day camaraderie with others like themselves.

South Beach wasn't considered fashionable, in the way of Miami Beach proper with its restaurants, swanky nighteries, and country clubs (many of them once labeled "gentiles only"), with *The Jackie Gleason Show*, and the world-famous Fontainebleau Hotel. Many of the aging South Beach resident hotels, built in the years following World War II, were paint-chipped and plaster-cracked and had seen better days; still, rents were reasonable, and on every corner there was a synagogue or a good deli.

For the transplanted Jews, it was paradise.

Andy Sweet preserved, in rich, lifelike color, a world that has long since vanished. The elderly Jews, the hotels with their makeshift shuls, sitting porches, and dining rooms, the community centers and their sprightly New Year's Eve parties, are just

Sweetness of Memory • 193

Art Deco retirement hotel, circa 1979, with retirees sitting on webbed lawn chairs on the porch. Photo by Andy Sweet, courtesy of Andy Sweet Photo Legacy, courtesy of Letter 16 Press, from the book *Shtetl in the Sun: Andy Sweet's South Beach, 1977–1980*, available from Letter16press.com.

memories in South Beach, dust and ghosts, replaced by preserved and renovated Art Deco hotels, trendy clubs, high-end price tags, and upscale young tenants.

Gone, too, is Andy Sweet, brutally murdered in his Miami Beach townhome back in '82, at the age of twenty-nine. Andy is a memory, as much a part of the past as the people he so happily danced with, as the South Beach he'd so lovingly chronicled.

His death shocked and saddened the community. When he died, the *Miami Herald*'s *Tropic Magazine* ran a cover story on his death and documentary photography, "Andy Sweet: A Portrait."

From the earliest days of his relationship with Ellen Sweet Moss, Stan Hughes remembers, she'd point to framed images on the wall of her south Florida apartment. "This is a photograph by my dead brother," she'd tell her new boyfriend, who wasn't sure how to react.

"There was tragedy under the surface," Hughes says, "and I didn't want to poke at it."

Andy's father, municipal judge Nelan "Chick" Sweet, stopped practicing law after his son's murder, citing a lack of faith in Miami's legal system. (It took several years, but Andy's killers were eventually tried and convicted.)

Andy Sweet is a memory, as much a part of the past as the people he so happily danced with, as the South Beach he'd so lovingly chronicled.

"The first time I met the parents," recalls Stan Hughes, "Ellen's mother was immediately asking me, 'What do you think we should do with his stuff?'" Hughes, a Chicago-bred fine artist and designer, recommended they digitize Andy's negatives to preserve them.

"I should have pushed harder," Hughes says. "It was such a new relationship. We were mostly concerned about each other. And frankly, the pictures that they had printed and put up weren't Andy's strongest. I wasn't bowled away by what I saw.

"It took me a few years before I realized there was real value there. That Andy had a voice."

After his death, the Sweet family kept Andy's carefully curated negatives in a climate-controlled art storage facility. They never were digitized. The company relocated and the negatives were lost. Much heartache, and a lawsuit, followed. Hughes remembers the day: Audrey, Ellen's mother, said. "Well, his negatives are gone. Lights out, sayonara. His work's gone and everything's awful."

It stayed awful until one autumn day in 2006 when Hughes—now married to Ellen and a well-integrated part of the family—went on an innocent exploration. "It was just one of those commercial storage spaces where you'd put Grandma's old couch," he recalls. "Ellen's son had a comic book collection in there. I hadn't paid much attention to what all these boxes were.

New Year's Eve, 1977. Photo by Andy Sweet. Used with permission of Andy Sweet Photo Legacy.

"But there it was: WORK PRINTS. I opened a box. It was all these big prints he'd made. All this stuff. And I was like, 'My God! Nobody's lost.' But I felt incredibly stupid, like I should have known it was there. Why didn't I look? We could have done this sooner."

Hughes had stumbled upon 1,600 printed photos—9×9 work prints, 8×10 contact sheets, and 16×20 finished prints—many with Andy's wax-pencil notes on the back.

There was the South Beach of the 1970s again, a beguiling population of suntanned old Jewish men and women, on the sand, in the pool, on the porch, radiant and in love with life. All those years, shuttered in storage, and now they were free once again to tell their stories.

Many of the prints had faded, their chemical colors dimmed with age. Hughes scanned and digitized each one, then set about enhancing the color palettes using Adobe Photoshop.

To get the hues right, he consulted with Gary Monroe. "What were Andy's colors like?" Hughes asked.

Monroe's reply was succinct. "Think beach ball," he said.

Sweetness of Memory · 195

It's impossible to tell the story of Andy Sweet without Gary Monroe. Recently retired after thirty years as a professor at Daytona State College, he famously brought the Highwaymen, Florida's historic African American landscape artists, to light. Monroe is a world-renowned photographer who won a Fulbright scholarship to document the impoverished residents of Haiti.

A Plan to Preserve a World

IN THE 1970s, he and Andy Sweet, both Miami Beach High School graduates, were inseparable.

"Andy was impetuous and irreverent, and I say this in the best sense of the word," Monroe explains. "Nothing was sacred to him. Everything was fair game. His was sophomoric humor, more often than not over the top, bordering on gross. But just about each of his observations were as insightful as they were poignant."

They both realized that the old-world culture wasn't going to last forever.

After studying photography at the University of South Florida, then at the University of Colorado, where they earned master of fine arts degrees, the two friends returned to their hometown to begin what they planned as a ten-year project documenting South Beach and the people who'd moved in and stayed. They received grants to support their work, including one from the National Endowment for the Arts.

Eight years after Andy died, a selection of their photos appeared in a hardcover book called *Miami Beach*. The limited edition was never republished and is out of print.

And then Andy's negatives were lost.

The Last Resort is part of a larger renaissance of interest in Andy Sweet's idiosyncratic, irresistible photos. A coffee table book, *Shtetl in the Sun: Andy Sweet's South Beach, 1977–1980*, was just published spotlighting more than 100 of his best pictures.

Over the past few years, used copies of the 1990 *Miami Beach* book began selling online for $150 and more.

Ellen and Stan have established the Andy Sweet Photo Legacy, encompassing a website, a Facebook page, the documentary, and the new book. "I'm doing this because his work is amazing," Andy's sister says. "My parents felt like this, before they passed away, that they wanted Andy to be known, for people to see his work.

"His photography was art, when a lot of people weren't doing it as art."

It's been compared to the classic photography of Diane Arbus, who memorialized less-than-glamorous, regular people with fabulously nonself-conscious images. Like her, Andy preferred spontaneity: click the shutter and look for the gold later.

Not that he looked at it that way, according to Monroe: "Andy was informal, like his photographs. We both made pictures that mattered, which found a resolve that was right for who we were.

A rabbi in a hurry, 1979. Photo by Andy Sweet, courtesy of Andy Sweet Photo Legacy, courtesy of Letter 16 Press, from the book *Shtetl in the Sun: Andy Sweet's South Beach, 1977-1980*, available from Letter16press.com.

South Beach scene, circa 1979: man in his personalized beach cabana. Photo by Andy Sweet. Used with permission of Andy Sweet Photo Legacy.

"Of course, this kind of discussion would bore Andy, and he never discussed his work or ideas about photography, at least not with more than a word or two, or a wise-ass quip. I don't think Andy had more than a handful of serious conversations in his life, and although committed to his art he was not at all interested in talking about it."

He wasn't a planner. He'd show up somewhere, smile and introduce himself, and with permission granted, put his black Hasselblad camera to his eye and begin shooting. "We were young and cute," Monroe smiles, "and reminded the seniors of their grandchildren." Usually, all it took was a few words of Yiddish, and the young men were accepted.

"People related to Andy," says Ellen Sweet Moss, Andy's sister. "Look at the photos. A lot of the people are looking back at him and smiling. I guess they realized he wasn't making fun of them. I thought he was. But he wasn't, and they seemed to enjoy him a lot."

From the **Spring 2019** edition of *FORUM* magazine, "Artful Revival: How the Power of the Creative Spirit Is Energizing Florida Cities."

Sweetness of Memory • 197

31 What You See When You Look at Me

A Haitian immigrant meets her neighbors.

Maude Heurtelou

Maude Heurtelou is vice president of Educavision Inc., which publishes Haitian-related educational materials for use in the Caribbean and North America. She is also an author, storyteller, and motivational speaker. She and her family currently live in the Fort Lauderdale area.

"It's amazing how you have become Americanized so quickly!"

I was stunned by this comment. Did my American neighbor see America in me? What part of me had become American "so quickly"? My husband and I had been in the United States for only about a year. I was still adjusting, looking for the right job, thinking of my dream house, and building a social life.

I was from Haiti. I was in my thirties and had already been an immigrant twice before, once in Guatemala, where I studied nutrition for four years as a fellow of the World Health Organization, and the second time for six years in Quebec, Canada, where I graduated with a master's degree in public health. In both cases, I had planned to return to Haiti. But in 1985, as the sociopolitical instability was boiling hot there and some of our friends were getting concerned for their safety, we decided to contemplate advanced university degrees in the United States—and possibly settle in for the long run.

It was my idea to move to Florida, the state that most reminds me of Haiti in terms of weather, flora, and multicultural life. Little did we know that many years later our daughter, Mia, would be raised here and would call Florida home.

My husband and I had much to learn about America. But among the first things we did upon our arrival in Tampa was to join a Haitian civic club. There we found people of all ages, grandma storytellers, grandpas playing cards and dominoes, children and grandchildren swimming and joking. The members of my generation became cultural bridges between our parents, who came from Haiti, and our children, who were born in America. We spoke to people in a blend of Creole, French, and English, depending on how long ago the person had left Haiti and how comfortable he or she was with one of those three languages. We taught Haitian folklore to the children. We also shared sweet memories of Haiti and compared our experiences in America.

But I was also eager to have a multicultural social life in America. A few weeks after arriving in our new home we became acquainted with Sheila and Chris (not

Maude Heurtelou in Haitian hat and beads in 1991. Courtesy of Maude Heurtelou.

their real names), the white American couple next door, with whom I shared the hobby of gardening. When we first met, they kindly asked to call my husband, Fequiere, by the name "Frederic," because they feared they would "mess up" his name.

One night, we had them over for what I thought was a typical American game: Monopoly. It turned out that Sheila had never played Monopoly, and Chris found it "too cerebral." So instead we chatted about the changing face of the neighborhood. Sheila was not at ease with the Hispanics who had moved into the neighborhood with their many children. She was nervous to see those brown and black faces now living so close to her. I interpreted her uneasiness as coming from a fear of the unknown and an uncomfortable proximity to people she may have seen as servants or labeled on television with some kind of negative stigma.

Sheila candidly explained how concerned she was when my husband and I had just bought our home and she heard that we were Haitians. Maybe they are living off social assistance, she thought. Or maybe they will be loud or gregarious or . . . ? She confessed her surprise at seeing us going to work and not being that different from her white neighbors. Then she said she began thinking, "Maybe they are nice people, and maybe they could eventually introduce me to the African-American culture."

"Really?" I said, raising my eyebrows and smiling with curiosity. "You really think I am Americanized, Sheila? And that I can introduce you, an American, to the Afro-American culture? How so?"

"Well," she said, turning to Chris, who was more a listener than a talker, "wouldn't you say, honey, that Maude and Frederic are really smart?" Alternately turning her

What You See When You Look at Me · 199

> *Sheila's candor mixed with her honest ignorance made me realize that the process of multiculturalism is a journey, and ours was just starting.*

face to me and to my husband, Sheila continued with a generous smile: "You are smart, guys; you really caught American manners very fast." And she snapped her fingers. "Wow!"

It was hard to grasp if Sheila meant to be condescending, implying that Haitians cannot have good manners or cannot be smart. Was she so deeply steeped in stereotypes that she didn't sense the level of discomfort my husband and I were experiencing as we listened to her? For my husband this was a "déjà vu" experience, but for me, it was an I-can't-believe-it moment. I wasn't prepared for this. I smiled politely, buying time, but Sheila interpreted my smile as an appreciative reaction to the compliment of being a quick learner.

And she went on, "You are my first Black friends, guys, I confess. I count on you to introduce me to the African American culture."

It became obvious to me that Sheila expected me to be more informed about or to relate more easily to the African American culture because I am Black. The truth is, since high school in Haiti and after reading many books on race and cultures in America, I was prepared to discover a cultural mosaic in Florida—but not this.

However, Sheila's candor mixed with her honest ignorance made me realize that the process of multiculturalism is a journey, and ours was just starting. We ate a blend of Haitian and American food that night: conch fritters, akra (a fried mix of malaga root and anchovies), fried pork, plantains, corn chips, slices of Cracker Barrel cheese, and raw veggies, with a five-star Barbancourt Rum as an alternative to Budweiser.

Heurtelou with her family on her thirteenth birthday. Maude (*left*) and her younger sister Denise stand at the top; in the center are her mother, Marie-Therese Pardo-Heurtelou, and father, Chevert Heurtelou; Maude's siblings are (*from left*) Eugene, Ghislaine, Raymonde, and Chevy. Courtesy of Maude Heurtelou.

200 · Maude Heurtelou

Sheila explained her idea of Haitians: poor Black people living in the muddy slums of Port-au-Prince who are so unlucky. She grew up in Ohio and never had Haitian friends; neither had Chris, who was from South Carolina. I talked about my life in Haiti. My father was an electronic engineer and my mother a homemaker. I grew up surrounded by members of my extended family, who taught me to write and read before kindergarten.

Since I was two years old, my maternal uncle had played a pivotal role in my life in many ways. For example, I wrote letters to Santa Claus that my uncle would mail for me. Every single year, Santa wrote back to me, thanks to my uncle's ingenuity.

When I turned six, my future as a professional was predicted, and I only had to focus on the path toward it. "She is my rising star," my uncle proclaimed with solemnity during a speech on my birthday.

When I came to America, my goal was to both realize the American dream and to fulfill Haitian dreams. My American dream was for my efforts to be rewarded with a stable life that wouldn't collapse because of political storms. My Haitian dreams were to give back to Haiti and to Haitians what I had so generously received growing up there: the love of family, the respect for moral values, and the appreciation of life with little money.

Heurtelou and a neighbor enjoy a Latin dance, 1988. Courtesy of Maude Heurtelou.

I am thankful for the stability in America, and I am blessed to make my Haitian dreams a reality through my writings and my volunteer work.

Sheila's jaw dropped when I said I was from a middle-class family and that strong values are widespread among Haitians, including good manners and self-empowerment, no matter how poor they are. The drive to succeed is almost always there, but too often opportunities are lacking.

I explained that I see Haitians who risk their lives to come to America as people with big dreams searching for opportunities. Chris eventually commented on the universality of the immigrant experience, remembering how as a young boy, he had given his bedroom to a distant uncle who had emigrated from Ireland.

The conversation became emotional that night, and it may have brought us closer because we shared personal experiences. It drifted later into Latin dances, Alvin Ailey's dance, Irish parades, and New Orleans carnival. That night was the beginning of a nice friendship that extended to other neighbors from other cultures.

If all this is part of Americanization, then, yes, I am Americanized, artfully crossing the bridge from my Haitian experience to the American melting pot.

From the **Fall 2011** edition of *FORUM* magazine, "¡Viva Florida! Marking 500 Years of Spanish Heritage."

PART VI

This State of Inspiration

At once dreamlike and forbidding, Florida is a heady elixir to the imagination of writers, artists, and musicians.

Marjorie Kinnan Rawlings on the sand dunes at Crescent Beach overlooking the ocean. Courtesy of the Marjorie Kinnan Rawlings Papers, Special and Area Studies Collections, George A. Smathers Libraries, University of Florida.

32 Finding a Literary Path Home

Learning to love Florida, through the writers who knew it first.

Lauren Groff

Lauren Groff is a *New York Times* best-selling author of the novels *The Monsters of Templeton, Arcadia, Fates and Furies, Matrix,* and *The Vaster Wilds* and the short-story collections *Delicate Edible Birds* and *Florida.* She has won the Joyce Carol Oates Prize for Fiction, the PEN/O. Henry Award, and the Story Prize and has been a finalist for the National Book Award three times, as well as many other honors. She lives in Gainesville with her husband and two young sons.

Image: William Bartram, portrait by Charles Willson Peale, circa 1808. Courtesy of Independence National Historical Park, Philadelphia.

I WAS BORN AND RAISED in Cooperstown, New York, a tiny village that is also the birthplace of the great early American writer James Fenimore Cooper. When I was a nerdy teenager, I read all of Cooper's work and was so delighted by the sense of depth and history that his books gave to my understanding of my hometown that, afterward, whenever I was preparing to move to a new city, I made it a practice to come to know the place first through literature, preparing for what I was to encounter through the eyes of the writers who had previously loved and written about it.

At seventeen I read Jules Verne to understand Nantes, France, where I was an exchange student after high school; I read Emily Dickinson for Amherst, Massachusetts, where I went to college; I read Thomas Hardy and Oscar Wilde and a panoply of greats before my study abroad in Oxford; then, after graduation, I read Edgar Allan Poe for Philadelphia, Mark Twain for the San Francisco Bay Area, and Wallace Stegner for Madison, Wisconsin, where I received my MFA. In 2006 I lived in Louisville, Kentucky, for a postgraduate fellowship and was reading the work of Louisville native Z. Z. Packer when my husband moved home to Gainesville, Florida, and a few months later, I moved to be with him.

Yet my reluctance to live in Florida was so great—and I was, honestly, so tired from my decade of peripatetic life—that I failed to do this most basic task of introduction when my husband and I bought a house in Gainesville. I came to Florida without having first experienced it through the visions of the master storytellers from our state. Because it wasn't my decision to move here, I felt trapped in Gainesville and, out of some sort of misplaced pique at having to live in this hot, humid, buggy, and wildly strange environment, for far too long I continued to resolutely ignore Florida literature, and I blame my first years of unhappiness in Florida on my own bizarre pigheadedness. Last, I found that I was so unhappy that I knew I had to do something to change myself; the place sure wasn't going to change itself for me.

And so I turned to the great solace and nourishment of literature. I started with *Oranges*, a slender, beautiful nonfiction book by John McPhee about the orange groves in the center of the state, and finished reading it in one sitting, having sustained a tiny revolution in my heart. I finally understood through McPhee that this place was worthy of close, precise, caring attention, which is another name for love.

From McPhee, I expanded to Zora Neale Hurston, whose *Their Eyes Were Watching God* slayed me and made me understand how difficult life in Florida might have been before air-conditioning or hurricane advisories. I read Marjorie Kinnan Rawlings's magisterial, slow-moving *The Yearling* and was so entranced by her vision of central Florida in the late nineteenth century that I made the pilgrimage multiple times out to her house in Cross Creek and even cooked a few meals from her cookbook *Cross Creek Cookery*. After Peter Matthiessen won the National Book Award for *Shadow Country*, his utterly gorgeous and wild novel about the Florida frontier, I let the book sit on my shelf for a year, a little cowed by the grand scope of his project, but when I finally read the book, I was so moved I could hardly read anything else for weeks afterward. It is still the most brutal, stunning, vicious, light-filled Floridian work that I know of. Slowly, I expanded my scope of reading to other writers and began to learn how to love Florida through the eyes of Joy Williams, Karen Russell, Marjory Stoneman Douglas, Cynthia Barnett, Jack E. Davis, and up to the relatively new Florida writers Kristin Arnett and Sarah Gerard.

Yet the Floridian writer whom I love the most fervently was one of the first Europeans to try to encounter Florida on its own terms: William Bartram, a Quaker naturalist who came through the South in the eighteenth century to describe it for a more cosmopolitan northern and English audience. I return to him often and take profound pleasure in his ecstatic, almost wild-eyed visions of the state. Bartram taught me many lessons in his *Travels*, but the ones I return to again and again in my own writing are these: that the eyes of the outsider can see things in the state that those who were born to it may miss, and that there is deep joy in the teeming wilderness here. After more than sixteen years as a Floridian, I rue the first few years I lived in the Sunshine State without the deepening and clarifying visions of the writers who taught me how to love this place where I have found myself.

Lauren Groff visits Paynes Prairie near Gainesville, 2019. Photo by John Moran.

From the **Spring 2019** edition of *FORUM* magazine, "Artful Revival: How the Power of the Creative Spirit Is Energizing Florida's Cities."

33 Many Voices from Afar

For 500 years, Florida's literary life has thrived on the state's complexity.

Maurice J. O'Sullivan

IN THE PROLOGUE to his influential *Ideas of Order* (1935), Wallace Stevens attempts to describe why he fled the seductive "ever-freshened Keys" for the "leafless . . . Wintry slime" of Connecticut. Titled "Farewell to Florida," this elegiac account of the poet's final return from Key West to life as an insurance executive in Hartford contrasts a turbulent, vital, ever-changing Florida with the cold, orderly North.

Such extravagant complexity, verging on chaos, has always characterized Florida's physical environment as well as its literary landscape. In today's Florida, for example, Cuban American poets mingle with the authors of Cracker cowboy stories at the Miami Book Fair, while southern Gothic novelists from Tampa and Tallahassee regularly vie for bookshelf space with writers of Florida noir and Space Coast science fiction.

This rich collision of writing and culture is nothing new. By the time the British founded Jamestown in 1607, we Floridians already had an extraordinary collection of poems and narratives, myths and adventure stories. Unlike the literary history of Virginia, however, no single strand of language, culture, or values knits our literature neatly together. While much of our earliest literature is in Spanish, for example, like the remarkable sixteenth-century poems of Bartolomé de Flores, Juan de Castellanos, and Fray Alonso Gregorio de Escobedo, one of our finest early works is an English book by a French naval captain. Jean Ribaut's exuberant *The Whole and True Discovery of Terra Florida* (1563) describes the French Huguenot expedition he had led the previous year. And even after almost two and a half centuries of Spanish and British rule, along with the increasingly powerful influence of the new, relentlessly English-speaking United States to its north, the first novel about Florida appeared in French, François-René de Chateaubriand's *Atala* (1801).

Perhaps more than any other single characteristic, this ability to embrace radically different traditions without forcing them to assimilate defines our literary history. The year after Wallace Stevens made his first trip to Florida in 1916, the elegantly patrician William Dean Howells fondly recalled *A Trip to St. Augustine*,

Maurice J. O'Sullivan, an award-winning teacher, writer, and filmmaker, is the Kenneth Curry Professor of Literature, Emeritus, at Rollins College and president of the Florida Historical Society.

while Ring Lardner's *Gullible's Travels* satirized our winter pretensions in his distinctive urban vernacular. As Stevens was shaping his allusively symbolic poems about Key West, Pulitzer Prize winner Stephen Vincent Benét described the journey of his Minorcan ancestors to New Smyrna in his poetic novel *Spanish Bayonets* (1926); James Weldon Johnson re-created the sermons he had heard as a child in his native Jacksonville in *God's Trombones: Seven Negro Sermons in Verse* (1927); Zane Grey took time from writing westerns to focus on fishing off Long Key; and John Dos Passos used his experimental styles to explore the Florida land boom in *The Big Money* (1936). Dos Passos introduced Ernest Hemingway and his spare understatement to the Keys, soon to be followed by the bohemian Elizabeth Bishop. At the same time, Zora Neale Hurston was capturing the African American voices of her childhood world of Eatonville and Marjorie Kinnan Rawlings the Cracker voices of her adopted Cross Creek.

These writers merely suggest the surface of our literary history during one brief window of time. Throughout our history, Florida has always experienced a vigorous competition of voices attempting to define its distinctive qualities. In the eighteenth century, Oliver Goldsmith lamented the effect of British emigration to Florida in *The Deserted Village* (1770), just as William Bartram was bringing a Romantic sensibility to celebrating our wilderness, Bernard Romans an engineer's eye to defining our topography, and William Roberts a naturalist's training to exploring west Florida.

After Florida became part of the United States in 1821, Ralph Waldo Emerson captured the contradictions of St. Augustine in his *Journals* with a distinct New Englander's ambivalence, George McCall boasted of his military and sporting life in *Letters from the Frontiers* in 1830, and in 1834 Davy Crockett's *Life* spun tall tales of his adventures pursuing Creek Indians in the Panhandle, while John James Audubon's *Ornithological Biography* offered a painter's view of the flora and fauna of what would soon be our southernmost state.

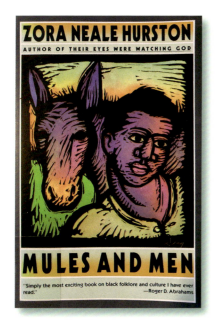

Zora Neale Hurston. The writer, folklorist, and anthropologist was photographed by the *Saturday Evening Post* working in her Eau Gallie cottage. Courtesy of *Saturday Evening Post*.

Many Voices from Afar · 207

Florida's ability to embrace radically different visions appears in two enormously popular writers who moved to the state late in their careers.

Harriet Beecher Stowe used some of her profits from *Uncle Tom's Cabin* (1852) to buy a cottage in Mandarin shortly after the Civil War. Her account of the pleasures of life along the St. Johns, *Palmetto Leaves* (1873), attracted not only Mark Twain and William Cullen Bryant to her riverfront home but also an enormous number of visitors who hoped to catch a glimpse of the woman they believed to have sparked the Civil War.

About 220 miles west of Mandarin, Caroline Lee Whiting Hentz, a Massachusetts native, lived in Marianna with her French husband, Nicholas. There she wrote a series of best-selling novels celebrating antebellum plantation life, including one of the most widely read rebuttals of *Uncle Tom's Cabin, The Planter's Northern Bride* (1854).

The Writers Arrive

In fact, since the 1880s it is almost impossible to name a major American writer—from Henry James, Theodore Dreiser, and Sinclair Lewis to John Knowles, James Michener, and Robert Ludlum—who has not spent time in Florida.

AFTER THE CIVIL WAR, writers flooded into Florida. John Muir walked to the Gulf, Sidney Lanier and Lafcadio Hearn toured by riverboat, and Silvia Sunshine pursued the state's legends. In fact, since the 1880s it is almost impossible to name a major American writer—from Henry James, Theodore Dreiser, and Sinclair Lewis to John Knowles, James Michener, and Robert Ludlum—who has not spent time in Florida. While many found the Sunshine State a perfect place to winter, others merely visited to fish with Papa Hemingway, party with Tennessee Williams, or dine with Marjorie.

Few areas of the country can match the talent that gathered in south Florida alone. Besides Stevens, Bishop, Hemingway, and Williams, it became home to an eclectic community of Pulitzer Prize– and National Book Award–winning poets like John Ciardi, James Merrill, Richard Wilbur, A. R. Ammons, and Donald Justice. Joining them were writers like Joy Williams, Thomas McGuane, Alison Lurie, Philip Caputo, Robert Stone, Thomas Sanchez, Peter Matthiessen, Marjory Stoneman Douglas, Rachel Carson, and Anne Morrow Lindbergh. And with Miami as its heart, the area has attracted the greatest concentration of crime-fiction talent in the world.

Ever since Davis Dresser, writing as Brett Halliday, introduced Mike Shayne in 1939, south Florida has nurtured or attracted Charles Willeford, John D. MacDonald, Ed McBain, Randy Wayne White, Elmore Leonard, Carl Hiaasen, Edna Buchanan, James Hall, Dick Francis, Les Standiford, Barbara Parker, Paul Levine, Carolina Garcia-Aguilera, and Stuart Kaminsky.

At the same time that classic and experimental crime fiction flourishes there, Miami has re-created itself as a vital center of Caribbean culture with writers like Carolina Hospital, Ricardo Pau-Llosa, Virgil Suárez, and Geoffrey Philp. Such odd couplings appear throughout the state. In the Tampa area, Jose Yglesias, Dionysio

Marjorie Kinnan Rawlings at the typewriter at her Cross Creek home. Photograph by Alan M. Anderson, courtesy of Marjorie Kinnan Rawlings Papers, Special and Area Studies Collections, George A. Smathers Libraries, University of Florida.

Martínez, and Nilo Cruz evoke the history of Ybor City, while Sterling Watson and poet Peter Meinke nurture young writers.

The Panhandle has witnessed Victor Nunez's remarkable trilogy of films as well as the vital Anhinga community of poets surrounding Van Brock and Rick Campbell. And central Florida has been home to the only two Pulitzer Prize novels set in the state: Marjorie Kinnan Rawlings's classic tale of Cracker culture, *The Yearling* (1938), and James Gould Cozzens's portrait of life at the Orlando Air Force Base, *Guard of Honor* (1948). It's also home to the first American novel published simultaneously in English and Spanish, Orlando attorney J. Joaquín Fraxedas's *The Lonely Crossing of Juan Cabrera* (1993), *La travesía solitaria de Juan Cabrera* (1995).

It's clear that Florida has a long, impressive, and diverse literary tradition, one that stretches from the stirring narrative of Cabeza de Vaca (1542) and the first poem by someone known to have lived in North America, Nicholas le Challeux's huitain (1565), to Nilo Cruz's 2003 Pulitzer Prize–winning play about Tampa, *Anna in the Tropics*.

Many Voices from Afar · 209

Absent from the Narratives

WHY, THEN, are we so rarely represented in histories? Aside from Zora Neale Hurston and Ernest Hemingway, Marjorie Kinnan Rawlings and John D. MacDonald, how many Florida writers can most people name? With the oldest literary tradition in North America, why are we so little known?

Part of the answer is that so much of our early literature is in languages other than English. But another part is that although many of those writers settled in Florida for long periods, we associate them with other regions. Robert Frost may have spent the last three decades of his life wintering in the exuberantly lush chaos of Miami and Key West, but we continue to identify him with the austere winters of New England. Although Nobel laureate Isaac Bashevis Singer moved to Surfside in 1973 and lived there until his death in 1991, his work continued to evoke Eastern European and urban American ghettos.

Tennessee Williams might epitomize this complex relationship between many American writers and geography. How narrowly can we define a writer born in Mississippi and educated in Missouri who adopted Tennessee for his name and became intimately connected with New Orleans despite spending much of his last forty years in Key West and New York?

While it is easy not to think of Frost, Singer, and Williams as Florida writers since they wrote so little, or in Frost's case, nothing about Florida, even many of those who have shaped our literature are rarely considered Floridians.

William Bartram's *Travels* framed the way the world saw this exotic Eden and inspired Samuel Taylor Coleridge to write *Kubla Khan*, Wallace Stevens's and Elizabeth Bishop's Key West poems helped define twentieth-century American literature, and the exiled 1956 Spanish Nobel laureate Juan Ramón Jiménez celebrated the city that reinspired him in *Romances de Coral Gables* (1957). But Bartram will always be the colonial Philadelphia naturalist, Stevens the Connecticut insurance executive, Bishop the Massachusetts and Brazilian adventurer, and Jiménez the most popular Spanish writer since Cervantes.

In this most mobile and diverse of all states, we certainly cannot expect our writers to be natives. But what if, like Albery Allson Whitman, the formerly enslaved poet who wrote our unofficial state epic, *The Rape of Florida* (1884), or Stephen Foster, author of our official state song, "Old Folks at Home," they never even visit the state? Florida may be unique in the number of writers like Oliver Goldsmith and Walt Whitman who have added to its literature without ever seeing it. It is unlikely that either our first novelist, Chateaubriand, or Hart Crane, whose posthumous *Key West* appeared in 1932, ever reached Florida. Even Stephen Vincent Benét first visited the state his family had helped settle in 1941 some fifteen years after publishing *Spanish Bayonets*.

As we continue attempting to comprehend and celebrate our ever-growing, ever-changing literary tradition, we need to recognize that it will constantly elude any

Tennessee Williams, on the front porch of his island home. Williams wrote many of his best-known works while visiting or living in Key West between 1941 and his death in 1983. Courtesy of the Ida Woodward Barron Collection, Monroe County Public Library.

attempt at simple definition or easy description. But the ability to live with paradox and contradiction has always been part of our history as Floridians.

If we can welcome both the mockingbird and alligator as official state symbols and relish both the Silver Spurs Rodeo and the Calle Ocho Open House as official state events, we can certainly embrace a literary heritage that connects Cross Creek to Key West, Lake City to Ybor City, and Marianna to Miami.

From the **Fall 2003** edition of *FORUM* magazine, "A Sunshine State of Mind: Florida's Place in American Culture."

34 Echoes in the Wind

In search of the poetry of Florida's Native people.

Maurice J. O'Sullivan

Despite our remarkably rich library of Florida literature, one shelf is far too short. The Natives who lived here for thousands of years before Europeans first sailed along our shores left behind some remarkable artifacts and a sophisticated canal system but no stories or poems, myths, or legends. Most of what we know about their culture comes from those who arrived as their rivals and remained as their interpreters.

One of those interpreters, Juan de Castellanos, has left an extensive description of the Calusa who lived along Florida's southwest coast in the first part of his monumental *Elegias de varones ilustres de indias* (1589). Using the ottava rima, an eight-line stanza traditionally associated with heroic subjects, Castellanos marvels at the communal lifestyle of the Calusa and their fearlessness in hunting what he called whales (*ballena*) but may well have been manatees:

No nada con tal impetus sirena,	No not even sirens can swim with such speed
Ni por las bravas ondas tan esperta,	Nor prove so expert among whitewater waves,
Pues cada cual y no con mucha pena	For all of them with no difficulty
Entre voracés peces se despierta;	Move among rapacious fish.
Matan en alta mar una ballena	After killing a whale in the ocean,
Para la repartir después de muerta,	They divide their catch among themselves.
Y aunque ella se zabulla, no se ciega	And when their prey dives, without fear
El indio, ni de encima se despega.	The Indian will ride its back under the water.
No puede con sus fuerzas no ser flacas	Even with its enormous power,
Desechallo de encima las cervices	It cannot shake its rider from its back.
El indio lleva hechas dos estacas,	The Indian carries two stakes
De durisimas ramas ó raices:	Created from sturdy branches or roots,
Y en medio de las ondas ó resacas	And in the middle of the rolling waves
Se las mete de dentro las narices,	Drives them into its nose.
La falta del resuello la desmaya,	The absence of air dismays it
Y ansi la hacen ir hacia la playa.	And forces it to the beach.

Maurice O'Sullivan's biography is found on page 206.

Image: (detail) Manatee, by Theodore Morris. LostTribesOfFlorida.com. Used with permission.

The few Native people who survived European settlement and diseases and who remained in Florida united with members of other tribes, especially Creeks, who migrated into Florida and formed the Seminole and Miccosukee tribes. Even they, however, left it to others to document their epic battles for survival, especially in the Second Seminole War (1835–1842), the longest, most expensive, and deadliest of all the nineteenth-century Indian conflicts.

As northerners grew disenchanted with the financial and human cost of that war, they became intrigued with Osceola, the charismatic warrior who consistently outfought and outwitted US forces. When the army finally seized him during truce talks, public outrage exploded. Unsure of how to deal with a captive who was widely seen as a hero, the military sent him to Fort Moultrie in South Carolina, where they treated him like a celebrity, allowing artists like George Catlin and Robert J. Curtis to paint him and even arranging visits to Charleston.

Osceola of Florida, circa 1838, by Robert John Curtis (1816–1867), oil on canvas. Courtesy of the Samuel P. Harn Museum of Art, University of Florida, Gainesville; the Florida Art Collection, Gift of Samuel H. and Roberta T. Vickers. Photo by Randy Batista.

Echoes in the Wind · 213

To memorialize one of those visits, James Burchett Ransom, who would later serve as secretary to the wonderfully named second president of the Texas Republic, Mirabeau Buonaparte Lamar, wrote "Osceola at the Charleston Theatre."

Osceola's death soon afterward inspired poets throughout the century. In 1891 the country's most influential poet, Walt Whitman, hearing a description of the Seminole's final day from one of the marines who had guarded him and familiar with Catlin's widely reproduced portrait, included a poem about him in the final edition of *Leaves of Grass*.

> When his hour for death had come,
> He slowly rais'd himself from the bed on the floor,
> Drew on his war-dress, shirt, leggings, and girdled the belt around his waist,
> Call'd for vermilion paint (his looking-glass was held before him,)
> Painted half his face and neck, his wrists, and back-hands.
> Put the scalp-knife carefully in his belt—then lying down, resting a moment,
> Rose again, half sitting, smiled, gave in silence his extended hand to each and all,
> Sank faintly low to the floor (tightly grasping the tomahawk handle,)
> Fix'd his look on wife and little children—the last:
> (And here a line in memory of his name and death.)

What may look like an odd fragment in a work already regarded as a literary landmark might well be less an incomplete poem than Whitman's tribute to an unfinished life and legacy.

Portraits of three Native men, by Theodore Morris. The artist depicts (*left to right*) two Ais Indians, "The Counselor" and "Yesterday's Hunter"; and a Timucuan, "Fisherman." Morris specializes in paintings of Florida's "lost tribes." LostTribesOfFlorida.com. Used with permission.

Much of our knowledge of Seminole poetry and song comes from the original song catcher, Frances Densmore, who transcribed and recorded their music in the early 1930s for the Smithsonian Institution. An ethnomusicologist who devoted her life to documenting Native American poetry and music, she published her transcriptions as *Seminole Songs* in 1956. While most of the songs—largely part of their games, hunting, and dance rituals—are in the Seminole languages, she does include a few translations.

One song re-creates "The Seminole Removal," the federal government's attempt to relocate the tribe to the western Indian Territories. Literary historians will, of course, note that without additional documentation, we can never know when the Seminoles first sang this song. Is it a contemporary response by someone walking their Trail of Tears or an imaginative re-creation years later? Seminoles undoubtedly find such questions naïve, irrelevant to the song's truth and beauty.

Much of our knowledge of Seminole poetry and song comes from the original song catcher, Frances Densmore.

> They are taking us beyond Miami
> They are taking us beyond the Calusa River
> They are taking us to the end of our tribe
> They are taking us to Palm Beach, coming back
> beside Okeechobee Lake
> They are taking us to an old town in the west.

Like "The Seminole Removal," a birth song uses a rhythmic chant, with its insistent repetition of words and phrases to emphasize the newborn's connection with both nature and the cycle of life.

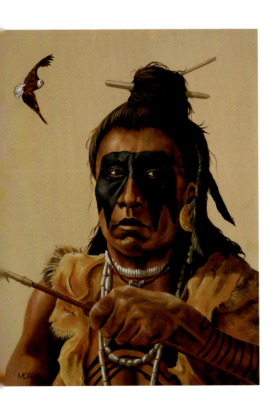

> You day-sun, circling around,
> You daylight, circling around,
> You night-sun, circling around,
> You, poor body, circling around,
> You wrinkled age, circling around,
> You spotted with gray, circling around,
> You wrinkled skin, circling around.
> Come.

A number of years ago I interviewed the legendary Miccosukee leader Buffalo Tiger for a Florida Humanities program on "Making Florida Home." We began by talking about the history of our families and the importance of passing stories down through the generations. Then I raised the question of why his ancestors and those of the Seminoles had left behind so few written records of their stories and songs. He told me that his people taught their children to find joy in the present because they had suffered so much in the past. Why remember such pain? Then he paused, smiled gently, and asked if spending so much time recalling our history had made

Echoes in the Wind · 215

An Apalachee, "Shaman," by Theodore Morris. LostTribesOfFlorida.com. Used with permission.

my Irish relatives or my wife's Jewish family happy. Could those memories, he wondered, imprison us and block light from our lives?

Perhaps the best responses to Buffalo Tiger's questions come from Seminole poets themselves. In "Native Poems," the introduction to his collection *Nightfall* (2006), the writer and painter Elgin Jumper sees himself as "a celestial writer / riding the orange tail of a shooting star glittering gold." His highly chromatic poetry helps him to "smile from behind dark clouds / allied with the long night of sorrow" and imagine a future which will allow "turquoise / poetry to come invade my silvery night."

For the Seminole Tribe's poet laureate, Moses Jumper Jr., poetry not only allows him to affirm his identity as he moves cautiously between the two cultures in which all contemporary Native Americans must live, it also offers him moments of transcendence. In the title poem of his collection *Echoes in the Wind* (1990), he sees language as a way both to collapse and to escape the boundaries of time and space.

> If but for a blissful moment,
> one feels caught with hope and pride, with time to spare
> and no emotion to hide.
> The experience begins to flow as one writes
> of perhaps a different place or time.
> Confuses a little, but soon the flow of
> words are jotted line for line.
> It is with moments like this that one expresses
> a place, a time of where he is going
> or where he has been.
> And then, silently he listens
> for the echoes in the wind.

From the **Spring 2015** edition of *FORUM* magazine, "St. Augustine: Life with History and Tourism."

35

Harriet Beecher Stowe, Florida Snowbird

Winters in a Mandarin cabin transformed her writing and sparked a tourist boom.

Michele Currie Navakas

Michele Currie Navakas grew up in Florida and is a professor of English at Miami University in Oxford, Ohio. She is the author of *Liquid Landscape: Geography and Settlement at the Edge of Early America*, which won the 2019 Rembert Patrick Award and the 2019 Stetson Kennedy Award from the Florida Historical Society, and most recently, *Coral Lives: Literature, Labor, and the Making of America*. Parts of her essay "Harriet Beecher Stowe, Florida Snowbird" are excerpted with permission of the University of Pennsylvania Press from *Liquid Landscape: Geography and Settlement at the Edge of Early America*.

"FOR THREE HUNDRED YEARS has Florida been open to settlement," wrote American poet William Cullen Bryant in 1873 to the *New York Evening Post*. How, then, is much of the state "still for the most part a wilderness"? On a trip to Florida after the Civil War, Bryant saw swamps, sandy plains, pine trees, and scrub palmettoes; he saw very few conventionally neat dwellings, sturdy fences, green lawns, or fertile fields. Echoing the sentiments of many northerners who visited post–Civil War Florida—the poorest, least populated, and arguably most undeveloped state in the South during that time—Bryant declared most of the peninsula the "despair of the cultivator."

Yet he found reason for hope just south of Jacksonville. For at Mandarin, a tiny village on the east bank of the St. Johns River, "Mrs. Stowe has her winter mansion, in the shadow of some enormous live oaks," surrounded by an orange grove.

We don't typically associate the author Harriet Beecher Stowe with Florida. Born at Litchfield, Connecticut, in 1811 to Roxana and Lyman Beecher, a prominent Presbyterian minister, Harriet Beecher married theologian Calvin Stowe, with whom she had seven children. The future author spent significant time in Hartford and then in Cincinnati, where she witnessed the nation's increasing racial unrest in the form of race riots, abolitionist meetings, African Americans escaping from slavery, bounty hunters seeking fugitive slaves, and other events that inspired her first novel, the abolitionist work and international bestseller, *Uncle Tom's Cabin* (1852).

Written as she raised children at home in Maine, where the family had relocated for Calvin's teaching position at Bowdoin College, Stowe's novel caused a groundswell of antislavery sentiment so powerful that some credit her book with precipitating the Civil War.

Yet after the war and during nearly every winter from 1868 to 1884, Stowe and her husband—accompanied by servants and an assortment of family members—traveled south from the family home in Hartford, by railroad and steamboat, to live in a renovated cottage at Mandarin.

Incorporated in 1841 and named after the orange variety, Mandarin would just begin to flourish by the time Stowe left Florida for good in the mid-1880s, when it boasted about 1,200 residents, a riverfront boardwalk, and several large estates and steamboat landings.

So what drew Stowe to Florida during the 1860s, and particularly to Mandarin, in the first place?

Her son Frederick was a Civil War veteran seeking a fresh start. To help him, Stowe leased a former cotton plantation called Laurel Grove, located on the west bank of the St. Johns River at present-day Orange Park. Stowe, her husband, and their son—accompanied by her nephew and his family—first visited Florida in 1867 and attempted to restore Laurel Grove to a fully functioning farm, assisted by recently freed African Americans hired as housekeepers, cooks, planters, and laborers. Stowe chronicles the experience in a short story called "Our Florida Plantation" (1879), published in the *Atlantic Monthly*. There she recounts Laurel Grove's brief success, followed by total failure due to a cotton-worm infestation.

The Stowe family abandoned Laurel Grove after just a few months. Yet there was one bright spot in that difficult winter of 1867: when rowing east across the St. Johns River to send and collect the mail in Mandarin, Stowe saw the cottage she would purchase as her winter home.

A Champion of Social Reform

In Mandarin, Stowe found a warm place to write in peace and a chance to expand her commitment to social reform by assisting African Americans who had been recently freed from slavery. She quickly began the complex process of planning and securing funding from the Freedman's Bureau for the construction of a combined schoolhouse and church. The school, built in 1869, served both Black and white children until it was destroyed by fire, at which point Stowe and her neighbors continued instruction in their homes until the Mandarin Schoolhouse was built in 1872.

To serve the community's spiritual needs, Stowe's husband, Calvin, offered Episcopal church services open to all denominations (with separate services for Black and white), while Stowe assisted him and led Bible study groups for women. By 1883 the congregation had grown enough to merit a separate building, and funds were raised for the Church of Our Saviour, which endures to this day.

Stowe entertained visiting family members, including her siblings Catharine, Charles, and Henry, her youngest son, Charley, and her daughters Hattie and Eliza.

Harriet Beecher Stowe, by Francis Holl, after George Richmond, stipple engraving, circa 1855. Courtesy of National Portrait Gallery, Smithsonian Institution.

She fished and boated on the St. Johns River and Julington Creek and visited St. Augustine and other tourist destinations by railroad. She observed agricultural experiments on orange trees, cabbages, cucumbers, and other crops growing on the small farm at her Florida cottage.

The Florida Writings

AND, OF COURSE, she wrote—sometimes from a desk in her yard where she could see the St. Johns River.

Stowe was a prolific writer in Florida. She published a number of letters about the state in the *Christian Union*, a New York newspaper owned by her brother Henry Ward Beecher, in which she promoted Florida settlement, tourism, climate, scenery, agriculture, and employment opportunities for Black and white residents.

Some of these letters appeared in her book *Palmetto-Leaves* (1873), and the success of her Florida campaign is evident in the many letters she received from northerners seeking additional information about Florida opportunities. Her writings are often credited with the significant increase in Florida tourism during the mid-1870s, when Jacksonville and the St. Johns River became popular destinations.

Stowe's Florida writings are wide and varied, but across all of them one thing is clear: the place to which she returned for nearly twenty winters ultimately transformed her. She grew to love and embrace the energy and vitality of the same natural features that other northerners, such as poet William Cullen Bryant, deemed "wilderness" or evidence of the state's resistance to civilized life. She delighted in swamps, orange trees, and the tangled roots of the scrub palmetto, a plant many settlers lamented but Stowe chose as the inspiration for the title and cover image of her published collection of Florida letters.

Her delight in Florida's resistance to conventional order is apparent in a letter to friend and fellow writer George Eliot in which Stowe describes her discovery and early renovation of the Mandarin cottage.

"The history of the cottage is this," she writes. "I found a hut built close to a great live-oak twenty-five feet in girth, and with overarching boughs eighty feet up in the air, spreading like a firmament, and all swaying with mossy festoons. We began to live here, and gradually we improved the hut by lath, plaster, and paper. Then we threw out a wide veranda all round, for in these regions the veranda is the living-room."

Stowe describes how the family had to build their veranda around the massive trunk of the oak tree and how they added on gables and chambers, just "as a tree throws out new branches," so that the cottage "seems as if it were half tree, or something that had grown out of the tree."

The tree architecture of Stowe's Florida home was a local attraction. In many of the photos and artistic renderings of the cottage, including Stowe's own oil painting of it, the live oak pushing through the roof takes center stage, as if to declare

Yellow Jessamine, by Harriet Beecher Stowe. The writer painted as well as wrote during her winters in Mandarin. Courtesy of Harriet Beecher Stowe Center.

the inhabitants' intention to adapt to the local landscape by disregarding any effort at symmetry, order, or intentional design. Stowe's winter home appeared "peculiar and original," she wrote to her friend. And yet, Stowe concludes, "we settle into it with real enjoyment."

At home in Mandarin, Stowe found beauty and vitality in Florida's opposition to familiar forms of cultivation. Writing to her son Charles, she reports that her garden is more like a "jungle" and that the lawn is "littered with fallen oranges" and covered with "rampant" roots. Elsewhere, she writes of the "raptures and frenzies of growth" and the "green labyrinths made by the tangling vines" of the swamp fronting her home. On the whole the place is "shockingly untidy," she declares, and yet, it is also "so beautiful that I am quite willing to forgive its disorder."

An appreciation for nature's resistance to order is similarly evident in a number of oil paintings that Stowe made while wintering at Mandarin, such as *Yellow Jessamine* and *Orange Fruit and Blossoms*, which portrays oranges so lively that they appear to push against the painting's frame.

This appreciation pervades Stowe's descriptions of life in *Palmetto-Leaves*, where she explains the difference between Florida and New England: in New England nature is a "smart, decisive house-mother" that sharply freezes and thaws at predictable "times and seasons"; Florida nature is more like a grandmother who "does everything when she happens to feel like it," alternating unpredictably between warmth and sudden cold snaps. But this atmospheric fickleness makes for a much more interesting life, a "tumble-down, wild, picnicky" existence filled with unexpected energy.

Harriet Beecher Stowe's Florida writings are wide and varied, but across all of them one thing is clear: the place to which she returned for nearly twenty winters ultimately transformed her.

Calvin and Harriet Beecher Stowe (*seated*) with unidentified man outside the Stowes' home in Mandarin, Florida, circa 1880. The house came complete with an oak tree growing up through the roof. Courtesy of Harriet Beecher Stowe Center, Hartford, CT.

Palmetto-Leaves is ultimately a settlers' guide, practical and whimsical. The book offers instructions for buying good land, building a home, hiring local laborers, and establishing schools for the recently emancipated. It also recommends impromptu picnics, twilight steamboat rides, and rambles through "magical" palmetto groves.

An important message is that while Florida may appear to resist settlement or progress, appearances can deceive. The same characteristics that sometimes make Florida seem averse to growth could actually be signs of its capacity for energetic development.

This message is most fully exhibited by Florida's orange trees and scrub palmettoes. In a letter about the frost of 1835, Stowe tells of a Mandarin grove that appeared to die that year. However, the trees soon "sprang up again" and vigorously bore fruit, thereby offering "lessons in perseverance" for people "struggling to found a colony here."

The same hidden resilience flows through the scrub palmetto. True, she reflects, this lowly shrub, native to the Florida peninsula, will never attain the "grace" or "perfect shape" of that other species, the tall sabal palm. Yet it possesses a hardiness that "these regions" require: "catching into the earth by strong rootlets, and then rising up here and there," the scrub palmettoes "burst forth into a graceful crest of waving green" leaves. Scrub palmetto leaves make an ideal cover image for Stowe's settlers' guide to Florida. Embossed in gold against red, the leaves attest that flourishing in Florida requires continual adaptation to its unique local landscape.

Stowe lived until 1896 but stopped visiting Florida after 1884 due to Calvin's failing health. Today a historical marker commemorates the site where her winter home once stood, while the Mandarin Museum features a permanent exhibit on Stowe in Florida. The 1872 Mandarin Schoolhouse still exists, maintained by the Mandarin Community Club. The Church of Our Saviour—destroyed by Hurricane Dora in 1964, then rebuilt on the site of the original church of 1883—continues to serve the community. And Stowe's letters, stories, and paintings of Florida remain as a testament to the vital possibilities of a place that has never been conventional.

From the **Fall 2019** edition of *FORUM* magazine, "What Does It Mean to Be a Floridian?"

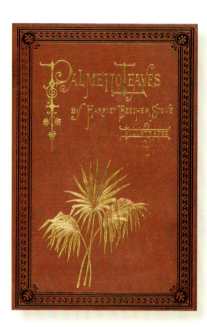

Palmetto-Leaves cover, 1873. Courtesy of Huntington Library, San Marino, CA.

36

Lift Every Voice and Sing

James Weldon Johnson's song for Jacksonville schoolchildren became an anthem for the ages.

Craig Pittman

ON A WARM AND WET September evening of 2021, the first football game of the year was about to start. The teams lined up on the field at Raymond James Stadium, each in their respective end zones—the Tampa Bay Buccaneers on one side, the Dallas Cowboys on the other.

Before the national anthem, they listened to a different song, one that some call the Black national anthem. It was a live rendition by the Florida A&M University's concert choir of "Lift Every Voice and Sing."

This was far from the first NFL game to feature the song. The NFL played an Alicia Keys recording of it before the start of all of its week 1 games during the 2020 season as well as ahead of Super Bowl LV and the draft in April.

The place where the anthem means the most, though, is Jacksonville, the Florida town where it was written and first performed more than a century ago.

> Lift every voice and sing
> Till earth and heaven ring
> Ring with the harmonies of Liberty . . .

The author of those stirring words was a Florida man, and a remarkable one.

The list of professions that James Weldon Johnson held is lengthy. The songwriter was also an educator, a novelist, a poet, a lawyer, a baseball pitcher, a diplomat, and a civil rights activist. And he did all that as a Black man navigating a post–Civil War world set up to extend white supremacy.

"He was a Renaissance man," says Liz McDonald McCoy, executive director at the Friends of James Weldon Johnson Park. Creating a park in his honor is one of the ways his native city has honored its most famous resident in recent years.

Johnson was born in 1871 in the Duval County town of La Villa, later annexed by Jacksonville. His father was the headwaiter at a hotel and pastor of a small church. His mother was the daughter of the first Black man elected to the Bahamian legislature, and she had become the vice principal of the segregated Stanton

Native Floridian **Craig Pittman** was an award-winning environmental reporter for the *Tampa Bay Times* for decades. He writes a weekly column for the *Florida Phoenix* and cohosts the popular *Welcome to Florida* podcast. He is the author of six books, including the *New York Times* bestseller *Oh, Florida! How America's Weirdest State Influences the Rest of the Country* and *The State You're In: Florida Men, Florida Women, and Other Wildlife*. In 2020 he was declared a Florida Literary Legend by the Florida Heritage Book Festival.

Finishing the lyrics gave him a feeling of "contentment—that sense of serene joy—which makes artistic creation the most complete of all human experiences."

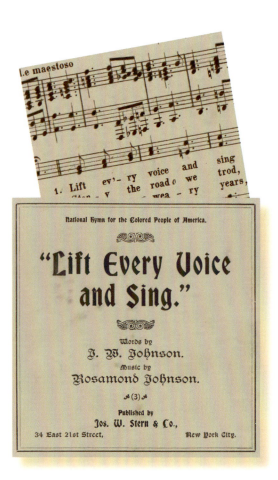

Sheet music for "Lift Every Voice and Sing," composed by J. Rosamond Johnson, with lyrics by James Weldon Johnson, [New York City: Jos. W. Stern & Co., ©, 1900] Notated Music. From the Library of Congress.

School. Johnson attended Stanton until he was sixteen. He had one brother, John Rosamond Johnson, whom he referred to by his middle name, and an adopted sister.

Johnson's father taught his children Spanish, which helped when a Cuban exchange student stayed with the family. When the teenaged Johnson took the train to Atlanta University, the exchange student went along. A conductor was ready to evict them from the "whites-only" section of the train until he heard them speaking Spanish to each other. That was Johnson's first encounter with racism.

In Atlanta, Johnson became a star pitcher for the university baseball team, a prize-winning orator, and a skilled woodworker. When he graduated, he was offered a scholarship to Harvard but turned it down to return to Jacksonville and become the principal of his alma mater. He pushed for the school to add high school classes, becoming the first high school in Florida to provide classes for Black students.

In 1895 he founded the *Daily American* newspaper, and in 1897, without ever setting foot in a law school, he passed the Florida Bar, becoming the first Black Floridian to do so.

Then, in 1900, for a celebration of Abraham Lincoln's birthday, he penned the inspirational poem "Lift Every Voice and Sing." His musically inclined brother, Rosamond, composed the tune to turn those lyrics into an anthem.

Johnson was not a fan of anthems. He often heard them in church, and even ones written by his brother stirred his dislike. In his 1933 autobiography, *Along This Way*, he joked that "it would not be gross injustice to give the composers of most anthems written for church choirs a light jail sentence for each offense." But this one was born of necessity.

Johnson was scheduled to give a speech for Lincoln's birthday. He thought about writing a poem about Lincoln, too. But he couldn't compose both in the short time before the ceremony, he confessed in his autobiography.

Then he had the idea of writing a song, to be sung by a Stanton children's choir. An anthem, in fact, with lyrics by him and music by his brother. The two had no great ambitions for the song, he wrote later. They regarded it as "an incidental effort, an effort made under stress and with no intention other than to meet the needs of a particular moment."

After that famous opening, which he judged "not a startling line," Johnson continued on "grinding out the next five." Then he came to the end of that stanza, where it says, "Sing a song full of the faith that our dark past has taught us / Sing a song full of the hope that the present has brought us."

At that point, he wrote later, "the spirit of the poem had taken hold of me."

He turned the first stanza over to his brother to compose the music while he kept going on the next two. As he paced back and forth, "I could not keep back the tears, and I made no effort to do so," Johnson wrote. "I was experiencing the transport of the poet's ecstasy."

James Weldon Johnson. Illustration by Winold Reiss. Courtesy of National Portrait Gallery, Smithsonian Institution; purchase funded by Lawrence A. Fleischman and Howard Garfinkle with a matching grant from the National Endowment for the Arts.

Finishing the lyrics gave him a feeling of "contentment—that sense of serene joy—which makes artistic creation the most complete of all human experiences."

Rosamond jotted down the musical score and then contacted a publisher he knew in New York to get it copyrighted and printed. Then the copies went to the children's choir members to memorize.

"A choir of 500 schoolchildren at the segregated Stanton School, where James Weldon Johnson was principal, first performed the song in public," the NAACP says on its website.

[The Johnson brothers] traveled to New York, where the pair composed hundreds of songs for Broadway shows.... They helped ignite the Harlem Renaissance that later would bring to prominence Zora Neale Hurston and Langston Hughes.

This should have been a time of triumph for both brothers. Instead, they soon left their native city, driven out by a near-death experience.

It happened in the wake of Jacksonville's Great Fire of 1901, explains Dr. Wayne Wood, historian-at-large for the Jacksonville Historical Society.

A spark from a small wood-burning stove caught some Spanish moss on fire as it dried outside a mattress factory. Over the next eight hours the blaze spread through 146 city blocks, destroying more than 2,000 buildings, killing seven people, and leaving almost 10,000 people homeless.

Johnson tried to convince the white firefighters to save the Stanton high school, Wood said. After all, the school was big enough to house Black families that were burned out of their homes. But the firefighters, looking dazed by the scope of the blaze, ignored his pleas and let the building burn, Wood says.

In the wake of the fire, Jacksonville had no civil authority. Instead, militias from all over the South converged on the city to impose martial law. Suddenly the city where Johnson was known and recognized, the city with a reputation for treating Blacks fairly, was a smoking ruin, and its streets were full of armed white strangers. They saw only his skin color.

A female journalist from the North came to visit the burned-out town. She had written a story about the fire and wanted Johnson's opinion about the piece. Johnson met with her in a riverfront park. She was Black but very light-skinned. Johnson's complexion was darker.

As they talked, Johnson wrote later, he became aware of men yelling and dogs snuffling around nearby. Uneasy, the pair got up and started back toward downtown, only to be stopped by armed men in uniform. A streetcar conductor had reported seeing Johnson, a Black man, consorting with what appeared to be a white woman.

"They seize me," Johnson wrote in his autobiography. "They tear my clothes and bruise my body, all the while calling to their comrades, 'We got 'im!'" Meanwhile, Johnson wrote, he could hear the crowd yelling things like, "Kill the Black son of a bitch!"

"As the rushing crowd comes yelling and cursing, I feel that death is bearing in upon me," Johnson wrote later.

Before he could become one of the 4,400 Black Americans who were lynched between 1877 and 1945, though, an officer intervened. He placed Johnson under arrest and took him to the provost marshal of the town. The provost marshal happened to be a member of the Florida Bar and recognized Johnson as a fellow attorney. He believed Johnson when he said the journalist was not legally white. He was released.

At first, Johnson was ecstatic about escaping his predicament. When he got home, the only person he told about what happened was his brother, who was horrified. Only then did Johnson fully appreciate the horror himself. The memory didn't recede after one night.

Atlanta University quartet, class of 1894. James Weldon Johnson is on the right. Courtesy of Jacksonville Historical Society.

"For weeks and months, the episode preyed on my mind and disturbed me in my sleep," he wrote. "Shortly after the happenings just related, Rosamond and I decided to get away from Jacksonville as quickly as possible."

They traveled to New York, where the pair composed hundreds of songs for Broadway shows. One of those songs, "Under the Banyan Tree," was performed forty years later by Judy Garland and Margaret O'Brien in the movie *Meet Me in St. Louis*. They helped ignite the Harlem Renaissance that later would bring to prominence Zora Neale Hurston and Langston Hughes.

Johnson became treasurer of the Colored Republican Club in New York and wrote songs that advocated for the election of his fellow New York Republican Teddy Roosevelt. That, according to Jacksonville activist and former senator Tony Hill, led Roosevelt, as president, to appoint Johnson as the United States' consul to Venezuela, in effect making him the ambassador. Three years later, Roosevelt's successor, William Howard Taft, named him to fill the same role in Nicaragua.

While he was a diplomat, Johnson married Grace Nail, the daughter of a wealthy Black real estate magnate from New York. "Her delicate patrician beauty stirred something in me that had never been touched before," he wrote of his first sight of her. After they wed, she learned Spanish and joined him in civil rights advocacy and served as a hostess for cultural gatherings in their home. They had no children. They remained a devoted couple until his death.

Diplomacy left him time to write, and in 1912 he published anonymously a provocative novel titled *The Autobiography of an Ex-Colored Man*. For its narrator, Johnson created a light-skinned biracial man who, after witnessing a lynching,

37

Jack Kerouac's Florida Farewell

He found a fertile place to work but no escape from his demons as his road reached its end.

Thomas Hallock

Thomas Hallock is professor of English and Florida studies at the University of South Florida, St. Petersburg campus. His publications include *William Bartram, the Search for Nature's Design: Selected Art, Letters, and Unpublished Manuscripts*, and most recently, *A Road Course in Early American Literature: Travel and Teaching from Atzlán to Amherst*. For more on his work with students recovering the early literature of Florida, go to EarlyFloridaLit.net.

Image: Photograph is in the Carol M. Highsmith Archive, Library of Congress, Prints and Photographs Division.

THE ST. PETERSBURG home at 5169 Tenth Avenue North sits empty. This brick-and-block ranch house, with low-slung ceilings to push through the central air conditioning, was the final dwelling of Massachusetts-born writer Jack Kerouac, "King of the Beats" and author of the celebrated novel *On the Road*. In November 1968, Kerouac returned to Florida with his new wife, Stella Sampas, and his aging mother, Gabrielle or Memère (*MAY-mare*), seeking asylum from another New England winter.

"Ti Jean" Kerouac (as he was known to family) packed an extraordinary amount of living into his forty-seven years. A printer's son from a tight-knit clan of French Canadian émigrés, he grew up in the factory town of Lowell, where he is buried. Kerouac attended Columbia University on scholarship for a year, dropped out, served as a merchant marine, wandered, and over a staggeringly productive two-decade spree, from 1950 to 1969, produced some two dozen books, including several volumes of poetry and his trademark autobiographical fiction. Florida fairly claims a major chunk of his work; he was in and out of Orlando and then St. Petersburg every few years, and his story in the Sunshine State is not just a tragic demise.

Kerouac settled into the St. Pete home late in his life, somewhere between snowbird and full-time resident, with hopes for artistic productivity.

The author squandered his final days in his living room nursing a favorite drink, scotch with a beer "wash." On October 20, 1969, he coughed up blood. Sensing his end, Kerouac dictated a peevish letter to his nephew, Paul Jr., speaking Quebecois to freeze out his Greek American wife and insisting that his estate remain in "my direct blood line." (Kerouac also had a daughter, Jan, from a brief marriage, whom he acknowledged only after a paternity test.) Early the next morning, at nearby St. Anthony's Hospital, the failing author died from esophageal hemorrhaging, what his biographer Gerald Nicosia calls "the classic drunkard's death."

Jack Kerouac, ready to take to the road, in Orlando, 1958. Kerouac and his mother moved to the area to be close to his sister, Caroline Blake. Courtesy of Florida Historical Society.

The Tenth Avenue North home, legally contested between families, is an aftermath of this shattered life. Initially the property passed on to Kerouac's mother, then to his wife, Stella, and then to his Sampas in-laws.

The estate remained mired in probate for decades as the sodden saga played out in courts. Meanwhile, Kerouac's ghost would continue to haunt St. Petersburg. His novels, some say, mysteriously fell off the shelves at a favorite bookstore, Haslam's, on St. Pete's Central Avenue. Fans called his telephone number, which stayed in the city directory until 1999. Mildew at the home crept around the toilets, critters

Jack Kerouac's Florida Farewell · 233

crawled through the soffits, and pilgrims broke in, leaving spent candles and cigarette butts. The estate's closest contact today lives in Greenwich, Connecticut, and somehow the overgrown yard still gets mowed.

Across Florida, Kerouac has left an ambivalent legacy. He and Memère actually held five Florida addresses, three in Orlando and two in St. Petersburg. In St. Pete, the 5169 Tenth Avenue North property piques either hometown pride or exasperation, depending who you ask.

For some, the author's death marks a local claim to fame; for others, the very name "Jack Kerouac" draws an eye roll, sharp rebuke, or exasperated sigh. His reputation polarizes. Kerouac was the chronicler of the Beat Generation, the boys' club of rebel-writers that included junkie-novelist William S. Burroughs (who shot his wife), poets Allen Ginsberg and Amiri Baraka, zen-naturalist Gary Snyder, and Lawrence Ferlinghetti (longtime owner of San Francisco's legendary City Lights Books). The Beats are credited for shaping the counterculture, a youth movement that Kerouac disavowed in slurred harangues.

College kids tracked him down in St. Petersburg, meanwhile, hoping to touch literary fame or more likely replicate the drunken sprees from his novels. Even after his death, visitors still came. Pilgrims left notes, until the mailbox itself disappeared. "Dear Jack," one admirer gushed, "your work is why I write and write to live."

The story of Kerouac's later years is historically hard to tell. Those seeking a fuller account might start with Orlando journalist Bob Kealing's book *Kerouac in Florida: Where the Road Ends*. The Sunshine State, Kealing demonstrates, loomed large in the last two decades of the author's life. Kerouac first moved to College Park, northwest of Orlando, in December 1956.

He had one novel behind him (the well-regarded but poor-selling *Town and the City*) and was making final changes to the book that brought him fame, *On the Road*.

Ti Jean and Memère squeezed into a brick saltbox in the Orlando suburbs, where his sister Caroline (or Nin) and his brother-in-law, Paul Blake, had moved. Paul, who moved to Florida to work in the burgeoning space industry, did not always welcome the ne'er-do-well author.

Jack Kerouac at work at his rental home in the College Park neighborhood of Orlando. Photographed in 1958 for *Time Magazine* by Orlando photographer Fred DeWitt. Photo courtesy of the Orange County Regional History Center.

Jack Kerouac's home in the College Park area of Orlando. The house where he wrote *The Dharma Bums* is now a writer's retreat. Photo by Maksim, WIKI.

But the Kerouacs remained formidably close, and Jack negotiated his place with family, constantly balancing steady contact alongside safe distance. "No writer ever traveled farther while staying so close to home," the critic Ann Douglas wryly observes. In July 1956 he and Memère settled into a sliced-up bungalow in Caroline's College Park neighborhood, at 1418 ½ Clouser Avenue.

The Clouser Avenue home, now a writer's retreat, is where Kerouac banged out *The Dharma Bums*. Fueled by backyard citrus and Mexican Benzedrine, working under a bare lightbulb on the back porch, he supposedly typed ten straight nights onto a 100-foot roll of teletype paper, following his usual free association of the "mind into limitless blow-on-subject seas of thought."

The Dharma Bums chronicles his explorations of western mountains and Buddhism with Gary Snyder, or "Japhy Ryder," though little in the novel betrays that at the time of writing Kerouac was actually in a rundown Orlando bungalow.

Florida remains invisible, though the Clouser Avenue apartment clearly served as his space apart, the retreat; nearly every one of the novel's thirty-four chapters sounds out a theme of artistic isolation. The narrator, Raymond Smith, longs for a mountain cave, a camp in the High Sierras, or "little temples hidden and forgotten," where the monastic writer can "take off by himself to live purely and true to himself."

That cave or mountain camp or hidden temple was Florida, his respite from the "mad sick sniffling" cities up north. Kerouac was rambling throughout North America during the 1960s, from New York to Berkeley to Mexico City, and four years after *The Dharma Bums*, his remarkable Orlando run continued. This time he set himself up in Kingswood Manor, a subdivision four miles from the Blakes in College Park.

Jack Kerouac's Florida Farewell • 235

Working nights in his bedroom of the new one-story ranch home, Kerouac took advantage of the "Florida peace" to polish off another major work, *Big Sur*. Set in northern California, *Big Sur* is rightly recognized for its evocative descriptions of Pacific fog and the twenty-two-page tone poem "Sea," which closes the novel. But it was the air-conditioned ranch house in Kingswood Manor, not the romanticized cabin on the Pacific, where the book got done.

Kerouac's Florida can be difficult to locate. He never wrote about the Sunshine State directly (except in letters), and he refused commissions to pen travel essays about the usual tourist destinations. His correspondence grouses about his isolation in Orlando and the "heatwave horror" of August. Friends repeatedly ignored his invitations to visit, to sunbathe on his back patio in early spring or grill steaks outdoors.

Amidst this same suburban self-exile, meanwhile, the lonely Kerouac would churn out roughly one-quarter of his fiction. "Dreary" and "DEAD," pre-Disney Orlando provided the solitude he needed to tinker with or finish up several well-known books, including *Desolation Angels*, *The Subterraneans*, and of course, *On the Road*. In St. Petersburg, where he lived on and off from 1964 to his death, Kerouac also dashed off *Satori in Paris* (a brilliant if flawed novella, diseased by alcoholism) and his piecemeal, posthumous publication, *Pic*.

Taking the author at his word, critics have downplayed the importance of the Sunshine State to Kerouac's literary output. The word "Florida" remains missing from most scholarly studies. Why?

The problem lies in how readers—popular and academic—approach him. Kerouac epitomizes the rebel traveler, riding the rails or hitchhiking from New York to San Francisco, tripping off to Mexico and Tangiers for wild adventures. Because the parties never seem to end in a Kerouac novel, we overlook the writer at work, sweating through drafts (or badgering his agent, the venerable Sterling Lord) from the bland comfort of a suburban block home.

Biographers especially paint his tight Quebecois family as an impediment to literary life. In this clichéd portrait, Memère comes off as a maternal buzz-kill, as a block, or Oedipal trap. Scholarship on the Beat Generation (like Kerouac himself) has never quite grown up. Discussions of the family are glaringly dismissive. Gabrielle Kerouac was "determined to hang onto Jack," the critic Gerald Nicosia opines, "even if she had to strangle him with kid gloves." Nicosia overlooks the extent to which this "strangled" artist depended upon Memère for emotional survival. The mother, in turn, protected her emotionally imbalanced son, also ensuring his productivity by providing a quiet, safe nest.

To recover the gaps in the story of Jack Kerouac's Florida we must explore two cities, Orlando and St. Pete, as well as two sides of a manic personality—the exacting artist and verbally abusive alcoholic. Despite the many addresses, today only

Working nights in his bedroom of the new one-story ranch home, Kerouac took advantage of the "Florida peace" to polish off another major work, Big Sur.

two homes are associated with his name. The first, the bungalow on Clouser Avenue, has settled into its niche as a writer's retreat. And the second, 5169 Tenth Avenue North in St. Petersburg, remains mired in court cases and a tainted legacy.

I managed to sneak in a visit to the Orlando house on Clouser Avenue in March 2020, shortly before the Covid-19 virus shut down all travel. The little bungalow, previously a "roach-infested hovel" (by Kealing's account) is now painted a tasteful light gray with misty blue trim. Holding down the corner lot in a gentrifying neighborhood, the home thrives as a writer's retreat. Certainly the neighborhood has changed. Most of the citrus is gone; a letter from Memère counts "9 orange trees, five grapefruit trees and 4 tangerines." But an ancient live oak still shelters the modest cottage, which holds the character of an older Florida, and Kerouac's tattered easy chair, donated by the Sampas family, reigns over the back room, where *The Dharma Bums* was created.

What succeeds in Orlando has struggled in St. Petersburg. Since 2013, volunteers with St. Pete's Friends of the Kerouac House have cooperated with the estate, hoping to establish a similar writer's retreat at 5169 Tenth Avenue North, the author's last home. He and Memère moved there in 1968, next door to their previous property, in what was his final north-south bounce. With early optimism, Kerouac set his rolltop desk in one of the home's three bedrooms and for privacy had a backyard weave fence installed. "I've got my office-bedroom all fixed up and tho it's small it's cozy," he explained to his friend Joe Caput. "I'se satisfied."

Jack Kerouac in Orlando. The author sits outside with his cat at his College Park house, where he lived in 1957–58, during the time *On The Road* was published. Photo by Fred DeWitt, courtesy of the Orange County Regional History Center.

The Yankee-*Quebecois* transplant could not get enough of mild Florida nights: "I can step out this very second into the moonlight piney tree night where my cats are already making girls."

But Kerouac could never turn away from a bender, and despite initial hopes for fruitful isolation, students from "Southern Florida U." (or University of South Florida) found him out. Kerouac fell into old habits, trading the hard work over his typewriter for show-off "belly busting" and barstool rants.

While writing *Pic*, his novel from the perspective of an African American boy, he got beat up at the Cactus Bar on racially divided St. Petersburg's Black side. Strangers cracked his ribs, and the belligerent author went to jail, bailed out by his mother for $25. One month later, the "King of the Beats" was dead.

Despite this tragic end, celebrations of Kerouac's legacy in St. Petersburg have never distanced themselves from alcohol. St. Pete's Friends of the Kerouac House commemorates his life twice yearly at the Flamingo Bar, one of several bay-area watering holes where he could be found. (Fundraisers at the smoky Flamingo Bar support maintenance for the Tenth Avenue North property.) A mural of the author covers the bar's south wall, and the owner preserves a small stash of memorabilia. For $2.50 fans can squat on Jack's favorite stool and throw down the "Kerouac special," a shot of Canadian Club with a beer "wash."

The accounts of Kerouac's drunken behavior from his own lifetime, however, suggest nothing to celebrate. "Sweet and tentative when sober," novelist John Clellon Holmes wrote, he grew "truculent, paranoic, garrulous, stiff-jointed, wild-eyed, exhaustless, and amnesiac when drunk."

This unheroic demise, perhaps, should raise questions about how Floridians honor a problematic legacy today. Can we come to terms with Kerouac? Scenes of open sex in *The Dharma Bums*, while celebrated in the 1960s, can raise hackles for #MeToo readers. Japhy Ryder has "a hard time convincing" his "favorite doll Psyche" to make love, a cringe-inducing passage explains, but "once she got drinking she couldn't stop."

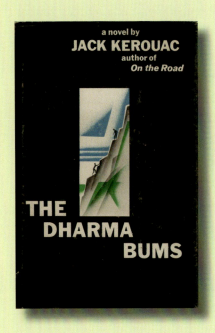

Footnotes in the biography are jarring. While in Orlando, as Kerouac's nephew Paul Jr. recounted to the biographer Nicosia, the two of them burned a makeshift cross outside the Black community of Eatonville. Paul would later say, "We almost did" that; still, only a naïve apologist can dismiss such episodes as outliers.

When I come across anti-Semitism in his letters, I wonder how a Jewish friend like Allen Ginsberg could still speak fondly of him. And how do we recognize the alcoholism, which was tantamount to suicide? A devout Catholic with unbreakable family bonds, Kerouac knowingly drank himself to death. So do I lay my $2.50 on the bar for a Kerouac Special?

His tombstone back in Massachusetts reads, "He honored life."

So how to honor that life? Rather than celebrating an author's tragic slide, I prefer to think about the work. The body went back to New England, not to mention most of his stuff, with Florida left as the place where Jack Kerouac came to die.

We get redeeming pockets of productivity. In spring 1965, at his first Tenth Avenue North home, Kerouac prepared for a journey to France, where he would track down his family name. The alcoholic had momentarily sobered up.

Athletic in his writing method, he used exercise to coax his brain back into shape. He was doing thirty push-ups daily and practicing handstands. In June he popped by the offices of St. Petersburg's *Evening Independent*, where he dashed off stories for the sports page, rightly predicting the Detroit Tigers to take the American League pennant and pegging a young slugger named Hank Aaron as our "greatest living ballplayer." One month later the part-time sports columnist was back with the *Independent*, this time commenting on Muhammad Ali's knock-out of heavyweight Sonny Liston: "Boxing matches are sad, and everything is sad anyhow," the story poignantly closed, "till that day when the Lion lays down with the Lamb."

238 · Thomas Hallock

The final home of Jack Kerouac, in St. Petersburg. Photo by Florida Humanities.

For brief moments in 1965, Kerouac recaptured his old form. That May, the *New York Review of Book*s reviewed his latest novel, *Desolation Angels*. The issue included a caricature by David Levine, who portrayed the King of the Beats in tattered pants, with a shock of black hair across his handsome face, and hobo stick angled for new adventure.

Soon afterward he journeyed to Normandy. Kerouac was forced to cut this trip short (brandy swallowed up his savings), but upon his return he sat down and typed up his "rare little hunk" of a novel, *Satori in Paris*.

Almost anyone who has ever followed Jack Kerouac indulges some vision of the author. As our conversations in America about gender, race, religion, and mental health continue to unfold, he remains someone with whom we should come to terms. I like to think of Kerouac in St. Pete that summer of '65, sober and moving in a new direction. This point in time helps me see beyond the suicide sips of whiskey and barstool rants. I like to think about the productivity and focus that a serious artist once found in my adopted home state. No one can write with the "delicious freedom and abandonment who has not practiced severe discipline," the novelist Henry Miller observed of *The Dharma Bums*.

Kerouac's Florida is a story about "playing the trade and never giving up," Kealing maintains. We might honor the "practicing" wordsmith rather than the fatalistic drunk, the disciplined artist who momentarily kept his demons at bay to push through another book, following the sacred calling of his craft. Florida was not just the "end of the road" for Jack Kerouac. It was where he worked.

From the **Summer 2020** edition of *FORUM* magazine, "Lights, Camera . . . Florida: How TV—and 100 Years of Filmmaking Here—Have Shaped Our Image."

38 Muse over Miami

How a hopeless kid from New Jersey became South Florida's "Queen of Crime."

Edna Buchanan

A police reporter for the *Miami Herald* for eighteen years, **Edna Buchanan** won the Pulitzer Prize in 1986. She went on to write eighteen books, including a fictional series about an intrepid Miami reporter and nonfiction accounts that include her best-selling true-crime memoir, *The Corpse Had a Familiar Face* (Random House, 1987). The *Los Angeles Times* dubbed her the "queen of crime." Buchanan was the 2017 recipient of Florida Humanities Lifetime Achievement Award for Writing. This story is based on her acceptance speech.

AT AGE FOUR I told everyone I would write books when I grew up. I was hooked on the stories my mother read to me. When she became too busy, I wandered the neighborhood, book in hand, and asked strangers to read to me. They were all too busy, even the mailman. So I decided I had to learn to read. Fast.

My textbooks were the newspapers my father read for the race results. I'd carry them down the street and read news stories to my grandmother at her kitchen table. She could not read English and was always shocked by the content. We lived in north Jersey, where I spent all my nickels on the *New York Daily News*, *Mirror*, and the *Journal American.* That is where I met the dark heroes of my childhood. Eagerly I followed the careers of Willie (the Actor) Sutton, the Babe Ruth of bank robbers; George Metesky, the mad bomber who terrorized New York; and Lucky Luciano, the man who organized the mob. Years later I interviewed two of them.

My goal: fiction. It was not easy. My mother was seventeen when I was born. My father took off forever when I was seven. Nearsighted and clumsy, I didn't mingle with other kids because my mom worked two jobs and I took care of everything else. I wore hand-me-downs that coworkers gave to my mother. I was laughed at, with good reason, and hated school.

An elementary school math teacher said, in front of the entire class, that I'd be nothing, not even a good housewife, since I'd be unable to count my change at the supermarket or measure ingredients for a recipe. I was so humiliated I never forgot her words. But recipes are not my strong suit, and I *never* count my change at the supermarket. I use credit cards.

Two gifts brightened my childhood: reading, and my seventh-grade English teacher, Mrs. Tunis. She said, in front of the entire class, that I could write, and asked the question that changed my life, forever: "Will you promise to dedicate a book to me someday?"

That triggered my eleven-year-old mind, and I began trying to sell short stories to the *Saturday Evening Post*. I showed Mrs. Tunis my first rejection slip and asked

> *I showed Mrs. Tunis my first rejection slip and asked why they didn't buy my story. She explained that it would be the first of many rejections but that I should never, ever give up, because someday I would write books. She was right.*

why they didn't buy my story. She explained that it would be the first of many rejections but that I should never, *ever* give up, because someday I *would* write books. She was right.

The Corpse Had a Familiar Face, published in 1987, was dedicated to Mrs. Tunis. She never knew. She died at forty-eight, when I was in the eighth grade. But Mrs. Tunis is still alive to me and always will be.

We moved frequently; I changed schools often. The summer I was twelve, I worked in a sweatshop, a coat factory where my mother operated a sewing machine. My job was to turn the long, fuzzy winter coats right side out after they'd been sewn together. Fuzz and lint swirled all around me.

When my mom felt too exhausted to report to her midnight shift, I'd go instead. I worked in a candle factory and an all-night sandwich shop. No one objected. At sixteen, I was old enough to sell socks at Woolworth's and baby clothes at W. T. Grant—and work as a telephone solicitor for a department store's photo studio,

Edna Buchanan with typewriter.
Courtesy of Edna Buchanan.

Muse over Miami • 241

selling parents on annual portraits of their growing children. I also worked at a dry cleaner's shop and as the world's worst waitress.

At eighteen, I became the youngest employee and union member at a Western Electric plant where I wired and soldered switchboards. What a gift to work with so many diverse and experienced people, listen to their stories, and share their lives! I learned far more about real life and human nature than anyone ever could in a classroom.

For my first week of paid vacation, I went to Miami Beach, took one look, and burst into tears. The sudden revelation was an emotional experience. I'd been born in the wrong place! That is what was always wrong with me! But now, home at last, I'd left behind the gritty black-and-white newsreel that was my life and stepped into Technicolor and CinemaScope where my future waited.

I began to job-hunt, joined a creative writing class at a local college, and could-not-stop-writing. The words flowed like a wild, rushing stream. Someone suggested I be a reporter. Great idea, I thought: I can report the news by day and work on the great American novel at night! Little did I know that daily journalism is a whirlwind that leaves no time to read a book, much less write one. I called the *Miami Herald*, one of the nation's best newspapers, to inquire about a job. The reply: "Unless you have a degree in journalism or five years' experience on a daily newspaper—don't bother."

So I applied at the *Sun*, a small Miami Beach daily. The editor had me rewrite a press release, then asked if I had a journalism degree. "No." Did I ever work for a newspaper? "No." Did I write for my high school paper? What? My school had no newspaper. My heart sank. Then he asked when I could start. "Now," I said. He shook my hand heartily. "Congratulations! Now you're a journalist!"

Isn't there a lot more to it than that? I wondered. The pay was lousy, but I loved it! I learned how to make up and lay out pages, set hot type, and read upside down, which came in handy later. The sole reporter for months on end, it was up to me to fill the paper each day. I interviewed Frank Sinatra, Joan Crawford, and Ray Milland; covered politics when Elliot Roosevelt was mayor; loved municipal court and the police beat; wrote a column; picked the horse and dog race winners for the sports department; wrote obits; covered tragedy, comedy, heroes; and sometimes, when no one else did, I wrote the Letters to the Editor. I started at 7 a.m. each day, often worked until 1 a.m., and learned to always fill my notebook with stories.

Once, at 2 a.m., hungry and exhausted, I slumped wearily over my typewriter. My editor waved his arms, cheered me on. "One more story! One more story!" I sighed, opened my notebook, and found one more story. I interviewed intrepid senior citizens whom I grew to love, learned to shoot pictures to illustrate my stories, and *always* took more notes than necessary. I rewrote and sold some of those stories to magazines. What a fabulous education. And they *paid me*!

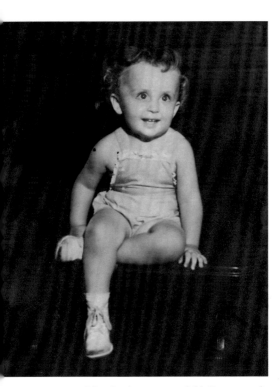

Edna Buchanan as a child. Courtesy of Edna Buchanan.

The *Herald* Years

Miami skyline at twilight. Photo by Bryan Katz.

Five years later, it crashed. A politician bought the paper to promote himself, then sold it to a buyer who only wanted to eliminate competition. I'd need a job soon and recalled the *Herald*'s chilly response years earlier. The paper was giant, but I knew the editors were aware that I existed because I'd won a number of press awards at the *Sun*, and they often assigned ace reporters to follow my stories. I plucked an editor's name from the masthead and gave it a shot.

Editors love brevity. My letter was just four sentences: "Five years ago I called the *Herald* to apply for a job as a reporter. I was told not to bother unless I had a degree in journalism or five years' experience on a daily paper. As of Aug. 14th, I have had five years' experience at the *Miami Beach Daily Sun*. How about it?"

A day later my phone rang with an invitation to a series of tests and interviews, one of them with the *Herald* shrink. "Do you ever have any irresistible impulses you find difficult to control?" His voice had a peculiar edge. I had to give him something.

"Yes." I averted my eyes.

He leaned forward, intense. "Tell me about it."

I sighed. "At least twice a week, I drive to a Dairy Queen for a Hawaiian Isle sundae with pineapple and coconut. I can't help myself." That was the best I could do on short notice. It was even true. Weeks went by. I heard nothing. The *Sun* building and presses were sold, the paper about to fold. The decision had been left to *Herald* city editor Steve Rogers. "Dear Mr. Rogers," my new letter began. The remainder was just one word in the center of the page. "Obits?"

A day later, he called to ask when I could start. Heart pounding, I told him, then said goodbye. "Wait!" he cried. "Haven't you forgotten something?" Bewildered, I had no clue. "Salary," he said, "you haven't asked me the salary!"

The *Herald* years were incredible. Who knew that the hopeless kid who'd lived in a rickety tenement, a rat-infested fire trap in Paterson, NJ, would go on to cover more than 5,000 violent deaths, 3,000 of them homicides, cover paradise lost, the cocaine cowboys, riots, and America's highest murder rate. Or that some of my stories would result in changes to Florida law or that I would win the Pulitzer Prize, the George Polk award, and scores of others; or be invited to the White House by Laura Bush; or lecture at newspapers, colleges, and journalism schools, even Columbia; or be profiled in the *New Yorker* by writer Calvin Trillin.

In 1981 we broke all records with 637 murders. I covered them all. My editors were not pleased. They told me to cover only "the *major* murder of the day." I understood but pretended not to. How do you *select* the major murder of the day? Every murder is major to the victim. They all wanted to live as much as we do. We're all in trouble when victims become mere statistics. I believed it was vital to report them all, all of their stories, in the newspaper of record, in black and white, where they would live in our consciousness forever.

Caught up in that whirlwind of violence, all I remember is going to murder scene after murder scene after murder scene. Numb and shell-shocked, I did it. I got them all in the newspaper.

My first trip to the morgue left me indignant, my consciousness raised by the plight of the downtrodden, the little guy pushed around, the victim of injustice. Death too soon at any age is an injustice. Who can be more downtrodden or pushed around than that? I wanted to know all their stories, what went wrong, why they were there.

I did things I never dreamed I could do—and never felt afraid, even when I should have. I was on a mission for the *Herald*, my deadline approaching like an avalanche. Nobody loves a police reporter. I've been threatened with arrest; had rocks thrown at me; guns pointed at me; and got threatening letters, subpoenas, and obscene phone calls, some of them from my editors.

When it was tough, I'd tell myself, "Mrs. Tunis said you could do it." And then I did. If she hadn't died young, if she were alive today, she probably wouldn't remember *me.* But I remember her. And that's what counts. In this vast tapestry that is life, some small thing we do, even a few words, can touch others, even change lives. The act of one person may resonate for years to come. We all can be somebody's Mrs. Tunis.

I know now, more than ever, how lucky I was to be a journalist. There is something noble and exciting about venturing out each day to seek the truth.

> *The police beat is all about life and death and what makes people become heroes or homicidal maniacs. It's all there: greed, sex, violence, comedy, and tragedy. Shakespeare in the raw.*

The police beat is all about life and death and what makes people become heroes or homicidal maniacs. It's all there: greed, sex, violence, comedy, and tragedy. Shakespeare in the raw. Every day I met Othello, Romeo and Juliet, Hamlet, or King Lear. On some bad days, I met them all. Sometimes you can reach out. One of the joys of journalism is that reporters are among the few people left in the world who can be catalysts for change, who can often bring about justice in cases where it would never triumph otherwise.

Learning to Play the "Tuba"

AFTER THE PULITZER, I decided to pursue my goal since age four and write my novel. An editor at a major New York publishing house wanted me to write a book, a nonfiction account of covering crime in Miami. But I wanted to write a novel. He declined and explained, "You have to have serious doubts when someone known for playing the violin suddenly announces plans to play the tuba."

But it wasn't sudden. It was my lifelong goal. I persisted. Doubtfully, he compromised. I wrote the book he wanted, then my novel. At last! Exhilarated, I began, but struggled, kept turning to my notebook, but it wasn't there. My heart sank. What if I couldn't play this tuba? But then, something happened! In the middle of chapter three my characters suddenly sprang to life, began to do things I never

244 · Edna Buchanan

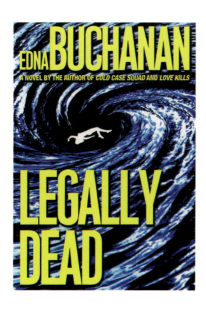

intended or even dreamed of. A few became aggressive, tried to take over the book. I had to promise one that he would return as a major character in a future novel. He became the dying detective in *Miami, It's Murder*, which was nominated for an Edgar, as was the first novel. My characters still whisper in my ear, seek attention, and demand to be heard.

Another reward for a life in journalism is your readers. They'd call, write, show up in the *Herald* newsroom, never fail to respond. Together, the good readers and I found missing persons; identified nameless, unclaimed corpses; brought home missing children; and helped solve many crimes. Half a million motivated readers can be far more effective than overwhelmed police. What a wonderful partnership! It's similar with novels, minus the instant gratification. It takes longer and is lonelier. But interacting with readers is pure joy.

Here are a few helpful thoughts for those who work at home alone, like me, and for everyone else as well. First, find your passion. Never give up the dream. Find your true home, the place where you belong. Learn everything you can about people, both good and evil. It's healthy for us all and the mother lode for writers.

Be brave. Follow your intuition, your gut feeling, that still, small voice, whatever you choose to call it. But never ignore it.

Other insights gained over the years: there is no one better than a good cop and no one worse than a bad cop. Sometimes they are the same cop, even on the same day. Their chief problem is that they must be recruited from the human race.

Real news should mirror real life. Every life matters.

And, of course, the three cardinal rules for a writer: *never* trust an editor, never *trust* an editor, and never trust an *editor*.

As for me, I still love to write fiction. But I still feel more comfortable knocking on a stranger's door to ask if he murdered his wife than I do making small talk at luncheons or parties with the literary set.

From the **Fall 2017** edition of *FORUM* magazine, "Florida through the Eyes of Its Writers, Artists, and Cultural Guides."

39 Once Upon a Time in Key West

Writer Philip Caputo laments what's been lost and what still stirs his soul.

Philip Caputo

Philip Caputo, a native of Chicago, began sampling exotic living spaces in the 1960s, at government expense. Later, as a writer, he covered Rome and Moscow, along with wars in Vietnam, the Middle East, and Ethiopia. The author of *Horn of Africa, Rumor of War,* and *Del Corso's Gallery,* he has won a boatload of prizes, including the Pulitzer.

Image: A typical conch house in Key West, with jacaranda, 2006. Photo by Dale M. McDonald, courtesy of State Archives of Florida, Florida Memory.

WHAT DREW ME TO Key West, and what holds me here, when, theoretically, I have the freedom to live anywhere I choose?

I think I can best answer that by giving some of the reasons why I don't live here and by listing a few of the things I dislike about life in Key West—the downside of paradise, so to speak. First of all, I did not move here and don't stay here because, as has been suggested recently, I am seeking to become the new Hemingway. I would be lying if I were to deny that I am flattered that some people regard me as heir to his "mantle," but I wish to stress that that is not my self-image. I do not compare with him, in terms of either physical or literary stature, and if I were to attempt to take his place, the world would find me a pint-sized Papa indeed.

Secondly, I don't live in Key West because of the quality of its politics and government services. We pay among the highest utility rates in the country and get for our money dirty drinking water and electrical power that frequently fails, while some of our streets and sidewalks resemble Stalingrad in 1944.

Thirdly—and this may surprise some—I'm not here for the climate. The weather in the Florida Keys is delightful from roughly December to March. After that, it starts to get as hot as Bangkok, and by August and September the air envelops you like a damp sandwich bag.

Finally, I don't live here because Key West has become—oh dreadful phrase—a literary colony. Termites, ants, and other insects flourish in colonies, but writers, in my opinion, suffer if they spend too much time in each other's company. Literary

Editor's note: This work was originally presented as a talk during "Writers and Key West," the Fifth Annual Key West Literary Seminar and Tour, partially funded by Florida Endowment for the Humanities, now Florida Humanities. Philip Caputo lived in Key West between 1977 and 1988. He currently lives in Norwalk, Connecticut, and Patagonia, Arizona.

Key West, circa 1849. This daguerreotype is one of the oldest photographs of Florida. It was likely taken from an observation tower or rooftop on the northwest side of Key West near the corner of Front and Whitehead Streets. The image is reversed. Courtesy of State Archives of Florida, Florida Memory.

friendships are important because writing is a solitary, at times a depressingly lonely, occupation, combining the worst aspects of sheepherding and monasticism. The cloistered, isolated struggle with language and character can drive even a stable personality half insane.

The temptation to immerse oneself in the doings of the so-called glitterati is powerful, but long rounds of dinner and cocktail parties can be harmful to the writer's waistline, liver, and, most important, his or her work.

Writers, at least those who are prose artists, are not abstract expressionists. They paint from life. If they start surrounding themselves with too many other writers, inevitably they will begin writing for their friends and not for their audience, producing the kind of arid, claustrophobic stuff currently being published by graduates of creative writing programs who sound as if they are trying to get an A-plus instead of their readers' attention.

Once Upon a Time in Key West · 247

Sun setting beyond docked shrimp boats in Key West, 1973. Photo by Dale M. McDonald, courtesy of State Archives of Florida, Florida Memory.

Characters of the Keys. Carvings of ship's captains, mariners, and a pirate, Key West, undated, between 1980 and 2006. Photo by Carol Highsmith, Photographs in the Carol M. Highsmith Archive, Library of Congress, Prints and Photographs Division.

In fact, Key West's lack of literary self-consciousness was among the things that attracted me when I first visited the island eleven years ago. Despite the living presence of Tennessee Williams and the lingering one of Hemingway's ghost, the island was not seen as, unfortunately, it now seems to be, the Hamptons with palm trees. To quote a close friend of mine, a local saloon keeper named Vic Latham, Key West in those days was "permissive without being faddy, creative without being trendy."

In those days. I sound as if I am speaking about the distant past. But Key West has changed so drastically in the past few years that the mid-1970s do indeed have an antique patina when I look back upon them from the present. The island was then in transition from a remote Navy and fishing town into the tourist mecca it is today. It had a stronger grip on its maritime heritage and lived up to its reputation as a salty, raffish, sinful seaport at the ragged edge of North America.

At the foot of Caroline Street, where there is today a yachtsman's marina, shrimp boats used to dock in such numbers you could almost cross the harbor by hopping from one deck to the next. The boats and their crews came from all over. When the fleet put in to unload their cargoes of "pink gold" or to ride out a norther, you could hear the skippers and deckhands speaking in the twangs of Georgia accents of the coastal Carolinas, in Louisiana Creole and the harsh drawls of the Texas Gulf coast. After long, dangerous weeks at sea, the shrimpers hit town with money in their pockets and big thirsts in their throats and did what seamen have done in port ever since the Phoenicians—raised holy hell. The more respectable, usually the captains, would go to a now-defunct bar called the Big Fleet and clog dance with their ladies to fiddles screeching "The Orange Blossom Special." The deckhands and rigmen got drunk, shot pool—and now and then each other—in dingy waterfront dives like the Mascot Lounge or in saloons like the Boat Bar and the West Key, the latter a topless joint that was closed after an irate stripper set it on fire in a wage dispute with her boss.

Shrimpers were not the only people on the island who earned their livelihoods from the sea. There were the lobstermen, many of them Cuban refugees whose boats bore lovely women's names such as *Dona Elena* and *The Maria Rosanna*. They gave a foreign flavor to Key West as they spoke in guttural Spanish at the docks, crowded with their faded traps and colorful marker pots. There were grizzled charter captains who had fished, or said they had, with Hemingway and Ted Williams: commercial hook-and-liners who would put to sea in yellow slickers when the nor'easters started blowing, pushing the immense schools of king mackerel southward to warmer waters.

There was also another class of seafarer, a colorful though criminal lot—the contrabandistas, drug smugglers, and gun runners who are direct spiritual descendants of the pirates, wreckers, and rum runners who had given Key West its outlaw reputation. I suppose it would be improper for me to stand here and speak fondly of dope smugglers; I'm not speaking of heroin traffickers or crack dealers, but marijuana smugglers, a less malignant lot.

Schooner Wharf Bar at the Key West Bight, Key West, circa 1990. Photo by Dale M. McDonald, courtesy of State Archives of Florida, Florida Memory.

The rough-and-tumble boat bar is now a hairdressing salon, and many of the other sailors' watering holes have been shut down, torn down, or tarted up in pastels and transformed into boutiques and T-shirt shops catering to the cruise ship trade.

But I found myself drawn to those renegades possibly because, to paraphrase something my friend Tom Sanchez once said, there is an element of the renegade in the writer, the contrabandista of the mind and heart, bootlegging forbidden thoughts and emotions into the reader's living room. I also admired the smugglers for the risks they took and for their skills as seamen. I met one of these high-seas brigands after he had single-handedly sailed an 85-foot Baltic trader from Belize to Key West. I don't want to romanticize these people, so I'll put it this way: if I am going to share a drink and conversation with a crook, I prefer the company of a man who can run through a hole in the reef at night without running lights to that of a yuppie plotting a securities swindle in a New York fern bar. Besides contrabanders, Key West also attracted (and still attracts) other kinds of social outlaws: rebels and runaways and refugees from middle America.

They were—are—in someone's phrase, the kind of people who led lives other people made movies about. "B" grade movies, but so what? That beautiful cocktail waitress you saw the other night used to be a career woman, and now she's in flight from a broken love affair or a bad marriage. Disbarred lawyers, quack physicians on the lam from malpractice suits, aging hippies, winos, heirs and heiresses, petty gamblers, macho fishermen, and gays—all were crammed together on ten square miles of marl and mangrove alongside the native conchs whose families had been in the Keys for six generations.

Though these disparate elements occasionally had their frictions, they managed to live together in more harmony than you would imagine, providing a stimulating environment for a young writer: a fascinating and varied human pageant. Daily life had a sense of adventure, by which I mean a feeling that the unexpected or the

Once Upon a Time in Key West • 249

Key West writing community, mid-1980s. Standing (*left to right*) are James Merrill, Evan Rhodes, Edward Howard, Alison Lurie, Shel Silverstein, William H. Manville, Joseph P. Lash, Arnold Sungaard, John Williams, Richard Wilbur, and James Boatwright. Seated are Susan Nadler, Thomas McGuane, William Wright, John Ciarda, David Kaufelt, Philip Caputo, Philip Burton, and John Malcolm Brennin. Photo by Don Kincaid. Courtesy of Key West Art and Historical Society, object ID 0000.00.1034.

unusual might happen at any moment; that you might meet a personality to whom you would not have spoken a word in a large city or in an average small town; that you might find yourself doing something you would not have done anywhere else.

I recall the morning eight years ago when I was having breakfast in my kitchen and Mel Fisher, discoverer of the *Atocha* treasure, came to my front door. One of his vessels had broken down, and he wanted to know if he could borrow my fishing boat. I replied that it wasn't suitable for such an expedition. Fine, said Fisher, if he could not borrow my boat, could he borrow me for a day or two?

He was short-handed and needed someone to toss marker buoys in waters he had just begun to explore for the *Atocha*'s gold, silver, and jewels. Off I went. Only in Key West could a man come to your door at breakfast time and ask you to help him in search for the treasures of the Spanish Main.

I am nostalgic for those times. The atmosphere of those freewheeling days has not entirely vanished, but it is vanishing rapidly. The shrimpers and lobstermen and outcasts are still here, but most of them now work out of adjacent Stock Island, which has become a blue-collar ghetto for an increasingly chic Key West. The raucous seaport is getting more and more respectable, turning away from the Caribbean northward to such places as Fort Lauderdale for its cues.

Much of the natural environment in the Keys has been devastated by greedy land developers and the short-sighted public officials who give them a free hand to do whatever they choose, which is to build huge condominiums and resort hotels. The raunchy deckhands who used to swagger off the shrimp boats, then stagger back, are being replaced by condo commandos and tourists garbed in Hawaiian shirts and armed with golf clubs. Most of the contrabandistas are dead or in jail, which, I suppose, is where most people want them. Hundreds of local conchs, Cubans and whites and Blacks of Bahamian descent, have had to flee skyrocketing living costs for the mainland and farther north. Lost with them is much of the island culture that made life here as rich and piquant as a Caribbean sauce.

The rough-and-tumble boat bar is now a hairdressing salon, and many of the other sailors' watering holes have been shut down, torn down, or tarted up in pastels and transformed into boutiques and T-shirt shops catering to the cruise ship trade, and it's sad and disturbing to hear the merchants in these establishments speak about their customers the way prostitutes do about their johns. I don't think Key West is in imminent danger of becoming a tropical Aspen, but I for one will not be unhappy if I never see again a sign that announces "Coming soon on this site! The Osprey's Nest! A new concept in time-share living! Own your piece of paradise for only $100,000 down!"

What, then, holds me here, to this fly-speck of land in the ocean, this coral rock at the end of the road? To quote from an article I wrote for *Esquire* magazine, most of my reasons for living in Key West are not on the island, but off it at sea. I love the sea. I love the smell of it, whether it's the scent of a salty tradewind or the rankness of low tide. I love to look at it, for it is always different yet always the same,

Strand Theater, Key West, undated, between 1980 and 2006, Photo by Carol Highsmith, Photographs in the Carol M. Highsmith Archive, Library of Congress, Prints and Photographs Division.

Aerial view of Ballast, Woman, and Boca Grande Key, 1968. Photo by Cory McDonald, courtesy of State Archives of Florida, Florida Memory.

providing at once both diversity and constancy. I love to walk along it in the early mornings and watch the sandpipers feeding along the shore, the royal terns wheeling above. I love to fish on it, sail on it, swim in it.

A short boat ride in any direction from Key West will take you to an entirely different world, far from the glitzy condos and discos and streets jammed with recreational vehicles. Due south a mere fifteen miles is the Gulf Stream, the mighty blue river in the ocean home to giant marlin and hammerhead sharks weighing half a ton. Westward are the wild Marquesas Keys, an atoll of mangrove islands girt by white sand and surrounding a three-mile-wide lagoon where seahawks and frigate birds nest and hundred-pound tarpon fin through the channels. Northward and eastward is the region called the backcountry, an immense sweep of tidal flats in which unpeopled islands are set like jade stones in a vast buckle of silvery green. Egrets, great blue herons, roseate spoonbills, and ibis breed there.

And when the tide moves over the flats, a riot of marine life moves with it: shrimps and crabs, bonefish and permit, bull and lemon sharks eight feet long, stingrays and eagle rays. Whenever I am there or elsewhere at sea I am aware that I am in nature's realm, not man's, and am subject to her rules and rhythms of moon and tide and wind, the same rhythms that governed the waters when the Calusa Indians fished in them, when the Spanish galleons sailed upon them.

As you probably know, the name Key West is derived from the Spanish, Cayo Hueso, Bone Key. When the Spaniards landed here, they found an enormous number of human skeletons, evidence that some sort of large tribal Indian war had been fought on the island. But what is left of the Indians now? Not even their bones remain. And what is left of the Spanish sailors who drowned on the *Atocha* and the *Santa Margarita*? A few rotting planks in the silty depths, a few bars of gold and jewels of no value to those sailors now. And yet the tides continue to ebb and fill, the trade winds to blow, the fish to follow the seasonal migrations they have for thousands of years, the ocean to heave and roll as if shrugging its vast shoulders at the petty triumphs and defeats of mankind.

It will be doing the same thing when we are gone, when our grandchildren are gone, and their grandchildren. In this skeptical age, the sea is what we have in place of God, said Hemingway's Thomas Hudson in *Islands in the Stream*. I don't know about that. I certainly don't want to offend anyone's religious sensibilities. But the sea is like a deity because it is mother to us all, and it is eternal.

The sea teaches what is enduring and what is transitory in this world, what is significant and what is trivial. Given the fashions and trends that plague American literature, I think that's an important lesson for a writer. I think it's important for everyone.

From the **Spring 1987** edition of *FORUM* magazine.

40 The Highwaymen

Painting fast and selling their dreamy landscapes cheaply, these young Black artists created a lasting vision of a Florida Eden.

Gary Monroe

Gary Monroe is a documentary photographer, writer, and lecturer who has written several books about Florida art, including *The Highwaymen: Florida's African-American Landscape Painters*, his first of five on that subject. He is a professor emeritus in the School of Photography at Daytona State College.

In the late 1950s, several Black teenagers in Fort Pierce taught themselves to paint Florida scenes. It was a money-making venture, a way they hoped to make a living, a better way than toiling in the citrus groves or doing the other menial labor available at that time to African Americans. They painted fast and just as quickly sold their framed oils from the trunks of cars, mainly on highways along the state's east coast. A fertile market existed for affordable and original art about Florida as families established themselves during the state's postwar population boom. This artistic enterprise went strong for twenty-five years, until the culture shifted and tastes changed.

Who could have guessed that decades later these entrepreneurs would be considered the visual artists of their time and place? Who could have known that they would leave a testimonial in the form of perhaps 200,000 oil paintings that would become the markers for the tropical version of the American Dream?

Years after they started their venture, this loosely organized and nameless association of what grew to be twenty-five men and one woman became known as the Highwaymen. As their art began to be recognized as something special, stories circulated about them.

The stories were little more than rumors when in 1998 I met with three of these artists—Mary Ann Carroll, James Gibson, and Hezekiah Baker. What they told me about their work didn't jibe with the few existing accounts about the Highwaymen. One of the myths, for example, held that several artists contributed to the production of each of the paintings. It was claimed that each artist specialized in producing certain images, with one painting in the birds, another painting water, another painting trees, etc. But the artists said this was not true. They each painted their own complete pictures. The artists also took issue with the notion that they were part of a school or movement. They didn't even have studios; they just worked in their backyards "like shade-tree mechanics," Carroll said.

The unfolding story was intriguing, ready-made, and ripe for the telling. It needed only a sympathetic intermediary. I decided to uncover their story and to tell it.

It begins in the mid-1950s, when young Alfred Hair took painting lessons from A. E. Backus, a prominent white regionalist painter. Florida's tropical beauty provided Backus ample inspiration; his time-tested aesthetic yielded paradisiacal images. Owning a Backus canvas was tantamount to claiming the land.

But Hair read the images differently; to him they provided a means to escape a bleak future and become wealthy. He decided to devise a way to use his painting skills to make money.

Another African American painter, Harold Newton, likely served as a role model, showing Hair how this could be done. Newton, a natural-born artist, sold his paintings door to door while Hair was still in school. Newton painted in the manner of Backus, rivaling the esteemed artist, in fact. Newton painted with more contemplation and greater formal resolve than would Hair. But Newton still painted fast, applying paint wet-on-wet with deft skill bordering on the magical, epitomizing what would become Hair's ideal: making glowing, exemplary images that seemed to form themselves effortlessly.

The Glades at Dusk, 3 Birds in Flight, by Alfred Hair. Courtesy of Collection of the Smithsonian National Museum of African American History and Culture, Gift of Robert and Flory Kahn in memory of Wolf and Tybe Kahn.

The Highwaymen · 255

When Hair was preparing to graduate from high school, he left Backus's studio and gathered a few of his friends. He suggested they join in a creative effort that might help them all rise above the inferior status to which "Negroes" were relegated at that time. By teaching them the conventional painting formulas that he had learned, he gave the others a way out of "Blacktown."

The Artist as Entrepreneur

HAIR DEVISED a system to mass-produce paintings and thereby be able to sell them relatively cheaply. This involved working on multiple boards—developing certain areas in phases—to minimize labor and material and hence maximize profits. Each artist was able to complete a group of paintings during the group's customary nightlong painting fests. In this way, by shedding the established modes in favor of mass production, he and his associates developed a fresh form of landscape painting. They created images that seemed almost like picture windows overlooking an idealized Florida landscape, a place where dreams would likely come true.

The quickness with which the core group painted altered the classical pictorial strategies that Backus, like other academic artists, incorporated. They arrived at their fluid style by necessity; time meant money. Hair's fast painting led to the distinguishing characteristics of the Highwaymen's art. Their facile process yielded images that linger in the memory, just as an image lingers after glancing at an expanse of land through the side window of a vacation-bound car. Florida-in-passing looked sketchy, half realized, ripe for people to lend their own meanings.

Instead of charging a price in accord with a Backus canvas, of say $250, Hair opted to charge $25 for one of his own paintings. He'd produce ten paintings in less time than it took Backus to complete a single painting and earn the same money. One might fairly reason that the Highwaymen's haste would have resulted in inferior paintings. Ironically, though, the speed—their painting in the moment—freed these artists to paint intuitively, allowing their ideas to flow along with their brushstrokes. The paradox was that their need for money, which required them to paint fast, contributed to rather than corrupted their art.

The painters were transparent, not wanting to draw attention as they traversed the state selling their wares. They did business without occupational licenses, but that wasn't the primary reason for their transparency. Rather, it was a calculated part of the fantasy they sold to their customers. People were attracted to the swift, free-flowing quality, the suggestiveness, of their paintings. Viewers could feel empowered by such surrogates for their own wondrously dreamt experiences, such metaphors for their ideal relationship to the land. Removed from its context, the landscape's significance was rendered mysterious, ephemeral, and up for grabs, just like Florida itself at that time.

The transitory nature of their imagery offered an intimacy that would have been lost in a more formal treatment. It left a void that compelled viewers to provide

Alfred Warner Hair, circa 1960s. Hair, who studied with prominent landscape artist A. E. Backus, was a founder of the Highwaymen movement. He died in 1970 at age twenty-nine after being shot in a bar. Courtesy of FloridaHighwaymenPaintings.com.

their own interpretations. Viewers were coauthors, finishing the pictures in their own minds. And given the paintings' varied symbols, sublime beauty, and willing collaborators, ascribing meaning was irresistible. So powerful was the draw that buyers personalized generic scenes with confidence. The river bend pictured was inevitably "the spot where this bass was caught" or "that place on the St. Johns where . . ."

Since making money, not art, was their goal, the Highwaymen needed to shower the state with paintings. And they did! It wasn't unusual for an artist to make ten, even twenty paintings at a stretch. The Highwaymen's landscapes took as little time as half an hour to complete; seldom did they spend much more than an hour on a painting.

Al Black, one of the Highwaymen, observed, "Alfred [Hair] could paint as good as he wanted and as fast as he wanted." Hair preferred his production mode. He was driven, determined to be a millionaire by his thirty-fifth birthday. He had to paint fast and paint a lot. To him and the other Highwaymen, a painting wasn't finished until it was sold. No painting was sold dry. With money in their pockets, everything was going better than planned.

Charismatic Alfred Hair may have acquired the wealth he desired. Cash rolled in, and he and other painters sported the high life. But at twenty-nine and on top of the world, Hair took a bullet during an argument in a juke joint. He died later that night at the Fort Pierce Memorial Hospital. He had succeeded in forming the unlikely atelier that was responsible for the creation of Florida's visual legacy.

The transitory nature of their imagery offered an intimacy that would have been lost in a more formal treatment.

James Gibson displays a piece of his art, 2017. Gibson was one of Florida's original twenty-six Highwaymen artists and among the group's most prolific. Photo by Jeffrey Isaac Greenberg, Alamy Stock Photo.

The Highwaymen • 257

> *The festival's credentials were held in the tight grip of the late "Cousin" Thelma Boltin, the folklorist who directed the festival from 1954 to 1965.*

Thelma Boltin, founder of the White Springs Folk Festival, circa 1950s. Courtesy of State Archives of Florida, Florida Memory.

make this a mecca for Florida songsmiths and folk music fans. Thousands make the annual pilgrimage to rural Hamilton County to commune among their own kind.

Prolific songwriter Stephen Collins Foster was the first name associated with Florida music. In 1851, Foster edited his original words about North Carolina's Peedee River into the international classic "Old Folks at Home," which describes a fictional Florida plantation "way down upon the Swanee River."

Although lore has it that Foster never laid eyes on the river he made famous, according to one account, Foster and his wife may have cruised the Suwannee by riverboat during their honeymoon that year, stopping for lunch at a cafe in Ellaville, where the river is wide and the boat could turn around. Passed down in the cafe owner's family through the generations, this account is attested to in a document in the possession of James Cornett, CEO of the nearby Spirit of the Suwannee Music Park in Live Oak.

In 1935 "Old Folks" became Florida's state song. The lyrics were penned in "darkie" minstrel dialect, but in 2008 the legislature passed a revised version, without the dialect.

Begun by area socialites in 1952, the festival came to hold the only real certification for state folksinger-songwriters. "You just weren't considered Florida folk unless you paid your dues at White Springs," explains Dale Crider, a Kentucky-born wildlife biologist, environmentalist, and songwriter who lives along Gainesville's Lake Pithlachoco. "Far as we knew, we were the main Florida folksingers and songwriters in the state."

That left out Jimmy Buffett, arguably the state's most famous folksinger, and hundreds of other songwriters and singers of all ethnicities across the Sunshine State.

The festival's credentials were held in the tight grip of the late "Cousin" Thelma Boltin, the folklorist who directed the festival from 1954 to 1965 and remained influential into the late 1980s. During the performances, Boltin sat on the main stage, clad in sunbonnet and pioneer-style dress, watching, critiquing, and protecting an event she defined according to her own traditional North Florida culture.

The talent lineup until the mid-1970s was almost exclusively from that region. It was once "Woodstock white," according to Peggy Bulger, who was hired as Florida's first state folklorist and administrator of the new Florida Folklife Program in 1976. "Thelma decided who was and who was not allowed on stage. I was hired to bring more diversity into the program," Bulger says.

Boltin's choices had left out many performers who have become valuable stitches on the Florida folk quilt. Unlike Texas, which promotes a sound immediately marketable as Texas music, Florida's folk music is a changeling, flitting all over the map. So many transplants and cultures make up modern Florida that the nature and definition of Florida folk can't be pinned down. As Ken Crawford, a festival director who succeeded Bulger, says, "In Florida, there are Chicago-style blues bands

"Cousin" Thelma Boltin and Gamble Rogers. Courtesy of State Archives of Florida, Florida Memory.

playing Florida folk songs. There are reggae bands playing it. And everybody has their own idea what Florida music is or isn't."

Over the next decades, with Bulger treading softly but firmly in the background—allowing Boltin and her able assistant, Barbara Beauchamp, to ease off the old values—the festival changed. Bulger traveled the nooks and crannies of the state, creating a compendium of folk talent and culture. Diversity blossomed.

BUFFETT AND ROGERS: A TROUBADOURS' FRIENDSHIP

Among true Florida troubadours, Gamble Rogers and Jimmy Buffett, his protégé, toured the farthest. From St. Augustine, Rogers roamed the country, carrying his expert Travis-style licks and his crafted tales of mythical "Oklawaha County, Florida" to audiences across the fruited plain. A former member of the nationally known Serendipity Singers, Rogers died tragically in 1991 while attempting to save a man from drowning off Flagler Beach. In 1998 Rogers was named to the state's prestigious Artist's Hall of Fame, becoming the third folksinger after Will McLean and Buffett to receive this honor.

In a letter read at the ceremony, Buffett paid homage to Rogers: "One of the untold but essential qualities of a life as a troubadour is that you teach your trade to those you feel deserve and can handle the knowledge of performing. Gamble was my teacher. Our classroom was his fastback Mustang, or a barstool at the Trade Winds, or a bench in Peacock Park in Coconut Grove. It was in these spots that Gamble offered up his wisdom to an up-and-coming folksinger from the Gulf Coast."

Singing the Songs of Florida · 261

In 1978 bluesman Blind Johnny Brown was rediscovered living in a St. Petersburg old folks home, after traveling the world performing with Jimmy Reed in the '40s and '50s. The writer of *I'll Be Glad When You're Dead You Rascal You* was invited to the festival main stage to sing *Nobody Likes Mexico Like I Do*.

Says Bulger, who went on to serve as director of the American Folklife Center at the Library of Congress from 1999 to 2011, "I knew the diversity was working when Ida Goodson and Diamond Teeth Mary [both famous Black blues artists] took the stage together." The crowd cheered.

Cousin Thelma could not help scoffing at such change. She had strong opinions not only about folk songs but about the singers. One of the state's best folksingers, the late Will McLean, became her nemesis. McLean and troubadours Gamble Rogers, Jim Ballew, and Don Grooms were respected as leaders of today's contemporary real Florida folk sound. McLean, an often homeless, hard-drinking man who wrote beautiful songs, defined Florida folk music, and Thelma knew it.

The Chipley-born McLean called himself "The Black Hat Troubadour" and roamed the state, in 1963 even performing at Carnegie Hall. McLean's songs borrowed from the traditional northeastern folk idiom but were roughed up with honest Florida grit.

"Times at night I gets to thinking, and the shivers colds my spine," he sings in his classic "Wild Hog," a precious string of words that songwriter Bobby Hicks declared "the finest single line ever written in a Florida folk song." (Hicks was too humble to nominate his own finest lines: "Well they cut down the trees and the mangrove keys, then they killed off the coral and the old manatee, and they put parkin' lots where the beach used to be and it's damn sure killin' me, it's killin' you and me.")

McLean's stature as the "Father of Florida Folk" forced Bolton to look the other way regarding his constant rule-bending. McLean messed with her lineup, bringing his unannounced discoveries onto the festival stage, giving up his own stage time to audition new talent.

Cousin Thelma could only look on disapprovingly. At one traditional Sunday morning group discussion, self-righteous performers, one after the other, complained about Diamond Teeth Mary McClain and her King Snake Blues Band stomping all over the Saturday-night stage.

Gamble Rogers rose to put the denouncers down forever. In the quiet voice of the southern gentleman that he was, he went to the Bible: "Would you deny," he lectured, "would you deny your brother a seat at the table?"

The whole hillside grew quiet and then resounded with loud applause. The festival was never the same. Why, with the waters broken, even Cousin Thelma relented, becoming best of friends with Diamond Teeth Mary; they sang Foster's songs in his original minstrel dialect and sat on the main stage together until Thelma died in 1992.

Will McLean at the 1965 White Springs Folk Festival. Courtesy of State Archives of Florida, Florida Memory.

New Voices... and Old

THE LATE LAKE WALES FOLKSINGERS Frank and Ann Thomas continued McLean's work by regularly introducing new talent at the festival. They served as mentors to a wide variety of folk musicians who made regular pilgrimages to their Lake Wales Rattlesnake Road "Cracker Palace" home. The Thomases hosted the state's first folk music radio show in the late 1980s, taped at their home. Any picker with a song and story was qualified to stop by. They were famously known to give songwriting assignments to young folkies who would return weeks later with their homework.

Now produced and coordinated by the Florida Park Service, the festival is more inclusive and eclectic than ever. And it's still the best gathering anywhere to hear and enjoy Florida folk music—the real thing.

Every year, many of Florida's folk musicians are there—and will be as long as God would leave 'em on earth.

Performers at the White Springs Folk Festival, 2018. Courtesy of Florida Department of Environmental Protection.

Singing the Songs of Florida · 263

Seminole singer-songwriters Chief Jim Billie and Paul "Cowbone" Buster are major ingredients in the Florida folk music stew. Both have written Florida folk lyrics in their native languages. Billie, once nominated for a Grammy for Native American music, remembers his grandmother singing to him, "the same song, over and over again. Years later I came to find out she was teaching me to count." The deep-voiced Vietnam vet used his grandma's Indian words when he wrote and recorded "The Counting Song," which now is used to teach Seminole children to count to ten: *Tahmee-hen, tow-gle hen, tata-chee, sha-tee-ta, choki-pun, e-papaw, nay-ounsch, cor-lee-ounsch, ee-yahwounsch, hah-pook.*

Gone, however, is colorful singing woodworker Whitey Markle, who carried recipes for his boiled peanut pie in his guitar case; he wrote "The Cracker Stomp." And so, too, is the environmental attorney known as Boomslang Swampsinger, who delivered his throaty lyrics with a deep bosso thunder, a result of years "eating roadkill at the Flamingo Cafe." And Don Grooms, a Cherokee, who taught at the University of Florida and famously sang, "If great-grandad had wanted me to be a Cracker, he'd have stole me some Seminole land."

Still going strong are the old-guard survivors: Virginia swamp cowboy Raiford Starke, named after a Florida prison, carries on, moaning about that "Girl from Immokalee"; and Dale Crider is still singing his ode to oysters, "Apalachicola Doin' Time." You can still hear the frailing banjo of Miami satirist Valerie Wisecracker's "Mouse That 'Et Orlando," Bob Patterson's exquisite river lullabies, and Marco Island sailor Fiddlin' J. Robert's shanty tales of cruising southwest Florida mangroves exploring the "Walkin' Trees."

In the late afternoon of the festival's last day, a tradition has cemented itself to the schedule: a celebration of the late songwriter Bobby Hicks and his legendary music on the old Marble Stage from a bluff above the Suwannee. Tradition says St. Augustine's Jimmy Carrick, Bobby's friend and frequent touring partner, will take the stage and soon "all y'all" will sense a crescendo of pride and nostalgia rising when Carrick sings the words that justify a Florida folk musician's existence.

"I'm Spaniard and I'm Frenchman, and I'm British and I'm Indian," he roars in Hicks's profundo. "I'm forest, I'm swampland, opportunities for all men / Proud as can be when I roar / I'm Florida, need I say more? I'm Florida, need I say more!"

From the **Winter 2004** edition of *FORUM* magazine and updated for the **Spring 2022** issue, "A Joyful Noise: Celebrating the Soundtrack of Our State."

The 41st Annual Florida Folk Festival poster.

42 The Great State of Rock

A star-studded group of Florida guitar masters electrified rock and roll.

Bob Kealing

Bob Kealing is the author of five books on Florida history and culture, a six-time regional Emmy Award–winning journalist, and a two-time recipient of the Edward R. Murrow award. University Press of Florida released his latest book, *Good Day Sunshine State: How the Beatles Rocked Florida*, in 2023.

Since 1969, four iconic bands have ruled American classic rock, their songs on a perpetual loop via FM and satellite radio. Each band includes two guitarists with deep Florida roots, supplying the gold and platinum riffs. Those eight artists, along with numerous others, make a compelling case for Florida as an incubator of great American classic rock guitarists.

Here's the honor roll of Florida's Eight Great Rock Guitarists, in order of the release of their first national albums: Duane Allman and Dickie Betts of the Allman Brothers Band in 1969; Bernie Leadon and Don Felder of the Eagles in 1972; Gary Rossington and Allen Collins of Lynyrd Skynyrd in 1973; and Tom Petty and Mike Campbell of Tom Petty and the Heartbreakers in 1976. Each one is a member of the Rock and Roll Hall of Fame.

Often those four bands' music may be broad-brushed as "Southern rock." In truth, they represent multiple, era-defining genres: country rock at its commercial peak; stretched-out, sophisticated jam-band blues rock; and hit-making rock and roll, with relatable lyrics, savvy as Sunset Boulevard via earthy, backwoods Florida.

The first electric guitar was designed by George Beauchamp in 1931. Innovators including Adolf Rickenbacker, Leo Fender, and Les Paul perfected the process by which the instrument was played and heard. The results were revolutionary. Previously, acoustic guitars were most often strummed as rhythm instruments, with their soft sounds relegated to the background. Electrified guitars, with their dynamic, pulsating sound, could steal the show.

In the 1930s and '40s, electric guitars started appearing in blues, jazz, and gospel records. An unlikely electric guitar influence on future rockers like Chuck Berry, Carl Perkins, and Elvis Presley was Sister Rosetta Tharpe, nicknamed by NPR "The Godmother of Rock and Roll." Mixing gospel and secular themes in songs that were daring for the time like "Rock Me," the African American Tharpe pioneered the use of distortion. By 1938 she had appeared in New York City's Cotton Club.

265

In the 1950s Berry made the electric guitar a star, bringing it to the forefront of his catchy, danceable music. Berry's opening riff to "Johnny B. Goode" is among the most famous in rock-and-roll history. Berry's stage antics, such as lifting the guitar over his head when he played, were copied by such 1960s luminaries as Jimi Hendrix.

But it took something unlikely and nonmusical to bring the electric guitar gods and classic rock to much larger audiences. An era of expansion in the National Basketball Association in 1966 and the National Hockey League in 1967 necessitated a building boom of sports arenas. On off nights, these massive venues could generate revenue hosting rock concerts.

Topping the roster of our Eight Great Florida guitarists is Duane Allman, raised in Daytona Beach Shores. Voted by *Rolling Stone* as the No. 2 Rock and Roll Guitarist of All Time (Jimi Hendrix was No. 1), Allman devoured the music of blues legends like Muddy Waters and B. B. King. Allman often jammed with Black artists around Daytona Beach at a time when segregation was the norm.

His formidable guitar counterpart in the Allman Brothers, singer-songwriter Dickie Betts from West Palm Beach, contributed his own countrified style in songs like "Ramblin' Man." Often overshadowed by Allman, Betts became an invaluable

The original Allman Brothers, on the cover of the 1971 album *Live at the Fillmore East*. Courtesy of Big House Museum.

266 · Bob Kealing

Eagles Bernie Leadon (*left*) and Don Felder. Photo by Bill Green, courtesy of *Reverb*.

part of the Allman Brothers, writing some of their best-known hits. Their earliest acclaim came with the 1971 release of *Live at Fillmore East*, which featured Allman's extended, ethereal slide-guitar jams. *Spin* magazine proclaimed it the greatest live recording of all time.

Allman's playing drew interest from England's own pioneering arena rocker Eric Clapton, whose band, Cream, in 1968 was the first rock act to play Madison Square Garden. In 1970, after the two recorded Clapton's *Derek and the Dominos* album at Criteria Studios in Miami, Clapton was so impressed he tried to hire Allman. "We cut a really super album together," Allman wrote in a letter home. "I'm really up in the air right now." After agonizing over how the increase in pay Clapton promised could improve his family's life, Allman ended up turning down Clapton's offer.

Bernie Leadon, son of a University of Florida professor, came of age in the garage-band scene of the mid-1960s. After moving out West, he sought his fortune in the nascent country-rock scene, most notably with the Flying Burrito Brothers. Leadon joined a backup band for Tex-Mex musician by way of Tucson, Linda Ronstadt. The backup players—Leadon, Glenn Frey, Don Henley, and Randy Meisner—soon realized they had the collective talent to strike out on their own. With Ronstadt's blessing, they did, and in 1971, the Eagles were born. Leadon was just as comfortable with a banjo as an electric guitar. The Eagles' good-time, laid-back sound,

The Great State of Rock • 267

Gibson 1952 Les Paul "Goldtop."

embodied in songs like Jackson Browne's "Take It Easy," brought them instant success in Vietnam War–weary America.

By 1974, as the popularity of country rock was waning, Leadon recruited his Gainesville garage-band buddy and coworker at Lipham Music, Don Felder, to give the Eagles' sound a harder, rock edge. The pinnacle of their success came in 1975 with the release of *Eagles: Their Greatest Hits*, the greatest-selling album of all time, with forty-five million units sold as of 2020, edging out Michael Jackson's *Thriller*.

Leadon left the Eagles that same year, and Felder helped feed the band's new era of arena-rock dominance, in 1977 cowriting the title track of its Grammy-winning album *Hotel California*. With singles like "Life in the Fast Lane," the album personified the cocaine-fueled hedonism emblematic of southern California in the late 1970s. When it came time to play live the daunting array of guitar sounds represented on the album, Felder chose to use a white double-necked Gibson electric guitar, one neck with six strings, the other with twelve. It became his signature look on stage. The iconic instrument was featured in a 2019 Metropolitan Museum of Art guitar exhibit in New York called *Play It Loud*.

Childhood friends Gary Rossington and Allen Collins grew up on the tough streets of West Jacksonville. In Lynyrd Skynyrd, the two guitar players forged a distinctive Southern rock sound, relatable to people struggling with everyday life. Their songs "Free Bird," "Simple Man," and "Sweet Home Alabama" are among the most played of the genre. Collins's precise, blistering guitar solo in "Free Bird" consistently ranks as among the best of the classic rock era. The band's leader, lyricist, and hard-drinking brawler Ronnie Van Zant, a Jacksonville native, recruited Californian Ed King from the hippie-trippy 1960s band the Strawberry Alarm Clock, and Skynyrd's triple-lead-guitar army was set.

In 1973 Skynyrd was known primarily on the circuit of southern clubs near Jacksonville. Producer Al Kooper plied his connections to give them their first big break. Pete Townsend, the Who's visionary lead guitarist and songwriter, asked Kooper if he knew of any hot young bands that could open for them on an upcoming American tour. Kooper suggested Skynyrd. While initially intimidated by the huge venues and crowds, Van Zant asserted his cocksure nature. Night after night, he told his band their goal was to kick the Who's ass in performance, regardless of their headlining status.

In 1976, with the top-10 hit "Sweet Home Alabama" now in their repertoire, Skynyrd's guitar army electrified a festival crowd of 100,000 in Knebworth, England. Most in the audience, including Paul McCartney and David Gilmore of Pink Floyd, were there to see the Rolling Stones.

Van Zant idolized the Stones. On May 8, 1965, when he was seventeen, he saw an early show at Jacksonville's Coliseum. At the time, he and Rossington were talented American Legion baseball players considering pursuing the sport professionally. The concert had a profound influence. "Ronnie was blown away by the Rolling

Lynyrd Skynrd (*left to right*), Allen Collins, Ronnie Van Zant, and Gary Rossington. Photo by Gijsbert Hanekroot, Alamy.

Stones," said friend Rick Doeschler, who wasn't old enough to drive but grabbed a ride with Van Zant in his red Mustang.

At the Stones concert in England, the stage had been outfitted with a long, wide tongue jutting out at the center, which Mick Jagger forbade any of the opening acts to use. Yet during the rousing guitar jam at the end of "Free Bird," Van Zant marched his guitarists, mid-jam, right down the center of the tongue. Skynyrd had come full circle on rock-star dreams ignited back home during the British Invasion.

Two days before Van Zant saw the Stones in 1965, Keith Richards had written their defining megahit "Satisfaction" at the Fort Harrison Hotel in Clearwater. The song's opening riff, which Richards said came to him in a dream, is arguably the most recognizable of any 1960s rock song.

Tom Petty was one of those kids whose life was never the same after seeing the Beatles on *The Ed Sullivan Show*. For the Gainesville eighth-grader, buying his first guitar and forming a band gave him the social structure he'd never had. But it also

The Great State of Rock • 269

sparked conflict. Petty had violent clashes with his crew-cut, insurance-salesman father, Earl, over the length of his hair and passion for rock and roll.

For six years Petty enjoyed regional success playing Beatles cover songs in garage bands like the Sundowners and the Epics alongside Bernie Leadon's little brother, lead guitarist Tom Leadon. In 1970 Petty met a shy University of Florida student, Mike Campbell. At a dilapidated farmhouse in Alachua County, he auditioned Campbell's roommate on drums, then asked Campbell to play something on his cheap Japanese guitar.

Petty didn't expect much—until Campbell ripped into "Johnny B. Goode." Soon afterward, Petty convinced Campbell to drop out of school to begin pursuing their dream. They named their new band Mudcrutch, after the hardscrabble rural property where they lived, and they earned $100 playing six nights a week at Dub's, a

The Mudcrutch–Road Turkey picnic, summer 1973. The occasion brought together Tom Petty (*center, with sunglasses*), then of Mudcrutch, and fellow musicians and friends of the two bands. Future Heartbreakers pictured are Mudcrutch guitarist Mike Campbell, Road Turkey drummer Stan Lynch, and Mudcrutch keyboardist Benmont Tench. Future Motels saxophone and keyboard player Marty Jourard, then of Road Turkey, stands beside Petty opening a beer. Photo by William "Red" Slater.

local steakhouse and nightclub. In 1974 Petty, Campbell, and Mudcrutch headed west to pursue rock-star dreams.

In 1976 Petty's producer Denny Cordell renamed the band Tom Petty and the Heartbreakers, with Petty and Campbell principal songwriters. It was what Campbell called "a throwaway lick" he added to their song "Breakdown" that helped make it their first top-40 hit. By 1979 they had their breakthrough album, *Damn the Torpedoes*. The reserved Campbell was comfortable in Petty's shadow, providing riffs to the band's most beloved songs like "Refugee," "The Waiting," and "Runnin' Down a Dream."

Despite their different styles and stories, the Florida Eight all shared talent and determination. In their formative years, the musicians spent most of their time jamming and playing gigs at youth centers, fraternity houses, backyard utility sheds, and even, for the Skynyrd boys, a rented cabin in Clay County without air conditioning they nicknamed "Hell House."

Despite their different styles and stories, the Florida Eight all shared talent and determination.... The leaders of these Florida-centric bands—Petty, Allman, and Van Zant especially—also had an unshakable understanding of their own identity.

The leaders of these Florida-centric bands—Petty, Allman, and Van Zant especially—also had an unshakable understanding of their own identity. Nonetheless, some record-company big shots tried to force-feed them lousy songs and dress them in ridiculous outfits. The most glaring example was packaging the Allmans in a contrived group known as the Hour Glass. It lasted two torturous years, 1967 and 1968, until Duane Allman walked out.

Allman cleansed his rock-and-roll soul in Muscle Shoals, Alabama, gaining employment from producer Rick Hall as a session player among cleancut, 9-to-5 musicians nicknamed "the Swampers," contributing to landmark recordings by Aretha Franklin, Percy Sledge, and Wilson Pickett. In the spring of 1969, Allman traveled to Jacksonville and met up with musicians from a local band, the Second Coming. After a legendary jam in a Victorian hippie crash pad known as "the Gray House," Allman knew this was it and issued an ultimatum: "Anyone who doesn't want to be in my band is gonna have to fight his way out of here."

He called brother, Gregg, back from Los Angeles to be the singer-songwriter for this formidable lineup, and the Allman Brothers Band was born. Gregg Allman started writing iconic songs like "Dreams" and "Whipping Post" in the Gray House.

Lynyrd Skynyrd personified the Southern rock mold but, like the Allmans, showed a progressive side. In the song "Saturday Night Special," Van Zant decried the danger of cheap handguns: "Ain't good for nothin', but put a man six feet in a hole."

Their biggest hit, "Sweet Home Alabama," written on the shores of Peters Creek in Clay County, Florida, is not necessarily the homage some believe it to be. In a reference to Alabama's one-time segregationist governor, George Wallace, Van Zant wrote, "In Birmingham they love the Gov'na." Immediately after that, as a show of what some commentators have called derision, backup singers add, "Boo, boo, boo." Still, it's hard to overlook Skynyrd's yearslong use of the Confederate flag in live shows and merchandising. Band members have said it was their record company's idea.

The Great State of Rock · 271

Tom Petty and the Heartbreakers in Chicago on February 7, 2008. Alamy.

Tom Petty stuck his neck out most, first to regain control of lucrative publishing rights to his music. In 1979, on the cusp of finishing *Damn the Torpedoes*, Petty refused to release the album. After his label, Shelter Records, was bought out by MCA, Petty grew unhappy with terms of the arrangement and declared he would not be "bought and sold like a piece of meat." Petty doubled down by taking on the cost, about $500,000, of recording the album himself. Then he declared bankruptcy and took his fight to court.

MCA caved, signing Petty to a multimillion-dollar deal. *Damn the Torpedoes* was released, went double platinum, and made Tom Petty and the Heartbreakers superstars.

The following decade, when he released the song that's often most closely associated with his ethos, "I Won't Back Down," anyone who had followed Tom Petty knew damn well he meant it.

Success and Sadness

A SAD COMMONALITY among these bands is tragedy. While the Eagles pursued the drug-addled lifestyle described in their 1977 anthem "Life in the Fast Lane," they narrowly avoided becoming celebrity casualties like their lead guitarist Joe Walsh's hotel-trashing party buddy, actor-comedian John Belushi, who suffered a fatal overdose on March 5, 1982.

Tom Petty and the Heartbreakers' bassist and talented harmony vocalist, Howie Epstein, died in 2003 at the age of forty-six, attributed to a heroin overdose. "Howie

Tom Petty stuck his neck out most, first to regain control of lucrative publishing rights to his music.

was never not a Heartbreaker," Tom Petty, who would himself die of an accidental drug overdose at the age of sixty-six in 2017, wrote in a *Rolling Stone* magazine eulogy. "He just couldn't do it anymore."

Duane Allman's love of fast motorcycles and living on the edge brought his rising star crashing to earth. In October 1971 a tractor-trailer turned into a lumberyard just down a hill Allman was cresting. To avoid hitting the rig, Allman laid down his bike and slid, incurring massive and ultimately fatal internal injuries. He was twenty-four. In an eerie coincidence, the band's beloved bassist Berry Oakley died nearby in a motorcycle accident the following year. Despite two devastating losses, the Allman Brothers soldiered on to an era of major success with the 1972 double album *Eat a Peach*.

On October 17, 1977, the members of Lynyrd Skynyrd were out promoting a strong new album, *Street Survivors*. One of the album's most memorable songs, "That Smell," included Ronnie Van Zant's commentary on their escalating drug use and Gary Rossington crashing his Ford Torino into an oak tree. That smell, Van Zant wrote, was the smell of death surrounding them.

> Say you'll be all right come tomorrow,
> But tomorrow might not be here for you.

Van Zant admitted he abused drugs to deal with the pressure of being the band's lead singer and vowed to get clean. Their upcoming tour included a headlining gig at the venue they had dreamed of, Madison Square Garden.

On the evening of October 20, both engines of the Convair 240 leased by their manager quit in midflight over Louisiana. Gliding in at high speed, the aircraft started striking scores of trees in a swamp near the Mississippi border. Survivors recalled what sounded like hundreds of baseball bats hitting the outside of the plane.

The aircraft cut a swath through the treetops before ripping apart. Among those killed were Ronnie Van Zant; the band's newest guitarist, Steve Gaines, and his sister and backup vocalist, Cassie Gaines. Without their lead singer-songwriter, Lynyrd Skynyrd could not continue.

Despite the tragedies that brought the original Lynyrd Skynyrd to a premature end, the band re-formed in 1987 with Van Zant's younger brother, Johnny, on lead vocals.

From aging Baby Boomers to kids just discovering them via digital download, the music of the Allman Brothers, the Eagles, Lynyrd Skynyrd, and Tom Petty and the Heartbreakers, remains timeless. The infectious riffs and lyrical themes of rebelliousness, yearning, and romance keep bringing new ears to their old songs.

From the **Spring 2022** edition of *FORUM* magazine, "A Joyful Noise: Celebrating the Soundtrack of Our State."

PART VII

Roots and Rivers

Nature, as it does, has the last word. On this peninsula, water binds all—history, literature, culture, and survival.

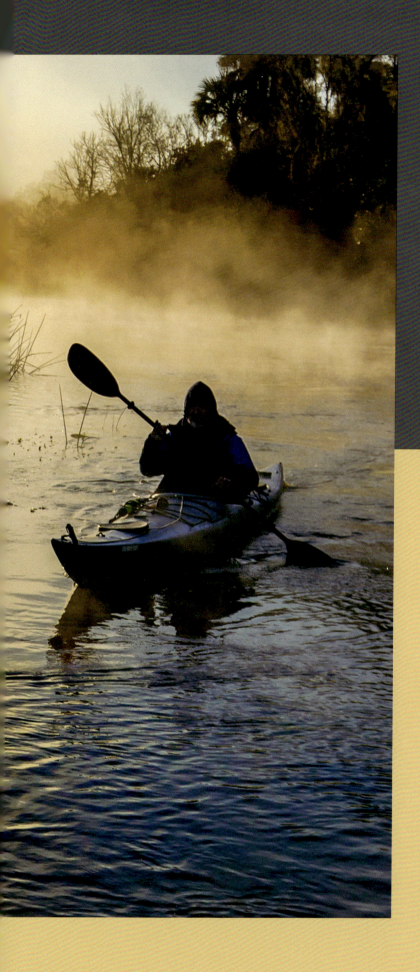

Jim Durocher paddles through a misty sunrise on Juniper Creek.
Photo by John Moran.

43

The Wondrous Gulf

*How its bounty and its bluster
have shaped the story of Florida.*

Jack E. Davis

Jack E. Davis is the Pulitzer Prize–winning author of *The Bald Eagle: The Improbable Journey of America's Bird*, *The Gulf: The Making of an American Sea*, and *An Everglades Providence: Marjory Stoneman Douglas and the American Environmental Century*. He is a professor of history and the Rothman Family Chair in the Humanities at the University of Florida.

SOMEWHERE AT THE bottom of the Gulf of Mexico lie the historical records of Spanish west Florida. They were lost in 1818 soon after General Andrew Jackson invaded Pensacola. Local Spanish officials responded to the invasion by fleeing to Havana on board the schooner *Peggy*. En route, they were intercepted by French corsairs, who learned the *Peggy* carried chests brimming not with gold and jewels but with the public records of the Spanish province. To exorcize their frustration, the pirates heaved the chests overboard.

This tale of historical archives lost to a seabed repository reflects a truth seldom considered: the Gulf of Mexico is a central force in the story of Florida. Rarely is this idea explored in history books and classrooms, and that's unfortunate. We cannot fully know Florida until we understand the Gulf as an elemental power to which people respond, much as they respond to ancestral cues or lessons learned. Put another way, nature has the capacity to shape human history, and in Florida the Gulf is nature supreme.

Yet, despite its power, its real and active presence, the Gulf retains a particular subtlety. As oceans go, it is not terribly big, the ninth largest in the world, to be exact. Fewer than 1,000 miles of ebbing and flowing sea separate Florida and Mexico. The drive from Pensacola to Key West is farther than the Gulf's north-to-south reach, which extends from barrier islands along the US coastal rim to the Caribbean and Atlantic shores of Cuba.

Rather officiously, the International Hydrographic Organization has designated the Gulf as part of the Atlantic Ocean. This reduction to mere appendage obscures important differences, however. Gallon for gallon, the Atlantic cannot compete with the estuarine capacity of the Gulf, one of the world's great hatcheries of finfish,

Editor's note: Davis recalls when he was asked to write about the Gulf of Mexico for *FORUM*: "At the time, I was considering the subject for a book. I wasn't able to fully conceptualize the Gulf as a book yet and was a bit intimidated by the subject. Writing that piece for *FORUM* gave me the confidence to do the book." Davis's *The Gulf: The Making of an American Sea* was awarded the 2018 Pulitzer Prize for History.

shellfish, and shrimp. By disposition, the Atlantic is often gray and disagreeable, whereas the Gulf is inclined to a cordial, blue-green serenity. The Atlantic is less "place" than entity, stolidly expansive and disengaged. The Gulf is manifestly the opposite. It draws you in. Humbly, it calls you to partake in its essential self, to dangle bare feet off the edge of a sun-faded dock; to peer down at fish that, like window shoppers, scrutinize the dock's every piling; to look up as a brown pelican in a death drop crashes down upon an unsuspecting offering.

None of this is to say that the Gulf is superior to the Atlantic or free of mood swings. Its warm, shallow waters, for example, naturally attract hurricanes that hurtle angrily in from the mother ocean. The argument here is that the Gulf is nothing less than a wonder in itself.

Postcard, 1940. A Tarpon Springs sponge diver shows off a day's harvest. Courtesy of State Archives of Florida, Florida Memory.

The Wondrous Gulf · 277

The Calusa of precolonial times understood this. They accepted the Gulf's ancient power and reaped prodigious benefits in return. Theirs was a flourishing civilization, with complex social and political systems and deep stakes in the wind-blown, water-washed coast of southwest Florida. Yet, remarkably, they were not farmers. Most sedentary peoples depended on agriculture to feed a permanently settled population. The Calusa harvested most of what they ate from estuaries. So perennially rich in protein was their diet of pigfish, pinfish, catfish, mollusks, crustaceans, sea turtles, rays, and sharks that they stood a foot or more taller than the Spanish.

Still, as mighty as the Calusa had been, they were defenseless against invading diseases from Europe, brought across the Atlantic and in through the Gulf. Eventually, they succumbed to conquest. Nature, not superior weaponry, had sealed their fate. In the form of an ocean stream fed by Gulf currents, nature also facilitated the transfer of New World wealth to the monarchy and cathedrals of the Calusas' conquerors. Spanish explorers spent sixteen years kicking around the Florida Straits before discovering the Gulf. They named it the "Spanish Sea," and it became the pathway to new conquests, including gold and silver plundered from Natives and mines in Mexico and South America. From its western shores, the Spanish Sea carried heavily laden galleons to the Gulf Stream, which, like a water carousel, flung them back to Europe. This extraordinary ocean current, which dramatically changed cross-Atlantic travel, is rarely mentioned in connection with the Gulf of Mexico, though the Gulf's warm waters and loop currents act as its wellspring.

Conquest was not always profitable; it was, however, always challenging. The Gulf did little to encourage the European occupation of Florida. Its mangrove-tangled shoreline, behind which Natives stood steadfast, frustrated one Spanish expedition after another. Similarly, the Gulf fare that nourished the statuesque Calusa provided scant comfort to would-be colonists. Many Spaniards could not stomach seafood. When distressed and starving, they would slaughter and eat their horses rather than touch a crab or oyster. That's exactly what the men of the red-bearded, one-eyed Pánfilo de Narváez did at Apalachee Bay after an aborted conquest of Florida. Once the Spanish finally established a foothold on the peninsula thirty-seven years later, they all but ignored the Gulf in favor of exploiting products of the land—food crops, cattle, timber, cotton, and indigo. The British followed their lead, and unwisely so. Neither power enjoyed a self-sustaining economy in Florida.

Not so for the Americans. Shortly after they acquired Florida, fishing wharfs in the Northeast buzzed with stories of the Gulf's potential. Stirred by possibilities, a seafaring family out of New London, Connecticut, set sail for Florida in 1835. A hurricane took one of their ships, but Leonard Destin, who was blown into the Gulf

A father and son watch pelicans, Marco Island, 1966.
Courtesy of State Archives of Florida, Florida Memory.

after losing his father and brother in the storm, was nevertheless impressed by what calmer seas revealed: fish aplenty. He made landfall on the Panhandle at a sandy point lapped by emerald-green water, built a house, and eventually launched a successful commercial fishing operation. Word got out about the area's equally good recreational fishing, and the town of Destin came to harbor one of the country's largest deep-sea charter fleets. It got a nickname, too, the World's Luckiest Fishing Village.

The Gulf's endowments were as vital as ever when the Georgia-born lyricist Sidney Lanier traveled to Florida forty years after Destin's eventful voyage. Like his predecessor, Lanier was awestruck. "The most marvelous stories are told," he wrote, "of the hosts of fish, even to the stoppage of vessels that have sailed into shoals of them." In later years, experts calculated that the Gulf yields more than the combined fisheries of the US east coast. The Apalachicola Bay–St. George Sound, nursery to plump oysters rated the best by chefs from New Orleans to New York, form one of the most productive marine ecosystems in North America. In 2009 it was a major contributor to the state's $6 billion commercial- and sport-fishing industry, which employed up to 60,000 people. Offshore of the five Gulf states, anglers that year landed 173 million sea trout, snapper, red drum, and other fish.

Sailing at sunset on the Gulf of Mexico. The Gulf's beauty and abundance are enduring hallmarks of the Florida experience. Photo by John Moran.

280 · Jack E. Davis

The Draw of the Gulf

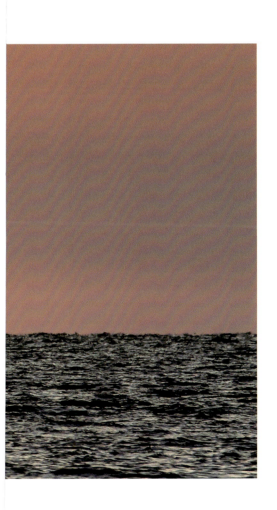

STARTING IN THE EARLY 1800s, the cornucopia spawned fishing communities up and down Florida's west coast. Their wharfs were crowded with sway-bellied trawlers that, with slouching nets suspended astern, lumbered out to sea on endless parade. Group charter boats of a similar anatomy joined them, their hopeful passengers standing shoulder to shoulder with hooks baited and ready for action. And luck was theirs. Countless big-fish stories were told, and most were true. The beginning of Major League Baseball's spring training can be traced to a nine-foot, 500-pound shark caught off Pinellas Point in September 1913 by Robert Hedges, owner of the St. Louis Browns. Excited by future game-fishing prospects, he took his team to St. Petersburg the next spring to train.

Good fishing attracts all kinds of people. In Florida, voices from Italy, Greece, Cuba, the Bahamas, Ireland, New England, the Deep South, Vietnam, Mexico, and Honduras could be heard over the years on commercial boats and wharfs and in boatyards and processing houses. A game fish gave Tarpon Springs its name, but Gulf sponges turned it into a Greek American city. Up at Apalachicola, the son of a German immigrant was the first to use the pasteurization process to pack oysters. After the Civil War, the sporting fight of tarpon and king mackerel off Fort Myers lured some of the state's first rod-and-reel tourists, wealthy men and women from the Northeast and Europe. Their hired guides and boat captains, like independent fisherfolk everywhere, drew on native instincts and working-class muscles to fulfill entrepreneurial ambitions.

The fear in those days was not a depleted bounty, but storms. Although hurricanes invite little enthusiasm for accepting nature's providence, few Floridians will deny the capacity of extreme weather to alter the direction of life. Before European contact, storms delivered early warnings of coming cultural change. Amidst the usual confusion of sea algae and driftwood, coastal Indians found the flotsam of wrecked ships, the "gear of foreign dead men," to borrow words from poet T. S. Eliot. On occasion that included the dead themselves, oddly clad, bearded men from an unknown land. Similarly odd was Florida's foul-weather gold and silver. It was the only precious metal the Spanish found in this new land, and it had been salvaged by Indians after conquistadors had lost it at sea.

The Spanish lost settlements to storms, too. Pensacola, not St. Augustine, would likely be the oldest city in the United States today if a September hurricane had not broken up the colony of Tristán de Luna y Arellano in 1559. The otherwise intrepid conquistadors avoided northwest Florida for the next 139 years.

Storms helped write the history of the Americans in Florida, too. During the early territorial period, legislators relocated the capital to the red hills of Tallahassee, with ominous consequences for local Creek Indians, and built a decent road across north Florida. They did so after colleagues had been shipwrecked while sailing around the peninsula between St. Augustine and Pensacola, the alternating sites of the first legislative sessions.

Many of these camps were no more than a rustic cabin along a remote lake or river, and others were built around landings for nineteenth-century steamers and paddle-wheelers.

river, and others were built around landings for nineteenth-century steamers and paddle-wheelers. By the turn of the twentieth century, the camps served not just as travelers' waypoints and recreational outposts but also as important stations for gathering climatological and geological data in a land primarily accessed by water.

Such informal camps expanded in the 1920s when road access opened Florida to more tourists and a growing population, and some fish camps even spawned towns, like Giant's Camp along the Alafia River near Tampa, which turned the Gibsonton community into the winter home of carnival sideshow performers. Fish camps grow by accretion. Like the bouquet of an oyster colony or barnacles on a boat's hull, they build up over time.

In their typical makeup of metal roofs and wood framing raised above the ground, they hew toward Florida's vernacular architecture as they also mix building types, blending dock with house and shed with shop. Fish camps are experiments in weathering. Utilitarian by design, they play at the absurd game of placing wood structures right next to the water and the weather that can tear them apart. As an architect and an angler, I love them for this mix of what is temporary and permanent. Camping, they connect us not just to fish but to nature as a whole. And as poet Wallace Stevens once noted about a fish camp in Long Key, they are paradise. Rustic, but a paradise nonetheless.

In early spring I visited Stegbone's Fish Camp on the St. Johns River near Satsuma. The camp's namesake and owner, Jim Stege, bought the place in 1998. There

Stegbone's Fish Camp on the St. Johns River, 2020. Photo by Aidan Hailey.

had been two previous owners. My copy of the 1957 fishing gazetteer lists R. A. Allender as operator of the camp and its ten boats (the "R" is for Robert, or "Bob" if you've come to fish). Allender left Kentucky in 1946 to start the camp across from a sandbar lush with eelgrass, where monster bass bedded down and stalked their prey.

Twenty-six years later, when its renown as the "Bass Capital of the World" still echoed across the tannin water between high cypress, the camp passed from Allender to Allen Norton, who in turn sold it to Jim Stege after another twenty-six years.

Fish camps are measured in generations. And one of those tall cypresses, which has seen about ten of those generations, is right here next to the campfire where Jim tells me stories about the camp.

We sit on rough-hewn benches, the river boils and swirls, and I listen. Jim tells me about the day he spent fishing a camper's dentures out from under the docks. Hooks and nets came up empty (the anglers later claimed it was the only time the fish weren't biting), and they finally called in an expert diving team. But it's not just older people at fish camps. Over Jim's shoulder, a grinning kid pulls a wriggling red-belly bream out of the St. Johns, as Jim recounts how all those years ago Bob Allender planted his family's Christmas tree that now rises high over the docks' low-slung roof. He points to the live well where anglers put their prize fish after a good day on the river and then to the white board where an honor system of tick marks records how many buckets of ice each of the camp's five cabins has used. He tells me about Stuart Pacetti, who had his own camp downriver and with perfect Minorcan form would throw his twenty-foot-diameter cast net from Stegbone's narrow docks and fill the fish-cleaning tables with clicking shrimp.

The day's fishing haul, caught in a photograph from Stegbone's when it was known as Bob's Fishing Camp, 1955.

Gathering over Memories

A FAMILY vacationing here from Georgia and Maryland joins us around the fire. Earthy and sweet and brackish, the smell of corn meal and oil follows them from the fryer that's boiling down on the dock. I met them earlier under the taxidermy catfish that swims below the surface of the metal roof. A cell phone snapshot proves yesterday's catch: dozens of sunfish, bluegill, and crappie. They scroll to another photo. It's the gar they told me about earlier, and its weight had gone up as the sun was going down. A woman holds up that gar that is easily forty pounds. It is as long as she is tall. Her husband has been coming here for more than two decades, and now around the fire he tells Jim he still wants to buy the camp. Maybe in 2024, when the next twenty-six years rolls around, but I doubt Jim will sell.

On the dock, which is really an outdoor kitchen with a stove and oven, a microwave, and assorted knives sheathed above the fish-cleaning table where a dinner bell used to hang, I join the family at the round dining room table. I taste the fried bream, and I'm back in Tennessee, a child fishing the Little Harpeth River and having a fresh-caught lunch with my neighbor on the riverbank.

I am convinced that each lake and every river in Florida has hosted its own fish camp at some point in time, a changing but enduring atlas of a truly aqueous state.

Stegbone's utility building. The fish camp shed that originally stored linens is now covered with signage brought by guests. Photo by Aidan Hailey.

By the turn of the century, the camps served not just as travelers' waypoints and early recreational outposts but also as important stations for gathering climatological and geological data in a land primarily accessed by water.

Fish camps do that. They bring back memories, just like they bring back people (another group from Kentucky has been coming here well into four decades). And Stegbone's is a living museum. On the ramp to the docks, faded photos of happy anglers line a glass-paneled cabinet across from a fire bucket stenciled "Bob's Fish Camp."

Another case on the old general store's wall holds a gator's foot, antique lures, gnawed boxes of Mustad hooks, and a "Fisherman's Ruler" where 20 inches is really 10. Behind the store's screen door I can still hear the old register ringing up gas, beer bottles clinking in the ancient fridge, and the radio crackling with the day's weather. At the end of the dock, a device known as the "Super Scaler" looks like an oversized lottery barrel. It runs on a washing machine motor and still has the coin-operated control for inserting quarters.

The fish camp's boat slips are narrow, designed for the beams of smaller, mid-century watercraft: skiffs easily powered by 5.5 hp Johnson outboards like the one clamped onto the dock's railing. Two rental boats float side by side; one is a 1960 Feathercraft with a 25 hp motor, named for Florida folk musician Gamble Rogers, and the other is named for James Harmon, the camp's longtime caretaker. The wake from a big cruiser out in the river channel rattles the boats against the heart-pine pilings that Jim traces back to Bob's Fish Camp and possibly further back to the time when paddle-wheelers carried citrus from the original grove to Palatka.

Up the hill from the dock, old salamander heaters that used to warm the grove during cold snaps lean against Cabin 3, and inside, an old popping float is the pull switch handle for the cabin's bathroom light. A rocking chair on the cabin's porch has plaques "in memory of" the Nicholson clan of fishermen: Charles, Roy, and Robert. On the dock, more rocking chairs with commemorative plaques tell their own fishing tales, and I think that the fish camp is really a porch to the river.

Traditions as Old and Young as the State

No one knows how many fish camps remain in Florida, and there's a wider definition now. "Fish camp" can describe bars and restaurants that prepare fish as easily as it identifies high-end glamping with all the amenities. In the 1950s there were nearly a thousand in Florida. Most were like Stegbone's, where the mix of fishing and camping meant rustic convenience, nothing too fancy but everything you needed to gather together and catch fish.

Names connected camps to people—Mary's, JB's, Ed and Bernice's, Paul's, Brown's, Elrod's, Hiley's, Pace's, and Honest John's—and to place—Pine Island, Highland Park, Oak Hill, Indian Mound, Twin Lakes, McIntosh, Spring Warrior, Pirate's Cove, Stump Pass, Dead River, Devil's Elbow, and Lake Griffin. I am convinced that each lake and every river in Florida has hosted its own fish camp at some point in time, a changing but enduring atlas of a truly aqueous state.

Stegbone's dock. Like conversations on a porch, the fishing stories at Stegbone's are told from rocking chairs on the dock, which retains the original pilings where paddle-wheelers loaded citrus in the 1880s. Photo by Aidan Hailey.

There is an ecology of the fish camp. It maps itself into the earth, which in turn transforms the camp. And the camp itself is a woven thing, tied up in the edges of water and land like Pacetti's cast net. Stegbone's occupies what's called a hurricane hole, a natural shelter where boats anchor during storms. The gentle but deep drop of the bank toward the St. Johns sends northeast winds over the top of the camp, and you can throw in a line as the barometer falls.

The sun is low when Jim lifts the lid on the cricket cases. As many as 20,000 crickets soak up the light from yellow bulbs and eat potatoes, and oranges born on trees grafted from the old grove.

The legs of each case stand in buckets of water to protect the crickets from the red ants that like to eat them, almost as much as the bass and bream hanker for the crickets. That's a lot like what running a fish camp entails, making do and knowing these networks of interconnections. Fragile but resilient, fish camps require

The Tales They Tell · 289

Meanwhile, Stegbone's has adapted the traditions of fish camping to twenty-first-century changes. His offerings on Airbnb attract Swiss, French, and German campers; a mast with sensors sends local weather info to Weather Underground; and Bass Pro Shops does photo shoots at the camp. But like the layers of ash and fish oil in this pit, where fires have been built for three quarters of a century, the fish camp endures.

the same ingenuity and craftiness and improvisation and dedication that fishing does. An architect and preservationist by training, Jim maintains the camp like you would an old boat, replacing parts when necessary, shoring up what still works, and sometimes wondering how much of the original remains, like the ancient problem of Theseus's ship: Is it still the same fish camp as more and more parts are traded out?

Sitting around the campfire at sunset, watching the flicker of the river in the dock's rafters, I think it is.

Meanwhile, Stegbone's has adapted the traditions of fish camping to twenty-first-century changes. His offerings on Airbnb attract Swiss, French, and German campers; a mast with sensors sends local weather info to Weather Underground; and Bass Pro Shops does photo shoots at the camp. But like the layers of ash and fish oil in this pit, where fires have been built for three quarters of a century, the fish camp endures. Or, more precisely, it stays afloat on Florida's saturated ground.

My son and I laugh at the fish-camp humor as we leave Stegbone's: "Catch Ya Later." Yes, I think so. On our way back to Gainesville, we will pass Kate's Fish Camp, where the highway crosses Prairie Creek. An easy paddle northward brings you to Newnans Lake and then on to the grassy shore where McGilvray's used to be.

Gary Simpson said he caught his first bass with an artificial lure at Kate's. The picture that Kate's friend Eleanor took of him as a young angler is the first photo in his fishing scrapbook.

Many years later, Gary tells me, the original owner of Kate's visited his tackle shop on Newnans, told him fish camp stories, and asked him a question: Did the sea cows still come up the creek? "I'm not sure what you mean," Gary remembers saying. The man went on to explain that manatee used to swim in the creek right by the camp.

This story still fills me with wonder. Imagine the manatee's journey: from the Atlantic, up the St. Johns, passing a slew of fish camps along the way—Pacetti's, Whitey's, Georgia Boy's, Shell Harbor, Stegbone's when it was Bob's, Anderson's, Sunset Landing, Bass Haven—and then up the Ocklawaha, into Orange Creek, through Orange Lake, the River Styx, and finally Prairie Creek, right by Kate's and into Newnans.

They swam right through Florida's watery veins, not yet locked and dammed. They connected a peninsula's center to its coastal edge. And the fish camps were witnesses.

From the **Fall 2020** edition of *FORUM* magazine, "Alone Together: Stories of Florida in a Time of Crisis."

45

The Marvelous, Misunderstood Mullet

Tracing the storied past of Florida's least respected and most important fish.

Terry Tomalin

IN GOODLAND, south of Naples, residents worship the simple herbivore, even crown a queen in its honor. On the Panhandle at the Alabama border, hundreds of people gather each spring to see who can "toss" a member of the species the greatest distance across the state line. As an adjective preceding the noun "wrapper," this fish has been used to describe many of the state's most prestigious newspapers. As a noun it has stood alone permanently embedded in pop culture as the hairdo favored by hockey players and country singers.

Some say as foodstuff, be it smoked, broiled, or fried, there is no better. Few would argue that as a key link in the estuary ecosystem, it plays a critical role in the circle of life.

Yet when the time came to pick a state fish, Florida officials fumbled and chose the largemouth bass, a boorish brute when compared to sleek, elegant *Mugil cephalus*.

"There is no doubt about it, when it comes to overall importance, nothing comes close to the mullet," says Ted Forsgren, former executive director of the Coastal Conservation Association. "Everything feeds on it—trout, redfish, dolphin, and birds. It is a building block in the food chain."

As an herbivore that converts plant matter to protein, the striped or black mullet has been critical not only to the diets of sport fish and waterbirds, but to humans. Archaeologists have long suspected that mullet played an important role in the diet of Florida's first residents. Many believed that the Paleo-Indians, circa 10,000 BCE, may have caught mullet, although any evidence left behind by these people has been under seawater for millennia and not accessible for study. The Native Americans who came later did spear and net mullet in the shallow estuaries and streams, as evidenced by bones found in the middens (debris mounds) they left behind. "They certainly ate mullet as well as pigfish, pinfish, and catfish, which were easy to catch in nets," said William H. Marquardt, curator emeritus of the South Florida Archaeology and Ethnography Program and director of the Randell

Terry Tomalin (1960–2016) was the outdoor editor of the *Tampa Bay Times*, and he taught digital journalism and led the Outdoor Leadership Program at the University of South Florida, St. Petersburg.

Image: Bernard Miller throws a cast net, Eastpoint, 1986. Photo by David Alan Taylor, courtesy of State Archives of Florida, Florida Memory.

Research Center at the Museum of Natural History at the University of Florida. "The Native Americans probably netted mullet and also caught them in tidal traps or fish weirs."

When Spaniards began settling Florida in the mid-1700s, they quickly learned that mullet could provide a ready source of protein to supplement domestic livestock. Plentiful and easy to catch, striped mullet travel by the thousands in large schools, unlike most other in-shore fish species.

This fact helped to sustain indentured servants from the Spanish island of Minorca who arrived in British east Florida in 1768 to work on a New Smyrna indigo plantation. But the conditions were so harsh they suffered near starvation and escaped to sanctuary in St. Augustine. Their freedom cry became "Mullet on the beach."

"When the mullet were running, word would spread fast," says Bob Jones, former executive director of the Southeast Fisheries Association and one of Florida's leading fisheries historians. "People would yell, 'Mullet on the beach! Mullet on the beach!' and everybody would just drop what they were doing and pick up their cast nets. People would stand there, shoulder to shoulder, and haul in net after net. That is how thick the schools were."

Once cleaned, the delicate flesh could be salted. This method of preserving the fish became important to Spanish Cubans who came by boat to southwest Florida starting in the mid-1700s. They came during the winter months, when roe-filled mullet congregated in the shallow bays before heading offshore to spawn. They established *ranchos*, hiring local Indian people as labor and supplying a burgeoning trade with Cuba. They returned to Cuba with boatloads of salted mullet to sell during Lent, when Catholics did not eat meat.

Some say as foodstuff, be it smoked, broiled, or fried, there is no better.

During the 1800s, mullet continued to play an important role in the lives of most coastal pioneering families. If you lived on the coast, you learned how to net, splay, and smoke mullet. This was especially crucial in times of hardship.

In 1885 a few fishing families from coastal North Carolina got word of the big schools of fat mullet on Florida's southwest coast. That gave birth to the modern commercial net-fishing industry.

"The Fulfords, Guthries, and Bells all fished for mullet in Carteret County, North Carolina," says Ben Green, author of *Finest Kind*, a book about the Gulf coast town of Cortez. "They were carrying on a tradition—fishing for mullet—that had started back in England."

Green, a descendant of the Fulford family, says those early commercial fishermen first moved to Cedar Key but then heard about a place called Hunter's Point on the south side of Tampa Bay where the mullet ran in schools larger than the eye could see. The families moved down there and established the fishing village of Cortez.

"It got to where if you were a boy growing up in Carteret County, North Carolina, as soon as you turned fifteen or sixteen, you would hop a train and head to Florida," Green explains. "Everybody knew about Florida mullet."

The Cortez fishermen learned that mullet were easiest to catch during the fall. The fish spend most of the year scattered about the rivers and bays, but once they get a hint of cold weather, they bunch up on the shallow grass flats, where they can be easily netted by the thousands, before moving offshore to spawn.

"You can almost set your watch to it," says Robert McCurdy, a St. Petersburg cast-netter who follows the schools as they move offshore to spawn. "When that first cold front comes through we set up and wait. There will be 100 boats just waiting at the pier for the fish to move down the bay. Once they do, it is a free-for-all."

Illustration of flathead gray mullet by Diane Rome Peebles. Courtesy of Florida Fish and Wildlife Conservation Commission.

Nobody knows how many mullet once inhabited the waters of a historic estuary such as Tampa Bay, but legend has it the fish were so plentiful people could actually hear the "roar" of a big school as it moved across the shallow sandbars.

While the striped mullet is found along both coasts, the bulk of the commercial fishery was located along the shores of the Gulf. The key fishing grounds were near Tampa Bay and Charlotte Harbor; both provided ideal habitat for a species that needs a steady flow of freshwater to survive.

The state of Florida began keeping records of the mullet catch in 1879, when 3,569,167 pounds of the fish were landed. By 1889 the catch had more than quadrupled, to 12,987,951 pounds. This dramatic increase came after the founding of Cortez. But biologists have learned that the size of the mullet catch is affected by more than just the number of fishermen pursuing the fish.

"This is a very cyclical species," says Behzad Mahmoudi, an internationally renowned mullet biologist with the Florida Fish and Wildlife Research Institute in St. Petersburg. "Over the years, fishing has had an impact, but there are also natural fluctuations in the [mullet] population that we still don't fully understand."

It wasn't long after the state began keeping records of mullet catches that the legislature began regulating the species. In 1883 the state legislature recognized the mullet's value as a food source and made it illegal to catch mullet for "the purpose of making oil, fertilizer, or compost."

In 1911 state officials took a bold step, one that would generate controversy for the next fifty years: they outlawed the harvest of mullet during the breeding season. Mullet roe, prized both at home and abroad, is said by some to rival the finest caviar. And during the roe season, the fish itself is good eating.

"There is no better thing to eat," says Thomas "Blue" Fulford, a Cortez net fisherman who made his living from the sea. "During the roe season is also the time you want to catch and fry some fish.... There's no sweeter meat."

No sooner had the mullet season closed than people began fishing illegally for the sweet red roe. One of those indiscretions led to an unusual ruling in the 1920s by Wakulla County Judge Roderick Donald McLeod.

When faced with the prospect of sending two local fishermen to jail for violating the mullet closure, McLeod noted the species was unique among fish because it possessed a gizzard, and he let the men go. Newspapers across the state reportedly rejoiced at the judge's ruling with headlines proclaiming, "Mullet to be a bird!"

This ruling is memorialized on a plaque in Crawfordville's Azalea Park.

Despite the restrictions, Florida's mullet fishermen continued to catch lots of fish during the open season. By 1918 the catch had nearly tripled, to 32,288,678 pounds a year. During World War II the catch shot up again, to 55,952,367 pounds. Food shortages during the war made mullet a staple for many.

"People needed protein," says Florida historian Gary Mormino. "Fish was one of the few things that was not rationed."

In celebration of a special fish, 1978. A young woman holds a mullet at the Boggy Bayou Mullet Festival. Courtesy of State Archives of Florida, Florida Memory.

Florida's mullet harvest eventually leveled off, and the net fishermen found a reliable market in fish houses and small restaurants around the state that specialized in smoking mullet.

In 1957 the Southeastern Fisheries Association, an organization that represented about 600 fish houses, finally succeeded in reopening mullet fishing during the lucrative roe season. The group did this by striking a deal with the Izaak Walton League, an environmental group named after the father of sportfishing.

"We sat down with the Izaak Walton League and cut a deal," explains Jones, of the Southeast Fisheries Association. "We said if you give us back mullet roe, we'll give you snook. That is how it happened. It was all done with a handshake."

Snook, now one of the most popular sport fish in Florida, was taken off the market. The state made it illegal to buy or sell and allowed commercial net fishermen once again to catch their beloved red roe mullet. Records show that the catch rose steadily for a few years and then leveled off. But in the 1980s something happened that would change the mullet fishery forever.

"That is about the time they discovered there was a market in the Orient for mullet roe," explains Mahmoudi, the biologist. "Suddenly it became very valuable." The mullet harvest increased during the roe season. But then sports fishermen, whose numbers had burgeoned along with Florida's post–World War II population, began complaining that this put too much pressure on the fishery.

In the early 1990s the sports fishermen formed a coalition with conservation groups to push for a ban on the entanglement nets most commonly used to catch mullet. In 1994 Florida voters approved a constitutional amendment banning the use of these nets.

A year after the vote, the mullet harvest dropped dramatically, from 14,972,738 pounds to 5,622,024 pounds. Many netters stopped fishing. Others targeted different species. Fishing villages like Cortez and Cedar Key were hit hard. Mullet stocks seem to be improving, and biologists like Mahmoudi are keeping a close eye on the health of the species.

They also continue looking for answers to the age-old question: Why do mullet jump? "That is a good question, one that I get asked a lot," Mahmoudi says.

One theory is that mullet jump to escape predators, he said. Another is that mullet jump to rid themselves of parasites. But Mahmoudi has a much simpler answer. "Maybe they are just happy," he says.

From the **Summer 2006** edition of *FORUM* magazine, "The Old Ways Are Vanishing along the Coast."

46 Florida's Deep-Blue Destiny

From the depths of a spring it is clear, we lose connection with the state's waterways at our peril.

Bill Belleville

Bill Belleville (1945–2020) was an award-winning environmental writer and documentary filmmaker who was the author of seven books, including *Losing It All to Sprawl: How Progress Ate My Cracker Landscape* (University Press of Florida, 2006) and *The Peace of Blue: Water Journeys* (University Press of Florida, 2014), and more than 1,000 articles and essays in publications such as *Audubon, Outside, Sports Afield, Oxford American, New York Times, Parade, Washington Post, Los Angeles Times, Denver Post,* and *Salon.com.*

I AM SOMEWHERE inside the vortex of Blue Springs, way past the "Prevent Your Death: Go No Farther" sign at 60 feet, and far beyond the muted glow of surface light.

The river that Blue feeds has been gradually warming, and the warm-blooded manatees that winter here have just left. Except for a few snorkelers back up in the shallow run, my dive buddy and I are alone in the spring.

The only illumination down here is portable, hand-held. And like the trail of exhaust bubbles from my regulator, it tethers me to the surface with my own limitations. Scuba tanks, face masks, containers of light, they are all reminders of how unsuited we humans are to immerse ourselves in the most primal and universal element of all.

Here, near the 120-foot-deep bottom of this limestone chasm, I am as aware as I have ever been of the pervasive power and magic of water. All but invisible, it arises from a slot in the rock, flailing me like a rag doll with its energy.

If underground water is the veins and capillaries that sustain our Florida physiography, then I am squarely inside a natural incision, a place where the liquid transports itself to the surface, where science meets myth and culture head on. Naturalist William Bartram sat on the banks of Blue once and later wrote in wonder of the "diaphanous fountain" that surged just below. He wrote likewise about Salt and Manatee Springs. In all of his travels, nothing seemed to touch him as fully. His descriptions inspired the romantic poet Samuel Taylor Coleridge to write of Kubla Khan, "where Alph the sacred river ran, through caverns measureless to man." I would give all I have if Bartram could be next to me today, could feel the full sway of this natural "ebullition" down here inside of Alph.

Looking closely in the soft rock around me, I see subliminal clues to the prehistoric sea that accrued to form first the platform and then the crust of Florida. The clues are fossilized shells, still ribbed like a cockle or cupped round like a clam. They are welded together by the dust of Eocene coral, whale skull, oceanic sand, an assemblage of calcium turned white as bone.

Even the manatees are a reminder of this oceanic genesis. I have encountered them underwater before, have seen the residual but distinct toenails on their front flippers, visual evidence of their own long and convoluted genetic journey from sea to land and then back again.

An Ancient Connection

BUT IF THE FOSSILS and the manatees are an *aide memoire* to the core fiber of both people and place, the most urgent reminder is the fierce upwelling itself. Isotopes of water have been dated in Florida springs. And although a water molecule seldom stays in the atmosphere for more than ten days, when hidden in the dark fissures and bedding planes in the rock, as it is here, it may remain so for 7,000 years or more.

It is inescapable. The water that pushes and shoves me around in the throat of Blue once fell on uplands as rain millennia ago, fell on and around the earliest Native Americans who lived here. They drank it, bathed in it, were nurtured by it.

How did they regard it? Of the Timucua, here along the St. Johns for at least 4,000 years before the Europeans arrived, we know at least shards of their language. Of their words, there were five different ones for trust, six for virtue. But there was only one root word for water.

Dew, rainfall, pond, river, lake, lagoon: it is all *ibi*. Perhaps it differed in context or pronunciation or modification. Nonetheless, it is *ibi* going in and *ibi* coming back out. *Ibi*, a liquid god that rendered this once-arid sandbar and savanna luxuriant, that made it a jungle, warm, wet, and wildly productive.

The Timucua had a reverence for this water, as they did for all of nature. Their deities were woven into it and not separate from it, not safely contained to a one-hour sermon one day a week. *Ibi* held fish and snails, fed wildlife, watered crops, floated dugouts, and gave life. In storms and in drowning, it also took life away.

So it was too for the Muskogean-speakers who migrated here when the Timucua were vanquished. The brave warrior Coacoochee hid out with a band of 200 in the wild swamps of the Wekiva River during the Second Seminole War. Coacoochee reported the spirit of his twin sister once visited him from the land of souls, offering him a cup of pure water from the spring of the Great Spirit. "And if I should drink of it," said Coacoochee, "I should return and live with her for'ever."

Water was enchantment, certainly. But it was also deeply feared and honored, held close to the heart in both mystery and awe. It was sacred.

Perhaps more than any single place on our continent, the new wet landscape of Florida was occupied almost as quickly as it had been formed.

Water has shaped culture in Florida from the very first moment humans stepped foot on this ancient sea-bottom terrace. When they arrived 12,000 years or more ago, the peninsula was dry and nearly twice as large as it is today. Few modern rivers or springs flowed as they do, and these nomadic Paleo-Indians encamped around limestone catchments on prairies and at mouths of coastal rivers, sites now inundated with the sea.

The glaciers began to retreat, the climate warmed, and water from the shallow seas was drawn up into the sky. The great hydrological cycle that sets Florida decidedly apart from other global deserts on this same latitude began to stir. Freshwater springs, charged by the new rain seeping into the soft sea rock upland, flowed effusively. Swamps and marsh were birthed, and rivers snaked through their lush and moist topography. The vast glade of shallow water and plants and limestone south of Lake Okeechobee took form, revealing what the Spanish would one day map as the "Lagoon of the Sacred Spirit."

What Water Fashioned

By 5000 BCE, millions of years after most of the North American continent had fashioned itself into mountains and valleys, Florida finally took the shape and substance of what it is today.

This new peninsula was verdant and biologically diverse, one giant organic marketplace of fish and game, and at last it had stabilized enough to offer sanctuary, to allow time for mythology to arise from the connection between people and place. Nomadic hunters could settle inland on rivers, build mounds, and grow crops. Tools, points, and pottery could become finer, more sophisticated, and tribal cultures and their art more complex. Leaders could evolve into chiefs and shamans, powerful men who could mediate with the forces of nature, especially the powers we moderns would one day call hydrology.

Perhaps more than any single place on our continent, the new wet landscape of Florida was occupied almost as quickly as it had been formed. It was as if the water-driven terrain and its people grew together, the environment shaping culture as quickly as it shaped itself.

When Ponce de León arrived in 1513, blundering westward of Puerto Rico in search of Bimini, he sailed along the mid-Atlantic coast, landing near Cape Canaveral. Soon, the first permanent geographic name on the North American continent was scribbled on his chart: "La Florida." It was springtime, flowers were blooming, and he noted this new land was "very pretty to behold."

Pánfilo de Narváez, following the conquistadors' quest for gold and glory, sailed around the Florida cape with ships loaded with horses, provisions, and 400 men and landed somewhere near Sarasota Bay fifteen years later. Over the next eight years, the first Spanish expedition to explore the New World by land would be whittled down to four men, and a decade before DeSoto, the survivors would cross the

Snorkeler at Fanning Springs on the Suwannee River. Beautiful beaches and rivers and lakes are found across the globe, but Florida alone is the Land of a Thousand Springs. Fanning Springs is emblematic of these pools of stunning blue wonder. Photo by John Moran.

Withlacoochee, the Suwannee, the Apalachicola, and then the Mississippi, building canoes or, when possible, swimming.

There was no gold in La Florida, but there was plenty of water, and as it does today, it enriched the soil, turning leaf and wood into humus and peat, composting the landscape. For the next 200 years, Spanish missions were built along major rivers and coastal lagoons, forcing the converted Indians to use the fertile land of La Florida as a breadbasket to fuel Spanish plundering elsewhere in the New World.

French artist Jacques Le Moyne, here for a brief time with the ill-fated French colony at Fort Caroline in 1564, left a more complete graphic picture of the same

Indians with his forty-one drawings. From Le Moyne, we learn the Timucua swam with children on their backs, rode in giant dugouts, performed ceremonies, captured alligators, dried fish, and planted crops, all behaviors made possible, indeed, even encouraged by the liquid nature of La Florida.

It was the ambitiously brutal conquistador Pedro Menéndez de Avilés himself, who after learning of the breadth of Florida's rivers and wetlands, felt sure there was some way the interior could be navigated by his large ships. It was he who first schemed of a cross-Florida canal to allow such a feat.

Meanwhile, with no technical solution to enable humans to commandeer such a soggy place, Florida grew slowly, lagging behind the rest of the dry and maneuverable continent. After all, the peninsula contained 12,000 miles of rivers and streams and no fewer than 7,700 lakes. Some 600 springs have since been identified, more than any other region in the country.

When they settled on the coast, Europeans usually chose natural harbors. Inland, they colonized high river bluffs and ancient Indian middens. Florida was one big swamp and marsh—what author John Rothchild has called "pre-dredged real estate"—and the best and surest roads were its waterways. It was a reality that would not escape the tourist steamboats that later arrived in the early nineteenth century. Fishing and boating, pirating and salvaging came with the territory; they are the natural antecedents of what is left of the Florida persona today.

How Bartram Saw It

BARTRAM, here in two separate trips in 1764 and 1775 and who lived on the St. Johns for two years in between, was among the first to see the water-driven ecological connections, to marvel at the strong rivers and the magic of the powerful springs. Our first spiritual naturalist, the gentle Quaker was an unlikely explorer. But he found his way farther into the interior of Florida than the Spanish ever had, sailing and oaring a boat all the way down to Puzzle Lake on the "grand and noble San Juan."

Bartram understood the promise this grid work of nature had—still has, even today—to hold mystery close to its heart. Unlike open savannas or mountains, you cannot see very far at all in a jungle, and every tree trunk, every vine-clogged pathway, every bend in the river conceals a new discovery. In contrast with the geological drama of continental mountains and valleys, this is a territory woven into the folds of biological nuance.

For 250 years, Florida had been a region to be exploited by Europeans, a place to be sopped up, trimmed, and tamed. But for Bartram, the man the Creeks called the "Flower Hunter," it was a natural cathedral, a place where we can "learn wisdom and understanding in the economy of nature, and be seriously attentive to the divine monitor within."

300 · Bill Belleville

Cave divers enter the labyrinth of Manatee Springs. Manatee, one of the state's first-magnitude springs, surfaces into the lower Suwannee River. Photo by Mark Long.

Perhaps nature as religion may have had a chance in Florida. But when technology finally developed to allow "submerged bottomlands" to be drained and sold for as little as twenty-five cents an acre in the nineteenth century, then Florida's destiny, which was once to flow, began to ebb.

In the long haul, humans have done more to disconnect themselves from Florida's water in the last century than they did in the 12,000 years that came before.

Afternoon clouds above sawgrass and lily pads. The Francis S. Taylor Wildlife Management Area covers 672,000 acres in the Everglades. Photo by Carlton Ward.

Seeking reinforcement, activists searched for a spokesperson with public appeal, one who carried the authority of local history and the truth of the Everglades. Douglas was their person. A remarkable speaker, she projected ideas with high-volume clarity despite her age. (A friend would dub her the "elocutioner"; she is truly one of Florida's finest orators.) For more than fifty years she had valued south Florida not as a slice of real estate but as a place to make a life. And her book, tucked like the Bible under the arms of local environmentalists, delivered the important truth, easily translated from the subtitle River of Grass. That was her lasting "genius," said her longtime friend Helen Muir, transforming with three words a debased wasteland into the country's most cherished wetland.

In 1969 the seventy-nine-year-old writer-turned-environmentalist founded Friends of the Everglades. After joining in the defeat of the airport, she guided her organization to press for the establishment of the Big Cypress National Preserve (1974), an end to agricultural pollution fouling Everglades water, reform in the expansionist impulses of water managers, and restoration of the channelized, diked, and otherwise arrested Kissimmee River–Lake Okeechobee–Everglades heart of the region. She spent her remaining decades moving the country toward a sensibility that assimilated the natural Everglades.

Much like her famous phrase, her name became synonymous with a valued place. In 1997 Congress attached it to a new 1.8 million-acre Everglades wilderness area, four years after President Clinton awarded her the Medal of Freedom. When she died in 1998, at 108, park rangers appropriately broadcast her ashes in the beloved river she gave to America, the River of Grass.

From the **Fall 2009** edition of *FORUM* magazine, "The Everglades: Life at the Edge."

When I lie down to die, I could not wish for a last memory finer than any of the days when I have taken my old golden retriever and my writing board down to the bluff overlooking the Suwannee.

I suddenly realized I had heard the rhythm his voice had taken in only one place before: church. And it held that rhythm while he told me I was sitting on top of the Suwannee River.

"River, you say?" I had no notion at all of what he might mean.

He said, "Suwannee River'll take this water our boat's floating on right now and pour it into the Gulf of Mexico. That Suwannee! It's rivers that's bigger but none prettier. I sawmilled over in that part of the country when I was a young buck. Lemme tell you about that river."

The boat stayed tied up the rest of the afternoon while he talked and smoked and I listened, understanding very little except his admiration for the river that turned to reverence as he talked the day into dark.

Uncle Cooter's been dead these past thirty years and I've grown long in the tooth and thin in the shank, but the Suwannee River still breaks free of the Swamp near Fargo, Georgia, then drops due south, its broad, shining expanse carrying no industrial traffic, veers west through White Springs, Florida, and flows on to the Gulf, the 240 miles of the river bordered right down to the water with trees that have never had an ax in them, opening at long and random intervals onto very little but very old communities and onto fish camps, where a man can fish all day or talk all day or do utterly nothing all day.

I'm proud to have had the use of the river and prouder still that we have managed to keep it as unspoiled as we have. When I lie down to die, I could not wish for a last memory finer than any of the days when I have taken my old golden retriever and my writing board down to the bluff overlooking the Suwannee and, after writing four or five hours, taken a pontoon boat upriver to Manatee Springs, where the water is so clear that I can flip a dime into it and tell whether the dime is heads or tails when it's resting on the sandy bottom.

I could flip a dime, but I almost never do. Usually, I sit in the sun and look at the Suwannee River rolling on down to the Gulf of Mexico while I remember my uncle Cooter and remember also his stories that I have made my own during the last quarter of a century by telling them, and retelling them, and telling them yet again.

From the **Spring/Summer 1993** edition of *FORUM* magazine, "The Suwannee River."

Opposite page: *Florida Swamp*, by William James Glackens, (American, 1870–1938), circa 1889, oil on linen. Courtesy of the Samuel P. Harn Museum of Art, University of Florida, Gainesville; the Florida Art Collection, Gift of Samuel H. and Roberta T. Vickers. Photo by Randy Batista.

Sanchez, Thomas, 208, 249
Sarasota: as the "Cradle of Golf," 116; location on pre-Disney Sunshine State postcard map, *xiii*; Spanish expedition by Pánfilo de Narváez, 298; Warm Mineral Spring in, 13
Schneider, Alan, as director of *En attendant Godot* in Miami, 175–76
Scholl, Dennis, 192
Seibert, Steve, 3, 6
Seminole (Creek Indians): children at the Brighton Indian Reservation, *178–79*; colorful Indian dress of, *175*; Creek Indian roots of, 19, 182, 213; settlements on lands previously occupied by the Apalachee and Timucua, 19; slavery practiced by, 180. *See also* Johns, Willie; Osceola
Seminole (Creek Indians)–poetry: Frances Densmore's *Seminole Songs*, 215; by Moses Jumper Jr., 216; "The Seminole Removal," 215
Seminole Wars, 44, 65, 181, 213, 297
Shepard, Alan, 100
Shoumatoff, Alex, 58
Simpson, Gary, 283, 290
Singer, Isaac Bashevis, 70, 174, *174*, 210
Skynyrd. *See* Lynyrd Skynyrd
slavery and slave labor: abolitionist work of Harriet Beecher Stowe, 217; advertisements for, *44*; cotton picking, 42–43, *42*; during the Civil War, 43, 44–45, 48; Florida railroads and canals built by leased bondsmen, 44; former slaves Charity Stewart and Ambrose "Uncle Doug" Hilliard Douglass, *43*; Fort Mose as a sanctuary for escaped slaves, 30, 33; Middle Florida holders of enslaved Africans, 42–45, *50*; practiced by the Seminole, 180; *The Rape of Florida* written by formerly enslaved Albery Allson Whitman, 210; rewards offered for runaways, *45*; St. Augustine and Fort Mose as sanctuaries for escaped slaves, 30, 292
South Beach, residents photographed by Andy Sweet, *185, 192–97, 193, 194, 196, 197*
Soviet Union: cosmonaut Yuri Gagarin's space orbit, 100–101; Sputnik launched by, 1, 99–101
space program: in Cape Canaveral, 15, 72–73; Friendship 7 mission flown by John Glenn, 1, 100, *107. See also* Challenger; National Aeronautics and Space Administration (NASA)
space program–Apollo and Apollo-Soyuz programs: Apollo 7, *106*; Apollo 11 launched from Kennedy Space Center (July 16, 1969), *52–53*, 72, 73, *105*; final flight of, 111
Spanish expeditions: by Cabeza de Vaca, 54, 209; by de Soto, 17, 18, 54; by Luna y Arellano, 18, 281; Narváez expedition, 32, 278, 298. *See also* Ponce de León, Juan
Spinner, Francis E., 65

sport-fishing. *See* fishing–sport-fishing
sports and sports arenas: hosting of rock concerts, 266, 268. *See also* baseball; golf
Stephen Foster Folk Culture Center State Park, Florida Folk Festival held in, 259–64, *263, 264*
Stevens, Wallace: "Farewell to Florida," 206; Key West poems, 207, 210
Stewart, Charity, *43*
Stowe, Calvin, 217, *223–24, 224*
Stowe, Harriet Beecher: biographical information, 217, 224; on Florida, 9, 57, 60, 62; Mandarin cottage, 208, 218, 220–21, *222–23*; "Our Florida Plantation," 218; paintings by, 221, *221*; *Palmetto-Leaves*, 56, 208, 220, 221, 224, *224*; portrait by Francis Holl, *9, 219*; *Uncle Tom's Cabin*, 208, 217
Summerlin, Jacob, 48, *49*
Sunshine, Silvia, 208
Suwannee County, Indian culture in, 16–17
Suwannee River: Fanning Springs, *299*; John Muir's study of, 282; in "Old Folks at Home" by Stephen Collins Foster, 176, 210, 260; stories told to Harry Crews by his uncle Cooter, 322–24; Suwannee Spring resort, 62–63; "Swanee" by George Gershwin, 176; waterfall on Robinson Branch, *323*
Sweet, Andy, *192*; brother-in-law, Stan Hughes, 194–95, 196; death of, 194; father, judge Nelan "Chick" Sweet, 194; *The Last Resort* documentary on, 192, 196, 197; photo legacy, 196; *Shtetl in the Sun*, 196; sister Ellen Sweet Moss, 194, 196; South Beach residents photographed by, *185, 192–97, 193, 194, 196, 197*

Tallahassee: Apalachee village of Anhaica located near the current site of, 17; convention vote by Florida's General Assembly (1861), 45, 60; demonstrators in front of the Florida Theatre (circa 1963), *137*; drive-in restaurant (1957), *153*; during the Civil War, 51; environmental movement in the 1970s, 73; location on pre-Disney Sunshine State postcard map, *xiii*; Pepper's base in, 74; relocation of the capital to, 281; Southeastern Regional Black Archives at Florida A&M University, 6. *See also* Florida A&M University (FAMU)
Tampa: Calusa town Tampa (present-day Pineland) distinguished from, *11*; Caribbean culture fostered in, 208–9; environmental movement in the 1970s, 73; location on pre-Disney Sunshine State postcard map, *xiii*
Tampa–Ybor City: cigar, manufacturing, 67, 69, *69*; writers on the history of, 208–9
Tarpon Springs. *See* Gulf of Mexico–Tarpon Springs
Telling Project: Steve Seibert on, 6; Taylor Urruela at, *5*
Tequesta Indians, 18, 19, 181

Timucua Indians: chief Outina, *14*; "Fisherman" painting by Morris, *215*; graphic pictures by Jacques Le Moyne, *17*, 299–300; *ibi* as the root word for water, 297, 302; Jesuit missions placed in settlements of, 19; settlements by the Seminole on lands previously occupied by, 19; settlements in eastern, central, and northern Florida, 16–17, 18, 181; shell rock digging by, 37–38; Taíno language compared with Timucua language, 304
tobacco: cigar-manufacturing in Ybor City, 67, 69, *69*; farming, 44, 70
Trillin, Calvin, 243
TV shows: *Burn Notice*, 131, *135*; *Dexter*, 128, *134*, 135; *Flipper*, 130, *131*; *Florida Girls*, 134; *The Good Place*, 129; *I Dream of Jeannie*, 128, *135*; *Karen Sisco*, 132; *Miami Vice*, 129, 131–33, 176; *Nip/Tuck*, 132, 135; *On Becoming a God in Central Florida*, 133–34, *133*; *Sea Hunt*, 130, *130*; showcasing of Florida in, 129–30, 135; *The Wonderful World of Disney*, 131
Twine, Henry, 160, 163, 165

Van Zant, Ronnie, 268–69, *269*, 271, 273
Venezuela and Venezuelans: immigrants in Florida, 76, *76*; James Weldon Johnson as ambassador to, 228

Walker, Charlie, 101
West Palm Beach. *See* Palm Beach–West Palm Beach
White, Eartha, 80, 81
White, II, Edward, 109
White Springs: bath houses in, *61, 62, 63*; Stephen Foster Folk Culture Center State Park located in, 259; Suwannee River, *323, 324. See also* Florida Folk Festival
Whitman, Albery Allson, *The Rape of Florida*, 210
Whitman, Walt, 210, 214
Wilbur, Richard, 208, *251–52*
Williams, John Lee, 60–61, 65
Williams, Joy, 205, 208
Williams, Tennessee, 175, 208, 210, *211*, 248
Women's Army Corps (WAC), training in Daytona Beach, 89–93, *91, 92, 93*
Wood, Wayne, 227
World War II: Norton Baskin's war duty, 84–85, 86; gas rationing, 89; mullet as a staple during, 294; Office of Strategic Services (OSS), 123; optimism following, 67; Marjorie Kinnan Rawling's correspondence with soldiers, 86–87, *87. See also* Women's Army Corps (WAC)
WPA Guide to 1930s Florida, Zora Neale Hurston's work for, 56–57, 77–78, *78*, 80–81
Wright, Richard, *Native Son*, 147

Ybor City. *See* Tampa–Ybor City;

330 · Index